EM_

This book includes:

Discovery, Learning and Protection for Highly Sensitive Empaths. A Psychic Survival Guide for Emotional Healing to Repel Energy Vampires and Reveal Dark Mystic Secrets.

By Crystal Gift

Table Of Contents

EMPATH DISCOVERY

A Survival Guide for Beginners for Understanding the Empathic Brain, Discovering Your Dark Side, Embracing Your Emotional Skills and Getting Stronger Daily. Healing Modalities and Personality Types.

By Crystal Gift

Table of Contents

Introduction

Congratulations on purchasing *Empath Discovery: A Survival Guide for Beginners for Understanding the Empathic Brain, Discovering Your Dark Side, Embracing Your Emotional Skills and Getting Stronger Daily. Healing Modalities and Personality Types* and thank you for doing so.

The following chapters will discuss empathy, what it means, how it affects so many various aspects of your life, and how to use it to your advantage in life. Empathy and empathic abilities can be useful in myriad ways. Learning about them will give you the tools you need to go about your life with successful and strong relationships.

Understanding empathy and empathic abilities in yourself or in those around you can give you tools to improve relationships and so much more. Be sure to complete the exercises within these chapters to get the very most out of what this book has to offer you!

There are plenty of books on this subject on the market, thanks again for choosing this one! Every effort has been made to ensure this book is full of as much useful information as possible. Please enjoy!

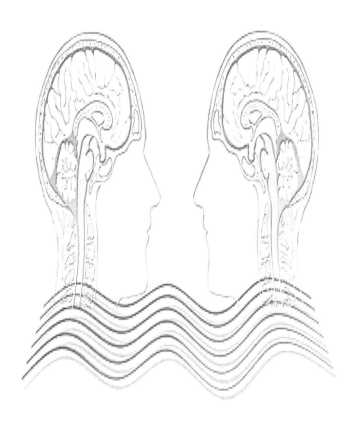

Chapter 1: Understanding Empathy

What is Empathy?

Empathy is a natural human response to things going on in one's environment. Most people are born with an empathetic response, and the severity or sensitivity of that response is varied amongst people. Think of empathy in the same way in which you would think of skin sensitivity. Some people have very sensitive skin that can't stand up to certain cleansers and fabrics that might be considered normal. Some people have skin that can't be irritated, no matter what.

Empathy, in general, is defined as being the natural response that one has to the emotions or feelings of another. It is characterized by an understanding of what someone else is going through, what those feelings are like, and how to respond to them in a way that makes the other person feel at ease.

People who have less empathy tend to "step on toes," and overstep the boundaries of what someone might consider polite, given their circumstances. You have probably experienced something like this while going through something that affected you adversely. Let's take a look and see if we can find something.

Have you ever had a bad day? Bad days happen to the best of us, and they seem like nothing we do will go right, no matter how hard we try. So, on that bad day, was there ever someone who seemed to be aware of what you were going through, but made no concessions for you, didn't treat you any differently, or even seemed to do more things to make your day worse? This is a *lack* of empathy.

That person either couldn't understand the feelings you were experiencing or didn't feel any personal connection to them. Empathy depends on being able to identify the emotions that another person is experiencing, and it depends on being able to relate to those feelings so we can "try them on," so to speak.

If someone loses a pet and is sad, they tend to look somewhat distraught. They don't laugh as readily, their eyes look sad, and there are a good number of other variable indicators. If someone is completely unfamiliar with any of those indicators outside of someone crying in front of them, they might have no idea anything is even wrong. Because of this, they could be cracking jokes, making statements about banal things that bear no importance to the person suffering the loss, or worse.

The person who is completely unfamiliar with the indications of sadness doesn't feel any malice toward the person who lost their pet. However, their lack of understanding of the emotion makes them completely unaware that they should be behaving differently, that they should be compassionate, or that they should at least ask how the other person is doing.

This complete lack of awareness can come across as malicious, but that is rarely the case. Hanlon's razor tells us, "Never attribute to malice that which is adequately explained by stupidity."

While the person who lacks the understanding of that emotion might not be completely stupid, there is a lack of emotional intelligence. Lacking that emotional intelligence and understanding of human emotion can gum up the works and can make one come across as being unfeeling or unkind. This is rarely the case, so we would all do well to brush up on our emotional intelligence and empathy!

It can be said that empathy is the sum of emotional intelligence, plus being able to imagine yourself in that emotional state. If you can imagine yourself in that emotional state, or at least understand the gravity of being in that state, you are much better equipped to respond to the other person in a way that will make them feel understood and more comfortable.

If you're talking to someone whose car was just stolen, you might be able to expect that the person will feel scared, angry, and a little bit panicked. Losing your car is a big deal, there are a lot of things to do to get it back or to get a new one in such an event. There is a lot of bureaucracy and red tape to deal with between the police, DMV, car dealership, and insurance, and there is a lot of uncertainty about how things will go for them in the coming hours.

If you try to speak with the person and say something like, "Hey, come on. It's not that big a deal, right? It's just a car, and you'll figure out getting a new one." This will only serve to make the person more upset or stressed. It will lead that person to feel like you're unconcerned with how upset this has made them like you feel that they are overreacting, and like you have no idea what they're going through. This will cause them to forcefully put distance between the two of you in order to get away from someone who is only serving to cause them more stress.

Instead, realize that this is the type of thing that causes a severe spike in stress levels. In the beginning, if you're not sure what to do, stay silent and allow that person to respond in the way they need to. The police should be called on an immediate basis, so if you can do that for them, that would be helpful. The sooner authorities are aware of the theft, the sooner they can work to resolve it.

When addressing the person, express your concern and your panic in a way that nearly matches the person. "Oh my gosh! Who does something like this? I'm calling the police right now. Let me know if there's anything else I can do for you. Just breathe, and we'll get through it, okay? I'm so sorry this is happening." Sounding calm in times of crisis isn't always the answer. Sounding like you understand the urgency and are rising to the occasion can often be more important and can take precedence when trying to be empathetic to the person suffering a crisis.

Let's take a look at another scenario that calls for empathy, but which is positive. Let's say someone has just been informed that they are going to be a parent and that they couldn't be happier about it. This person is fighting the urge to leap out of their cubicle at work and is telling everyone who will listen to the news. Now, this person doesn't need you to be excited for them, it's not a life or death situation, and not everyone is going to be as invested in this news as they are. However, showing a complete lack of investment or empathy could drive a divide between you. Let's take a look at some possible outcomes.

This person who has gotten the news, we'll call them Paige. Paige comes to Brad's desk and tells him the news. Brad can see that she is happy and excited, but Brad doesn't really understand *why*. He's not particularly excited about children, and he's not really sure why Paige would feel the urge to tell him about it, so Brad just gives Paige a very flat, "Okay," along with a head nod. Brad isn't rude, he isn't angry, and he didn't say anything negative about it. Because of his lack of empathy, however, Brad said the only thing he could think to say. His pragmatism tells him that his response doesn't lessen the excitement that Paige should feel about this news, he didn't say anything *mean*, and he didn't react negatively. These factors tell Brad that his response was perfectly acceptable.

Paige, however, expected Brad to be happier about the news. Why wouldn't Brad say something more supportive and with more excitement than that? Is Brad concealing some ill will toward Paige? Would Brad prefer that Paige didn't get this wonderful news? Is Brad annoyed with Paige for being so excited about where life is now headed for Paige and their significant other? Being parents is no small thing, of course.

In reality, we know what Brad was thinking about the situation. We know what Brad intended with his response: simply to respond. So where does this leave Brad and Paige? Brad is confused by Paige's hurt facial expression, and Paige is hurt by Brad's confusion and stoicism. It would take a third person stepping in to ask, "Gee, Brad. Would it kill you to be a little excited about Paige's news? It's pretty clear that this means a lot and that your flat response takes the wind out of the sails."

This would cause Brad to say something like, "Oh, I didn't know that my opinion meant that much to you in this subject. Of course, I am happy for you and I'm glad that you're so excited about the new addition coming to your family." This response, while it isn't very effusive, tells Paige that Brad doesn't wish anything but the best for Paige and Paige's family.

A lack of empathy can serve as a red flag to people who are looking for it. If someone seems to find emotional connections hard to make, who doesn't know how to respond in such a way that the other person feels heard and understood, or who doesn't seem to understand emotion on a fairly basic level, it can serve as an alarm to those who are very effusive, empathetic, or emotionally sensitive. Emotional understanding and sensitivity can serve as the indicative antithesis of sociopathy or narcissism. If someone possesses all the abilities mentioned above, the likelihood of sociopathy or narcissism is historically and categorically much lower. People who deal with sociopathy often cannot understand or process emotion on the same levels as others. This can stunt the growth of personal relationships and can occasionally cause issues of crossing boundaries and harming others without remorse. This gives those suffering from sociopathy and narcissism a reputation that may or may not necessarily fit their usual behaviors.

When you're looking to size someone up at the beginning of your relationship with them, part of what you're taking into account is the way in which they respond to you. Do they seem cold and unfeeling, or do they seem warm and welcoming? A warmer, more welcoming demeanor is generally indicative of a more empathetic person. This is because they know how someone would generally prefer to be greeted. They know what it means to be new somewhere and how they would like to be treated, and make an effort to treat them in that way.

Having empathy and showing it for the people around you is far from a sign of weakness. It can make you seem like you're too kind, or that you wouldn't react badly to someone taking advantage or otherwise harming you. This is rarely the case, however. You may have heard the saying, "don't mistake my kindness for weakness." This applies here. Those who are generally more empathetic to people around them can detect malicious intent or anger toward them. This being said, those who have empathic abilities can generally get a feel for this type of inclination in the very early stages of knowing someone.

Thanks to this internal alarm, so to speak, it's easier for those who understand emotions, people, interpersonal relations, and empathy to make proper assessments of risk and danger with someone they've met and brought into their lives. Knowing what people are thinking is a superpower. Knowing what people are feeling can be exceedingly useful and can come pretty close to that superpower.

Knowing what empathy is, understanding it when you're feeling it, knowing how to hone that skill, and improving your sense of empathy can help you to improve your relationships with others in more ways than you can imagine. It's not until you start to grow your empathy response and use it often, that you really realize how much that ability permeates your entire life, your relationships, your work, your community, your family, and so many more aspects of your life.

How does Empathy Help us Survive?

Having empathy gives us the ability to know what is going on in the hearts of the people who are close to us. Having a very high empathic response means we know what's going on with those who are close to us in proximity. Having an average empathetic response means we know what's going on with those who are close to us in an emotional sense.

Sensing the anger, resentment, sadness, happiness, excitement, frustration, elation, or boredom of the people we're with can give us an upper hand we may not have even previously realized. For instance, if you can tell that someone is mad at you when they walk through the door, that could save you a little bit of trouble, couldn't it? You would know, walking into the conversation, that there was some frustration, upset feeling, or anger to address.

Knowing how someone needs to be addressed when you go into a conversation can cut out so much guesswork, and it can save you a lot of time. You don't need to dance around the issue. You won't end up ignoring the fact that they're mad and making it worse, and you'll be able to get the problem addressed in short order.

In many cases, when someone is upset, simply acknowledging that the person is upset can do a lot to diffuse that anger. Let's take a look at a scenario and how that works, shall we?

Steven walks into the room to talk to Phillip, his roommate. As soon as Steven walks into the room and sees Phillip's face, Steven knows that Phillip is upset. In order to test the waters, Steven says hello and asks how Phillip is doing. Phillip's response is that he's "fine," and then he immediately asks what Steven wants. "Fine; what do you want," is a pretty clear indicator that the person in front of you is mad at you, right? They're not asking how you're doing, they're not trying to make you feel welcome, and they aren't concerned with pleasantries.

From this response, Steven knows that Phillip's anger is directed toward him. It's not a general anger at something else going on in Phillip's life. This is an assumption, but it is safe to make this assumption until proven otherwise by statements or behaviors from Phillip.

This is the point in the conversation at which Steven deploys the ever-useful question: "What's wrong?" When you ask this question instead of "What did I do," it shows more concern for Phillip than it does self-preservation. Asking what you've done shows a defensive response for one's own behaviors and can make the person who is already upset, feel like they're attacking.

When asked what is wrong, Phillip tells Steven that he's just so angry at him for eating the last of the pastries his mother sent to the house. Phillip had been polite by offering some of those baked goods to the other people in the house, but that he didn't expect Steven to eat the last one without saying anything to Phillip.

Now, in the grand scheme of things, this could seem like a fairly banal problem, but it means a lot to Phillip. Knowing this and seeing how adversely this misstep has affected Phillip, Steven takes the initiative to appropriately and thoroughly apologize to Phillip for eating the last of the baked goods without saying please or thank you.

"Wow, I didn't even realize that it was the last one. I'm very sorry about that, Phillip. I never would have taken it if I had known that you wanted it, and I should have thanked you for sharing them with us in the first place. It was a very nice thing for you to do, and I did enjoy those pastries a lot. In the future, I'll be sure to ask before taking something that isn't mine. I'm very sorry for the misunderstanding."

This tells Phillip that he's been heard, that a mistake was made, that there is regret on Steven's part, and that he wishes to smooth things over and do better moving forward. This tells Phillip that he won't have to worry about it in the future and that his feelings on the subject do matter to the people who live in the house with him.

Had Steven not sensed that Phillip was upset with him, he might never have asked what was wrong, and might never have had the opportunity to apologize and make it right. Arguments that start over something this small end friendships and relationships all the time. Being vigilant and assuring that all parties are healthy and happy is a huge part of maintaining a friendship or personal relationship, no matter how low-maintenance they are.

Another important thing to realize about empathy is that we will tend to feel it more with certain parties than with others. It's possible to feel empathy for your best friend and none for your neighbor. It's possible to feel empathy for your mother and not your father. Your closeness with a person and your connection to that person have a good deal to do with your ability to tell what they're thinking, how they're feeling, and how best to approach them in every scenario.

Connecting and dealing with the people around us is a hefty part of our existence here on Earth. It's a good deal of what keeps our lives moving, and it's fairly impossible to go about life without dealing with at least a couple of people here and there. The more people you deal with and connect with, the more experience you will find that you have.

Surviving and having a life worth living should be considered synonymous in order to get along well in life. One can consider that the things they do, which contribute to a healthier, happier lifestyle, to be a survival tactic. You are surviving very well if your life is going very well. Your quality of life should directly correlate to how well you're surviving, right?

Using empathy to help you in life is innate, to some degree. Since empathy is a natural ability that we have, it can weave in and out of many varying parts of our lives. When you go to get an oil change and you can tell that the guy behind the counter is having a rough day, you might find that you'll ingratiate yourself to him by simply asking about it.

If you find that someone you see at the bank is quite happy, telling them that their smile brightened your day is a sure-fire way to keep that good feeling rolling for both of you. Making friends is a pretty great byproduct of being outgoing and empathetic at the same time as well. Using those two traits in tandem can bring you more success than you may previously have realized.

Sharing in the emotions that are felt by the people around you does so much to connect you with that person. It's part of why similar interests can bond people. Certain media, hobbies, or places can inspire similar emotions or feelings and that gives you a common ground. Understanding how someone's feeling gives you a lot of insight into that person's thought process as well. You don't have to worry about how they will take things that you tell them and you can rely on their mood behaving in a way you can predict.

Conversely, you can see how much stress someone adds to a relationship when they behave erratically, unpredictably, or have a volatile disposition. Someone who blows up at the most random, benign triggers introduces quite a lot of stress into the relationship. When you don't know what things someone will take issue with, misunderstand, yell about, or get upset over, it's impossible to adjust for those responses and take them into account. You will inevitably be taken by surprise when it comes to their emotional or verbal responses to various things in the environment.

As previously mentioned, one of the abilities that an empathic person has is the ability to know when someone around them has ill intentions. If someone near them is dangerous or means them harm, it's something that comes across in their emotional pattern. There is usually a base level of anger or resentment that can be picked up in such cases. People who are empathetic and who have honed that skill may also pick up on this.

This is something that can save you a lot of heartache, and it's something that can keep you from getting too close to the people around you who might not want what's best for you. In such cases, your empathy response can literally save your life.

Journaling Prompt:

If you were highly empathetic to someone around you and found that they were very upset, how would you handle it?

How to Recognize Empathic Abilities around You

People who have empathic abilities can tend to stand apart from the crowd if you know what you're looking for. In general, you will find that empathic people tend to be better listeners, better friends, less judgmental, more understanding, and they can usually tell how you're feeling without you telling them anything. Have you ever experienced this? Mothers usually have this uncanny ability to know that you're feeling a certain way in spite of efforts to hide them.

Let's take a look at an empathic person's response to someone around them who is stressed. Let's say that Tim is at work and he's stressed out because of a deadline at work that is approaching much faster than the project seems to be going. He plans to arrive early to work, stay late, and work weekends in order to make this deadline that's looming overhead.

Right as he begins to feel the stress, his supervisor Elliott is aware. He senses the stress that comes from having to buckle down for several days, burn the midnight oil, and keep his supervisors from seeing this scrambling. Because of this stress arising in the environment, Elliott calls a small department meeting to get an update from each of his team members on where they stand.

This gives him the opportunity to see each person, hear the way they talk about the projects that they have going on, and see the things they feel as they talk about them. During this meeting, he's in the room with several people, but he's taking care to address each of them individually, to connect with them, and to get a feel for the emotions that are occupying their mental space at that time.

Upon speaking with Tim, Elliott feels stress. He feels an urgency and he might even feel a little bit anxious or harried. Elliott gives Tim a kind smile and asks him to please take a seat in the conference room, make himself comfortable, and relax for a moment. Elliott's demeanor, control, and ease with the stress immediately imparts a little bit of calmness to Tim's mental space.

As each of the members of Elliott's department gets up to speak about the things they're working on in the current quarter, he is made aware of the things that are causing hiccups for his staff. He is made aware of the projects that are causing difficulty for them, and he's able to redistribute effort as is needed to ensure things are getting done in a timely manner and with as little strain on each member as possible.

When Tim describes each of the things he's working on, Elliott sees, hears, and feels the stress surrounding the most urgent project, its deadline, and the actions involved in completing that project on that deadline. Given that this is something the company needs by that deadline, that Tim is a human being with a life outside of work, and that he doesn't deserve to kill himself for the job, Elliott makes some impromptu adjustments.

Elliott asks Tiana to move some meetings around to help Tim with some of the research aspects of his project. He assigns one of the interns to Tim to help with coffee, copies, supply runs, etc. He assigns Keith, who has an eye for numbers, to help Tim check for the discrepancies that tend to hide from tired eyes. He extends their deadline by one day to give them as much time as possible to adjust, complete, and deliver.

Immediately, Tim has the resources he needs in order to deliver the project with more than enough time for everything they need. What does this mean for Tim? This means he arrives on time for work, that he leaves for home right at five, and that he will not be working weekends for the next two weeks. It might also mean some quality time to get to know Tiana and Keith!

This empathic person is able to assess the things that caused trouble for the people in his department. From there, he is able to tell who is well enough emotionally to jump in and help. This reallocation of resources means that no one works late, everyone gets paid for their efforts, and that everyone is able to have their lives outside of work with no worries.

Let's take a look at that same situation, but let's imagine that Elliott is simply empathetic, as opposed to empathic. Let's say that Tim is at work and he's stressed out because of a deadline at work that is approaching much faster than the project seems to be going. He has arrived to work early for each of the last several days, including weekends, has stayed late, and is still convinced that this deadline is going to get the best of him.

When his supervisor Elliott arrives, he sees Tim in the break room grabbing his third cup of coffee for the morning. Tim has been avoiding Elliott because he is concerned about what repercussions await him if Elliott finds out that things are not moving along as quickly as they ought to be for the deadline that's currently in place.

However, Elliott is well aware that he's been being avoided. He doesn't particularly know why, but he knows that he's been seeing Tim slink around corners just as Elliott enters a space, and he knows that all attempts to find Tim have happened to take place right as Tim found himself needing the restroom. Elliott, concerned for the person working in his department, makes it a point to arrive ten minutes early to catch Tim on his way into the office.

Of course, when Elliott sees Tim, he notices that his eyes are red, his hair is just slightly out of place, his tie is off-kilter, and that Tim looks worse for wear. Knowing he's been spotted and that there isn't a possibility to run away, Tim inadvertently takes on a look of fear and nervousness. All of which is glaringly obvious to the supervisor who knows what stress looks like.

This project that Tim is working on is due in just under one week, but Tim has been able to make an astronomical amount of progress in the time that he's spent on the project. The question in Tim's mind is whether or not he'll be able to last long enough for the project to get completed. One more week of sleepless nights just might be enough to put Tim out of commission for a while.

Elliott, aware that Tim is looking like he might keel over any moment, asks Tim to follow him into his office. Being an empathetic person, Elliott knows that healthy and happy people don't have eyes that are quite so red, and he knows that the kind of stress he can sense coming from Tim can't be healthy. He asks Tim to take a seat and tell him how he's doing this week.

When Tim describes how he's doing, he's not very specific. He says he's doing fine, which is an attempt to put a stop to the questions. From here, Elliott tells him that he is concerned by the color of his eyes. He tells him that it looks like he might not be getting enough rest and asks if that's the case and why that might be.

After some roundabout questioning, Tim lets it slip that the project is one week from the deadline, but that he's not certain of his ability to complete everything within the next 40 hours that he has allotted for it. He assures Elliott that he doesn't need to worry because Tim will be continuing his 12-hour days and weekends until it's completed.

Elliott feels immediately exhausted simply by hearing that notion and refuses to allow Tim to continue this unhealthy regimen of constant work and takes the coffee from his hands. He tells him that he should know for future reference that Tim is more than welcome to come to Elliott with things like this in the future. He tells him that if he knows in advance, he can reallocate resources and staff to get things rolling at a faster clip. He tells him, "I can't help if I don't know there's a problem." He tells him that if he had known a week and a half ago that if this was a problem, it would have been possible to ask the client for an extension.

All that being said, Elliott informs him that all is not lost and that there are still some things to be done to help with the project. Elliott rolls up his sleeves, has Tim lead him to the files on the project, and dives in with both feet. Over the course of the day, Tim, Elliott, and two interns get a good deal of progress made on the project and get through some major hurdles.

Over the course of the remaining time for the project, Tim, Elliott, and the interns work very studiously together to complete the project during business hours, ensuring that everyone gets a proper amount of sleep between shifts. By the time the deadline approaches, the project has been completed, the department head has signed off on it, and it's been returned to the client with an invoice for services rendered.

The company is happy, Tim, Elliott and the interns are happy, and the client is happy.

The differences between these two scenarios are largely on the focus of the empath and on the stage at which detection occurs. The empath is well aware of the problem as it approaches and is able to make provisions to avoid it. The empathetic person seems the problem as soon as he can and jumps in to get it resolved as quickly as possible.

Jumping in to resolve a problem is known as compassionate empathy. It's an empathetic response that causes us to spring into action to alleviate the troubles or strife of the people around us. It's the Good Samaritan response, it's the helping hand's response, and it's the things that drive us to resolve things for others.

Some people don't experience this calling or this compulsion and that's okay. One can be empathetic and can even care for others without jumping in to make changes to the things they're going through for them. People can even feel the compulsion to jump in and help without obeying that urge. To do so is sometimes the most logical response, depending on how dangerous circumstances may be, how much investment they may require, and how much you may have to contribute.

For instance: if someone is out of money and you're struggling to pay your own bills, you're not going to send that person money, right? If someone is terribly ill and needs someone to bring them some groceries for the week and you have a compromised immune system, you couldn't just walk in there and bring that person groceries. This is in spite of feeling that call to help. Sometimes staying removed from the solution for a problem is the best option.

There are often steps that you can take to help produce a solution without having to be directly involved. It's possible to call someone who is able to help, it's possible to have proper authorities handle something, and it's possible to simply talk to the person to let them know you're thinking of them. These things can all lead to potential solutions for problems that people are going through and you shouldn't feel like doing these things isn't the same as helping.

Just like Elliott said, "I can't help if I don't know there's a problem." Sometimes telling someone that there is a problem that needs to be addressed is the catalyst that gets the struggling person the help they need in order to get back up on their feet.

Knowing the person, their situation, what they need, and what they would prefer is a great first step to getting them the help they need.

Exercise:

Do You Know Someone who is Empathic?

Make a note of someone who you believe might be empathic, based on the information in this chapter. As you continue to learn more, use this person for the exercises to determine if you are correct.

Chapter 2: Empathy, a History

A Medical Investigation of Empathy and its Origin

When identifying the things that characterize compassion and empathy, and the parts of the brain that affect those responses, we are left to wonder if it's a matter of internal wiring or discipline. Is it possible to learn how to be compassionate? Is it possible to learn empathy? Or are we born with a specific threshold for these things that cannot be surpassed, no matter how many experiences and life lessons we have?

If there these can be learned or affected over time, are there daily habits, exercises, or regimens that can stave off or change selfishness, narcissism, sociopathy, and psychopathy? Are there daily habits that can reinforce or strengthen these conditions as well? If we can teach our children to think and act with compassion and empathy, then we owe it to future generations to do so.

In October of 2013, a study was done on the neurobiological roots for specific behaviors. This study by the Max Planck Institute for Human and Cognitive Brain Sciences discusses the ways in which the neurobiological roots of the feelings and experiences one has had can affect one's capacity for both empathy and compassion.

In September of 2013, a study that had been done by the University of Chicago shed light on the neurobiological roots of behaviors indicative of psychopathy. In tandem, the information we get from the premises of these two studies offers key clues for ways in which we can reinforce and improve empathetic and compassionate responses on a neural level. From these two studies, researchers learned that empathy and compassion *can be learned.*

In that first study mentioned above, conducted in October of 2013, the *Journal of Neuroscience* reported that Max Planck researchers concluded that the inclination toward egocentric behavior is innate in human beings. Immediately following this conclusion, however, was the conclusion that one has a part of the brain that identifies a lack of empathy and forces a course correction in such cases that are influenced by one's egocentric behaviors and thought processes.

The part of the brain we have to thank for our humility in such cases is known as the right supramarginal gyrus. In situations in which the right supramarginal gyrus doesn't kick in, or in cases in which it doesn't have the opportunity to do so (quick thinking and snap decisions), researchers found that the presence of empathy in such decisions was dramatically reduced. This portion of the brain is responsible for the analysis of emotion and helps us to make a distinction between the emotional state imposed by our own thinking and circumstances and the emotional state of someone else. This portion of the brain is responsible for both empathy and compassion.

The supramarginal gyrus, a portion of the cerebral cortex, is located right about at the junction of the parietal, temporal, and frontal lobes. Claus Lamm, one of the authors of the paper written following this study explains, "This was unexpected, as we had the temporoparietal junction in our sights. This is located more towards the front of the brain."

The team of researchers taking the reins on this study was led by Tania Singer and had this to say: "When assessing the world around us and our fellow humans, we use ourselves as a yardstick and tend to project our own emotional state onto others. While cognition research has already studied this phenomenon in detail, nothing is known about how it works on an emotional level. It was assumed that our own emotional state can distort our understanding of other people's emotions, in particular, if these are completely different from our own. But this emotional egocentricity had not been measured before now."

The right supramarginal gyrus is the part of the brain that works to show us the differences between our perceptions of ourselves and the perceptions of others. During the course of the study conducted by Singer and her team, neurons in the right supramarginal gyrus were disrupted while the participants completed tasks assigned by the team. Throughout these tasks, the participants displayed great difficulty in keeping themselves from projecting their own emotions and circumstances onto others. The assessments made by participants also appeared to be less accurate when they were made to decide very quickly on something.

One of the more interesting conclusions that the study by Max Planck Institute for Human and Cognitive Brain Sciences was that those who are living a more luxurious, more lavish lifestyle tend to have a lower threshold and a diminished capacity for empathy. When one finds oneself in the "lap of luxury," so to speak, one finds oneself having more difficulty with empathizing with someone's struggles, their inabilities to get by, and their hardships.

Those who have found themselves exposed to more agreeable or pleasant stimuli on a consistent basis were found to have a lower neurobiological response to hardship on those around them. This means that on a chemical level, their supramarginal gyrus wasn't found to be functioning properly. Thanks to this, putting oneself in the shoes of another to experience what they're experiencing is much more difficult when life is exceedingly easy for one.

The way Singer's team tested this was by pairing their participants. Each set of participants was subjected to a perception experiment, wherein one half of each pair was exposed to stimuli that were either pleasant or unpleasant. One person would be subjected only to pleasant visual and tactile stimuli that were presented simultaneously. The other participant would be subjected only to unpleasant visual and tactile stimuli that were presented simultaneously.

In the experiment, participant A was given a soft, plush fabric to feel with her hands while she was shown pictures of puppies. When participant B underwent the experiment, she was handed a slimy substance and shown pictures of bugs and larvae. A was given the pleasant stimuli while B was given the unpleasant stimuli. The reason it was important to combine tactile and visual stimuli is that with visual stimuli only, the brain has a way of detaching itself from the experience. It's not registering any feelings to go along with the visual that's causing disgust or disturbance, so the body is okay, and it can move on from there. By introducing the tactile element to the experiment, this immerses the brain in a situation that is either positive (enjoyable) or negative (uncomfortable). Another very important aspect of this experiment is that the participants could always see the stimuli to which the other was subjected. Participant B could see the puppies on A's screen and the plush fabric in her hand, and vice versa.

In order to gauge the empathetic response from both sides, part of the experiment also focused on the subject of commiseration. This would come about by subjecting one participant to one set of stimuli that were unpleasant, whilst simultaneously subjecting the other participant to another set of unpleasant stimuli. This gave the participants a chance to see the same nature of experience from a different perspective.

In the experiment, each participant was asked to give a short assessment of their own emotions in comparison to those of the person sitting next to them. In cases in which the participants were exposed to the same types of stimuli, the participants found it easy to assess how the other one was doing. If both participants were exposed to varying types of negative stimuli, A could very accurately assess how the negative stimuli were affecting B. The same was true of B for A in cases where both were exposed to negative stimuli as well.

The largest change in empathetic response came from the portion of the experiment during which the participants were subjected to different types of stimuli. When one participant was given pleasant circumstances, and the other participant was given unpleasant circumstances, the participants' capacity for empathy plummeted when provided with pleasant stimuli. The emotions of the person with pleasant stimuli were causing a distortion in their perception of what the other participant was going through.

What this means is that when participant A was experiencing pleasant stimuli while participant B was experiencing unpleasant stimuli, participant A had a tendency to underestimate the severity of B's circumstances. Their assessments of B's conditions were a good deal more positive than what B was exhibiting. In contrast to this, participant B's assessment of the circumstances and the feelings of participant A were much less positive than they were.

Historically, the assumption has been that people rely solely on their own emotions as a point of reference for empathy. However, this appears to be the case solely in cases wherein the right supramarginal gyrus isn't functioning to curtail the egocentric processes to which we are naturally predisposed. Otherwise, we must count on being in the exact same neural state and circumstances as our counterparts in order to be able to put ourselves into their shoes with no help from the right supramarginal gyrus.

From this study, we can deduce that the supramarginal gyrus is an essential part of developing empathy and compassion for the people we encounter in life. In addition to this, we can deduce that someone who has a lower amount of activity in their supramarginal gyrus might not feel as much compassion or empathy for someone who is in a situation that is even remotely dissimilar to their own.

Now, when we investigate the neurological basis for lack of empathy, we are directed to the personality disorder psychopathy. This disorder is characterized by a lack of remorse or empathy, as well as glibness, callousness, manipulation of others, as well as something called shallow affect.

Shallow affect is when someone exhibits a very low response to emotional stimuli or situations. Things like joy, anger, sadness, surprise, happiness, and other emotions that are usually very visible, seem to produce very little physical effects on the person. They can come across as emotionally monotonous or even very apathetic about things that would generally invoke an emotional response.

Researchers who have conducted experiments on participants with psychopathy were looking for the brain's response to certain scenarios. For instance, brain function was monitored when these participants were asked to imagine someone in severe pain. The portions of the brain that are typically necessary for feeling empathy, concern, and compassion for others failed to activate in such cases, which affected the connected regions that are involved in affective processing and compassionate decision making.

One study that was done by the Department of Psychology at the University of Chicago in September 2013 may have found the neurological roots for psychopathic tendencies. This study was published in the journal *Frontiers in Human Neuroscience* in that same year.

In this study, when participants with severe psychopathy imagine situations in which pain was inflicted on themselves, they showed the neural response that would be considered typical for producing empathy for those in pain. The areas that showed increased activity included the anterior insula, the anterior midcingulate cortex, somatosensory cortex, and the right amygdala. The responses produced in these regions of the brain were not negligible in scale. These responses were generally quite pronounced, which suggested that the psychopathic participants are as sensitive to the idea of pain as neurotypical subjects, but that the psychopathic participants were unable to imagine themselves in the place of another and experiencing that pain for them on any sort of automatic basis.

When the same highly psychopathic participants imagined the pain being inflicted upon or befalling others, these regions failed to become active. Interestingly, when highly psychopathic participants were asked to imagine others in pain, they showed an increase in the ventral striatum. This is an area of the brain commonly active during moments of pleasure.

The tool used to determine these things was the PCL-R, which is a diagnostic tool that is typically used in a wide number of studies to determine varying degrees of psychopathic behavior. Based on the assessment conducted with this tool in this particular study, the participants were divided into groups of about 40 people each, which were then given the designations of highly, moderately, and mildly psychopathic.

The previous theory about psychopathy in prisons vastly overestimated the percentage of the general population with psychopathy. It was previously estimated that about 23% of prison inmates were psychopathic, while more recent data points to an average of only 1%. In order to get a better understanding of the neurological basis for lack of empathy, or dysfunctional empathetic response in those with psychopathy, neuroscientists utilized functional magnetic resonance imaging on the brains of over 120 inmates in a medium-security prison.

This study required that participants be shown an array of photographs so their neurological responses could be measured. Visual scenarios were provided to illustrate physical pain like getting a toe stuck under something heavy or a finger caught in the door. Once they were shown these things, they were asked to imagine that this incident had occurred to them personally or to someone else. Among the visuals given to the inmates were images of a benign nature, such as a hand on a doorknob.

Researchers and neuroscientists believe that finding answers as to the neurobiological origins of the empathetic response and the psychopathic tendencies could shed valuable light on an area that is overwhelmed by therapeutic pessimism. This means that psychopathy has more or less been written off as untreatable or treatment-resistant in past studies, which has caused many researchers and neuroscientists to do less to pursue answers and treatment for those patients.

Understanding the neural pathways that are key and most active in the empathetic response could be the answer to targeting those areas of the brain and treating them, so psychopathic behavior is significantly lowered. Treating and mitigating psychopathic behavior could mean a lower rate of violent crime and a better quality of life for those suffering from psychopathy.

The authors of the paper on the above research experiment had this to say: "Imagining oneself in pain or in distress may trigger a stronger affective reaction than imagining what another person would feel, and this could be used with some psychopaths in cognitive-behavior therapies as a kick-starting technique.

The goal of these experiments and indeed of neuroscience, in general, is to see into the human brain, understand what's going on inside it under certain circumstances, and to better understand the human mind. With the knowledge we gain from the experiments done in neuroscience, we can make changes to our daily habits, behaviors, routines, and shape our mindsets and neural circuitry to better accommodate effective and positive human interaction on a consistent basis.

One's capacity for empathy and compassion is never a static thing, thanks to neuroplasticity. Neuroplasticity is your brain's ability to reform synaptic pathways and patterns based on new information, new skills learned, or even following an injury. Practicing certain actions over an extended period of time is the way for your brain to decide what pathways need to be reworked, rearranged, and changed. By this logic, we would all do well to practice putting ourselves in someone's unique position on a consistent basis to allow those neural networks to rearrange to allow for a more consistent empathetic response to the people around us.

This isn't a guaranteed change, but efforts in this direction will often do more than doing nothing. There aren't simple, clear-cut answers for how to elevate consciousness and the empathetic responses. Outlook, however, for those who dedicate themselves to the pursuit of those daily tasks that will bring them a little closer to the people around them, is pretty positive. As with many pursuits, utilizing as many techniques as possible will only improve your results and the longevity of those results. Treating one's brain like a muscle that needs to be worked out on a routine basis is a great way to keep yourself going in the right direction and improving the areas that are important to you.

Historical Information

The concept of empathy, when compared to other concepts, is relatively new. As such, the very definition of empathy, its place in society, and its importance to the progress of mankind are still the subject of debate amongst philosophers, scientists, economists, journalists, doctors, and more. In fact, it was only between 2014 and 2015 that two articles were published arguing the subject.

In a column for *The New York Times*, journalist Nicholas Kristof named the "empathy gap" in society as a problem with understanding the myriad circumstances that could thrust someone into the throes of poverty and their numerous complexities. Psychologist Paul Bloom, however, submitted an article that was posted in the *Boston Review,* which stated that a sense of empathy can be too narrow of a view. Because of empathy's general focus is on the people closest to us, and to the situations we can conceive of on an individual basis, it precludes us from being able to fully grasp the impact of things that may have a larger scale of impact. Bloom stated in his article that a sense of empathy can be "parochial [and] bigoted," which could lead to a situation in which "the whole world cares more about a little girl stuck in a well than they do about the possible deaths of millions and millions due to climate change."

Now, this statement isn't to spur an argument about a hot-button issue, or even to say that those who are deeply empathetic are incapable of being understanding the gravity and impact of something on such a large scale. This is to say, however, that the general concept of empathy has been defined and focused in such a targeted way, that we can miss out on the bigger picture if we aren't careful.

For Nicholas Kristof, empathy is defined as a willingness and the capability to grasp the situation and circumstances of someone. This is an exercise in cognitive and emotional ability that can spur compassion for the people in those situations when it's warranted. For Paul Bloom, empathy is an emotion. In addition to this, it's an emotion that can cloud one's thinking and can preclude one from achieving more analytical and rational thought about things that are going on in society and the world around one.

Kristof's theory suggests that having more empathy makes us more able to think of people as individuals and less prone to seeing other people as background in our lives. Bloom's theory suggests that seeing people on such an individualistic basis can keep one from being able to conceive of the scale on which many of our actions as a society will have an impact. How you perceive empathy and what it means for you will shape your opinion on this and it will give you more of an idea of how empathy can benefit or hamper you.

Now, looking at the origin of the word "empathy," we find that it's a relatively new one. The word came into being just at the beginning of the twentieth century and was the result of a translation of a German paper on psychology, which contained the word *Einfühlung*. Literally translated, this word means "feeling-in."

Once this paper was released in English-speaking psychologist circles, the word was retranslated into things such as "animation," "aesthetic," "play," "semblance," and "aesthetic sympathy." It wasn't until 1908 that two psychologists from the University of Cambridge and Cornell suggested that word *Einfühlung* should be translated as "empathy," which they took from the Green "em" for "in" and "pathos" for "feeling." This translation made the most sense, given the context, and it has since stuck with the community.

In spite of how well this translation and derivation fits today's concept of empathy, the concept was quite different when the term was first coined. In the early 1900s, if a patient had empathy, they were projecting imagined feelings onto things and people around them. Projection as a concept gained its own place in psychology and was discovered to be quite a different response from empathy in later years.

It was about mid-century when empathy's definition began to come into its own and shift as more social relationships and interactions were studied. It was 1948 when sociologist Leonard Cottrell and experimental psychologist Rosalind Dymond Cartwright collaborated to conduct tests to measure empathy on an interpersonal basis.

In this pursuit, Dr. Cartwright made it a point to reject the contemporary definition of empathy and to center the focus of the concept of interpersonal connection. As it happens, what was originally called "empathy," is now known as "imaginative projection," and has been studied at length as well. Thanks to Cartwright's rejection and pursuant refocusing of the concept, we now have a greater understanding of the mechanics of interpersonal relations, their importance, and we are even coming to understandings of how to improve all of those elements.

This new focus inspired a slew of experimental studies of the newly defined concept of empathy. From here, psychologists began to pointedly differentiate between true empathy—which was stated to be an appraisal of the thoughts and feelings of someone else, which was typically accurate—and projection. Following these studies, the concept of empathy began to enter the purview of general society when *Reader's Digest* defined the concept for its readers in 1955. Before this point, the concept of empathy had simply been known in medical and doctoral circles as an esoteric and abstract concept. Rightly so, since they hadn't quite nailed it down until such time as the definition was explained to the public.

The definition provided to readers by *Reader's Digest* in 1955 was "the ability to appreciate the other person's feelings without yourself becoming too emotionally involved that your judgment is affected." Now, when we think of empathy, we tend to deal with the emotional and physical responses that come about as a result of that understanding you get from the other person. Sometimes we spring into action, sometimes we talk to the person, and on rare occasions we do nothing with it at all. However, it might be foolish to think that our personal judgments are not affected in any way by our understanding of what is being experienced by the people around us.

When the person we're thinking about is particularly close to us, our empathetic response can often cause us to make judgments as a result. This is not to say that the things we do will be negative as a result of that judgment, but it is to say that those judgments would be impossible to make without that empathetic response in the first place, you see.

In the decades since that publication, more interest in the subject of empathy has been generated among people outside of psychological circles and has spread into primatological, and neuroscientific circles. In the 1990s, neuroscientists began studies on monkeys and discovered mirror neurons. These are cells in their brains that fired when the animal moved, as well as when the monkey saw another make the same exact movements. This discovery prompted much new research into empathy and related brain activity. This was then expanded into the same studies conducted with humans as well. As studies have continued on brain activity and empathy, the concept of empathy has spread into other fields that were previously thought to have no connection. As we've been learning more about what empathy is, what it means, how it's used, and what it influences, people in fields such as economics, literature, politics, art, and more have seen a rise in this topic of discussion.

As we can see in debates that have taken place as recently as 2014-2015 (as illustrated by Bloom and Kristof), there is still quite a bit of cultural debate surrounding the subject of empathy, what it means, and its impact. In the psychological field, this is no less accurate. There are critics who question the theory behind mirror neurons, their location in the human brain, and whether or not the simulation of the gestures of someone else is a display or indication of empathy in any capacity.

Social psychologist C. Daniel Batson has researched the topic of empathy for decades and makes the argument that the term empathy can apply to eight different subjects or concepts. Those concepts are:

1. Knowing the thoughts and feelings of another.
2. Imagining the thoughts and feelings of another.
3. Adopting someone else's posture.
4. Physically feeling the sensations of another.
5. Imagining how you would personally feel in another's place or situation.
6. Feeling distressed because of the suffering of another.
7. Pity or compassion.
8. Projecting yourself into their situation.

You may have thought of all these concepts as being a part of empathy, or some of them might be new to you. Understanding the path was traveled by psychologists who strove to understand the human mind and how it works gives us a context that can help us better understand the concepts of empathy, human emotion, and how far-reaching that subject really is.

Classification of Empaths

In the years since psychologists have delivered a more relevant and workable explanation for empathy, the understanding of people with a more heightened empathetic response has been made possible. It is prudent to mention that, like with the subject of empathy, the subject of empaths is still up for debate in the world of psychology and psychiatry. Those who have first-hand experience with empaths, their abilities, proclivities, and tendencies tend to have a firmer belief that what is being experienced is deeper than the base level of empathy that is considered to be typical.

There is a good deal of scientific data from psychological studies and experiments that point us in the direction of understanding the mechanisms that are at work in the empathetic and empathic responses we experience.

In the section above, we mentioned the subject of mirror neurons. These neurons are a specialized group of brain cells that are networked and wired to be responsible for the compassion we feel for others. It wasn't terribly long ago, in the grand scheme of things, that these neurons were discovered. It is these cells that enable one to "mirror" or "reflect" the emotions that are felt by someone aside from ourselves. By being able to simulate these emotions, we're more able to understand them, their effects, and how to deal with them.

Empaths put these systems to work overtime. These neural pathways and networks have been discovered to be much more active in people who consider themselves to be or who have displayed traits of being empathic. Thanks to the hypersensitivity in this neural network, empaths tend to experience a much deeper resonance from the emotions experienced by those around us. Mirror neurons are specifically triggered by outside stimuli. This means that things happening in our direct environments are the only things that will cause these neurons to fire. They aren't influenced by how badly we want to feel what someone else is feeling, and they're not influenced by our perception of the outside events.

This is the data that amounts to empaths feeling the things that others feel. This is what causes empaths to feel hurt when others do, to cry when others cry, to laugh when others laugh, etc. as a matter of contrast, when someone who is considered sociopathic or psychopathic is tested on this same basis, those mirror neurons aren't firing except for at a fraction of what empaths' do. Since these personalities are considered to be deficient in empathy and compassion, we have taken to studying the parts of the brain that contribute to or are connected to these responses.

The mirror neuron system is indicative of how much empathy is being felt. The right supramarginal gyrus is a part of the brain that influences how much empathy is being felt. Think of it as part of your car. The speedometer is telling you *how fast* your car is going, but it doesn't contribute to accelerating at all. The gas pedal, however, is the thing that tells the accelerator to move in one direction or the other. The mirror neurons are your speedometer, and the right supramarginal gyrus is your gas pedal.

Empaths have a notably higher read on their speedometer and a notably more sensitive gas pedal.

Another current theory behind the cause for higher sensitivity in empaths has to do with sensitivity to the electromagnetic fields that are naturally produced around the brain and the heart. According to the HeartMath Institute, there is information regarding our thoughts and feelings in these naturally-produced electromagnetic fields that could be picked up on by highly sensitive and empathic people.

Something that lends some credence to this theory is that people who are considered to be empathic tend to have more sensitivity in the shifts in the electromagnetic fields that surround the Earth and the sun. Shifts in these fields have been found to affect the feelings, behaviors, and wellbeing of empathic people.

Understanding empaths, how they work, what they do, and what they deal with becomes a little bit easier when we take into account, the theory of emotional contagion. This is the phenomenon wherein the highly sensitive or empathic person picks up on the emotions of the people around them. This has also been found to affect people who do not consider themselves to be highly sensitive. It has been found that people who are neurotypical can pick up on how someone is feeling simply by being near them, whether they are cognizant of that or not. For instance, one could be in the presence of someone who is elated while having no idea what they're in that presence. However, they can find themselves suddenly feeling much happier and brighter without any known cause. This is the theory of emotional contagion at work. Unfortunately, this phenomenon works for the more negative side of the emotional spectrum as well.

Groups tend to exemplify this phenomenon, as well. In general, you will find that one group of people that are all co-mingling will generally share the same emotion or "vibe." When one person in the group gets excited, the rest tend to follow. When one person gets upset, the rest of the group tends to respond in kind. One article in *The New York Times* suggested that this emotional synchronicity is vital to healthy personal relationships.

So, what is the lesson that empaths should take from this phenomenon? Being more prone to taking on the emotions of those whom they keep close, it is prudent for the empath to be very selective about the types of people they allow into their circles. Allowing negative people into one's circles if one is empathic can lead to a good deal of pain, difficulty, or worse. Having positive people in one's circles when it is quite sensitive or empathic will give one a more positive starting point. In addition to this, it is vital for the empath to keep a keen eye on which emotions are their own and which are coming from another while offering help to someone who is going through a rough patch in life.

Another notable trait of the empath in a scientific sense is an increased sensitivity to dopamine. Dopamine is a neurotransmitter that causes an increase in neuron activity, and which is commonly associated with the pleasure response. Research on this topic tells us that empaths who tend to be more introverted have a higher sensitivity to dopamine than those who are extroverted. In layman's terms, this translates to an introverted empath needing far less dopamine to be much happier. This could explain why people who are more introverted tend to get a "battery recharge" from solitary activities like reading, games, puzzles, meditation, and other activities that don't depend as much on outside stimulation and interaction.

Conversely, people who are generally more extroverted tend to pursue interactions and more live events that bring on a much more intense "rush" of dopamine within the brain. Those who are extroverted tend to seem as though they are always looking for things that will increase that dopamine output, as they thrive on a steady, or at least regular flow of dopamine through their system on a consistent basis.

When one considers the concept of synesthesia, one might not immediately think of the empath and their abilities. Synesthesia, for those not in the know, is a condition characterized by the pairing or close association of two different senses within the brain. Some common experiences of synesthesia are seeing particular colors when certain musical pieces are heard, tasting certain things when certain words are spoken, and more. Billy Joel and Isaac Newton are two prominent people who have this fascinating condition.

There is a type of synesthesia that is called mirror-touch synesthesia. This is the neurological condition in which one can actually feel the emotions and sensations of another person as though they are one's own. This was an extraordinary finding that seemed to lend a good deal of credence to the things highly sensitive people and empaths have been experiencing for centuries. Having a name to put to the experience and having professionals in neuroscience who understand this phenomenon has contributed a great deal to the confidence and improvement in mental health for those who deal with the emotions and sensations of those around them on a daily basis.

Being made to feel things that you have no other connection to or to deal with those sensations when you have no personal connection to them can be frustrating, confusing, alarming, and more. There has been little support for those who are dealing with these things until very recently and there has been very little understanding of this condition, which has been and still is lumped in with mysticism and more fanciful or fantastical subjects than neuroscience. Having that understanding and support makes a world of difference for those who are more sensitive to these happenings than others.

Chapter 3: How to Spot an Empath

The Many Traits of an Empath

1. **Strong emotional content on television has a profound impact on you.**

   Have you ever been minding your own business, watching television or scrolling through social media, only to find yourself bawling your eyes out in the next moment because of something that happened on the screen? If you're like me, the things that do it the most are people paying surprise visits to loved ones, cute animal videos, and television shows that have a lot of love or death in them.

   This type of content is definitely meant to evoke an emotional response from the people who watch them, but those who are highly sensitive know what it's like to be sitting there trying to enjoy a television show and suddenly feel overwhelmed with emotion.

2. **People are always asking you for advice.**

   Having a lot of friends who want to "pick your brain," "bounce things off you," or "get your take," can tell that you're in-tune emotionally and consciously. They can tell that the things you see are things that others cannot see, and they wish to take advantage of your unique vantage point.

This is not to say there is anything disingenuous about their interest in your view, but they do want your take on things, and they want to know what you would do in this situation. Being a sensitive person or an empath gives you the reputation of being trustworthy and emotionally intelligent.

3. **Intimate relationships can overtake all of your thinking, and the energy you get from them flows throughout your entire life.**

Some who are empaths or highly sensitive decide to stay single because of this. Personal relationships take a lot of work, maintenance, investment, and communication under the best and most "normal" circumstances. When one of the parties is an empath or a highly sensitive person, it can put a little extra weight on things.

You will find that empaths and highly sensitive people will do their best to very quickly address and resolve any emotional conflict in the relationship because, when those come up, they envelop every aspect of that person's life.

If this is you, you might find yourself having trouble eating, sleeping, thinking, working, or doing *anything* while there's an unresolved conflict in your relationship. Finding someone who is as ready to resolve conflicts as you are is a very key part of making a relationship work as an empath.

4. Your sensitivity could be mislabeled as anxiety or shyness.

Empaths and highly sensitive people can often—as discussed elsewhere in this list—find themselves being very introspective or can have sudden and seemingly adverse reactions to very mundane or minimal stimuli. As a result of these factors and some others, it can be possible for doctors, loved ones, friends, or acquaintances to assume that there is something mentally askew or unbalanced. Autism, anxiety, shyness, introversion, and depression are among some of the false suggestions that have been made for those who are highly sensitive to the emotions and sentiments of the people around them.

5. Regardless of introversion or extroversion, you withdraw often.

Being highly sensitive and being an empath can make personal interactions very taxing and exhausting. As a result of this, as well as other factors, the empath will find a great amount of benefit in creating some time in which they can be by themselves and "recharge their batteries."

Solitary relaxation activities like coloring, reading, meditating, personal hygiene and care regimens, journaling, listening to music, and games can all be great recharging activities.

Because of this semi-frequent need for solitude and seclusion, people may perceive you as reclusive or introverted, in spite of being very interested in talking with others, being outgoing, and making friends when you go out.

6. When thinking of leadership roles, you always assume that means putting the team first.

As an empath, not putting others first is a pretty foreign concept as a general rule. It is hard for an empath to be centered on themselves, and they perceive leaders as the people who are supposed to help the group get to where it needs to be. This means that the leader must ask the team to complete tasks they would not be unwilling or unable to do themselves, in order to achieve a goal that they could not do as individuals.

When a leader shows narcissism or self-preservation, it can elicit a disgusted or outraged response from an empath or highly sensitive person. By the estimation of such a person, a leader should be the guardian and custodian of the group they're leading before anything else.

7. The world you've created in your mind is rich and vibrant.

Many empaths and highly sensitive people have been thinking, daydreaming, imagining, thinking, positing, and hypothesizing since their childhoods. Because of this, they have unspoken theories and mental models regarding the world around them, they have little stories in their minds, and they may have characters they think about on a regular basis.

The imagined ecosystem in the mind of the empath is vibrant, teeming with life that's both new and old, and is always coming up with something new to throw out in the event of downtime, or just a little too much silence in the room.

8. Others find your very presence to be calming.

Due to the empath's ability to "tap into" the emotional frequency and thought patterns of the people around them, it can tend to have a very calming effect on the people who are near them. If someone is sad, scared, agitated, or experiencing a negative emotion, they will feel an alleviation from your being there.

This is due in part to the fact that when others who are not highly sensitive experience someone who is feeling a deeply troubling emotion, they have questions. They're curious, scared, put off, or otherwise unaware of what's happening.

Someone who is an empath or a highly sensitive person knows exactly what's happening and knows how the person wants to be responded to in that moment. That alone does so much to calm the mind of someone dealing with a strong, negative emotional response.

9. Hunger very quickly turns into anger, sometimes even before hunger.

You've probably heard the term "hangry" before. This is a colloquial term to identify that irrational anger that people can tend to feel when their blood sugar has dipped a little too low, and they need to eat something right away or they will bite someone's head off over something mundane.

This is very uncharacteristic behavior for the person, but it's something they seemingly can't control in traffic, or at the grocery store when they've just gone a couple of hours too far without a sandwich.

People who are highly sensitive to their own feelings, emotions, and bodily stimuli might find that this happens to them a little more often than they might be comfortable with admitting.

10. You're highly sensitive to wardrobe malfunctions.

This is one that bothered me a lot as a child. Did you ever get to school and notice something like the scratchy tag inside your shirt, itchy wool in your sweater, a popped seam on your sock, or underpants that were just a tiny bit too tight?

For most people, things like this will eventually fade into the background of the day when something that's more pressing or important takes the stage. For some empaths and highly sensitive people, this feeling does not ever go away.

We can tug at the clothes, re-fold the tag, turn up the music, really throw ourselves into whatever it is we're doing, and it will feel like the volume on these issues just gets cranked up another notch as more mental stimuli creep in over the course of the day.

11. Criticism is painful beyond reason.

For the empath and the highly sensitive person, criticism can feel like a slap in the face. Rest assured that every empath has worked on seeing it differently, looking at it from a helpful angle and trying to get help from it that there is to get. Some have succeeded, but it's a large hurdle that many have to really try to get over.

Those who offer constructive criticism of our creative pursuits are rarely trying to hurt us with that criticism. We do know this on a cognitive level, but there's always going to be that initial shock and sting from the delivery of that statement.

12. You feel an overwhelming love for pets, animals, or babies.

You may be familiar with something called "cute aggression," or you might know someone who gets tears in their eyes when looking at something that's "So cute I can't handle it." This is a trait of a highly sensitive person.

There is an overwhelming feeling of excitement, happiness, joy, love, and about a million other things that bubble up when you see someone or something that is adorable, and you freak out a little bit.

Some people might view this response as a little "extra," but how can you not gush over how cute the little tiny corgi puppy is!

13. You're exceedingly perceptive, and minor details don't escape you easily.

As you go through your day, there will often be small details that stick out to you like a sore thumb. When you bring them up to the people around you, you might say things in response like, "how did you even see that?" To you, however, it might seem like something that you couldn't possibly have missed.

Those things that you notice tend to make others see you as a detail-oriented person who has an eye for the minutia or projects. In the workplace, this can be a great advantage and it looks great on a resume.

14. You're prone to jumping or startling easily.

If you find that sudden loud noises make you jump more than they should, you should be a highly sensitive person. Furthermore, if you find that this trait lessons when you're particularly drained, exhausted, tired, or depressed, that jumpiness is rooted more in your higher sensitivity.

It would be nice if being more sensitive to things, being more aware of small or minute details, and being less able to be lied to meant we weren't easily startled. Instead of this, however, we find ourselves so completely immersed in the things that we do in every moment that when something comes up to snap us out of it, we can become quite jarred or unsettled.

15. Once startled, you may be shaken for a while or experience "aftershocks."

Have you ever been startled in a really big way, perhaps as a joke by a friend or loved one, only to feel "aftershocks," or shivers afterward? It might feel like you're anticipating it happening again, every part of you tenses up for just a quick moment, then you can go about what you were doing.

Being an empath means you're aware of a lot of things. Being aware of so many things comes to be something that we rely on from day to day and when we're suddenly and loudly confronted with something of which we weren't aware, it can catch us off-guard in a big way.

The systems in the body can sometimes seem as though they're trying to overcompensate for that lack of awareness by being hyper-aware after the fact. Cognitively we know that this wasn't the intention of the person who startled us, we know that being hyper-vigilant now won't help, and we know that it won't likely happen again. This does not, however, quash that response.

16. Stimulants are very effective in short measure.

An empath or a highly sensitive person might find that one cup of coffee can do a great deal to "light a fire under them," so to speak. With all the nervous responses being more highly tuned in and with all the sensitivities being raised, it makes sense that a little bit of a stimulant would go a long way.

Be careful of the stimulants you take into your body and be sure not to overdo it. Overuse of caffeine and other stimulating substances can cause anxiety and other issues in the mind and body if left unchecked. Try to limit how much you take on and see if you notice any differences.

17. Depressants are very effective in short measure.

Just like with stimulants, depressants will take effect very quickly and will often last. Alcohol might hit a little harder for people who are highly sensitive. In addition to this, certain substances in the body could fail to have the intended effect and just make you feel ill.

It's prudent to be dubious of new substances and take only what is prescribed by a medical professional.

18. It's easy for you to get a feel for where someone is coming from when telling you something.

When someone is explaining something to you, you might have an idea of exactly what they mean within the first few seconds of them talking. This can trip you up from time to time when you're ready to move onto the next phase of the conversation, but the person in front of you is still working on explaining things that you've already grasped.

It's important to recognize this mechanism at work and to be kind in such an event. Most people don't understand how you could possibly know the things you know and cutting off the communication of someone who is trying to work with you is a very fast way to complicate the relationship.

19.You do a lot of introspection and deep thinking.

People might find you "zoning out," or "spacing out" on a semi-regular basis. People who are highly sensitive and who are empaths will often find that there's a good deal of things going on behind the scenes, so to speak. There are a lot of thoughts about the things going on in your life, the things that are going on with your friends and family, or the scenario in your head could be completely hypothetical.

20. Pain sets in more easily.

Without any medical diagnosis like fibromyalgia, arthritis, dermatitis, or anything else, it would seem that things just hurt you a little more easily. I have met someone whose legs in particular, if touched just a little too hard, she would flinch from pain.

No bruising or otherwise alarming indicators of anything wrong with her body, other than pain that occurred very quickly and in a very sharp way. Hip checking a table while walking past it could thoroughly ruin her afternoon, or at least part of it!

Are there any areas of your body that are particularly sensitive?

21. You ask the big questions in life and seek a lot of answers about the status quo.

"Why are things the way they are," is a pretty common big question to ask. It's very broad, it has a lot of answers, and it could keep you busy pondering for days on end. However, the questions that an empath will find themselves asking have to do with life's deeper subjects, as well as some that might be hard to articulate until they've been mulled over for a good long while.

Have you ever wondered about something, but you had no idea how to broach it with someone to discuss it with them? Or thought that you could figure out how to word the question, but you doubted very much that they would be interested or see you normally after you asked it?

22. You find cruelty and violence to be abhorrent.

Being in-tune with the emotions, feelings, and pains of others, it's easy for us to put ourselves in the shoes of someone being brutalized, without ever meaning to. When we watch the news, we see people going through worse pain than can be imagined, but we're right there alongside them.

Watching someone who is at a severe disadvantage being neglected, harmed, or otherwise sustaining any measure of cruelty will often rattle someone who is highly sensitive. This might be the kind of thing you choose to remove from your television watching, or it might be something you do your best to avoid even in conversation.

When these things happen around you, you might find yourself overwhelmingly compelled to jump into the thick of it and do something about it.

23. You feel ailments or illnesses as someone you love is going through them.

It's possible that you've hears of "sympathy illness," or "sympathy pains." This is when someone with whom you're very in-tune is going through something painful or sickening and you, as someone who's very connected to that person, will feel some of the effects of that as well.

This is something that can happen to just about anyone who happens to be strongly connected to someone who is going through something. For empaths, however, this can happen with just about anyone you've even just met.

Being in a nursing home or hospital might be difficult for you as an empath, because you leave feeling more ill, less vibrant, or just exhausted at the very least.

24. Deadlines and time limits leave you feeling shaken or rattled.

Keeping to deadlines and time constraints isn't necessarily difficult for you to do from a work effort standpoint. However, you might find that time limits on things tend to make you feel more harried, pressured, and less effective. It can seem like all the energy you originally had to work on your project is completely occupied by the time limit that's been imposed on you.

Things you should have easily been able to achieve otherwise, seem to be slammed up against that timeline and can only be accomplished with stress, a furrowed brow, and terrible personal care practices.

Don't allow yourself to skip meals to get to those deadlines; you need to eat, sleep, bathe, and breathe. Let yourself do those things.

25. Your greatest efforts are expended on not messing up.

Empaths and highly sensitive people have a tendency to be concerned with being a burden on others and with messing up. Because of this, there is a good deal of pressure exerted from within one's own self that tells us not to mess up or that we should concentrate on messing up less.

The Catch-22 here is that when you're hyper-focused on not making mistakes, it opens the door to a lot more mistakes than would have occurred if you had simply been able to relax.

This can be changed, thankfully, but it is quite an exhausting thing to deal with in the interim.

26. Change is jarring or even upsetting.

We perceive change everywhere, on even the tiniest scales. It's up to us to see when things are going differently with the people around us at work and in life, and as previously mentioned in this list, tiny details always seem to snag our attention on their way past.

Thanks to this, large changes that could seem normal to others around us, could seem completely cataclysmic to someone who is an empath or a highly sensitive person.

This doesn't mean that we can't adapt to change and that nothing should ever change around an empath or highly sensitive person. What it does mean, however, is that those around us could stand to give us a little warning, or at least give us a minute to get adjusted to how things will be since the change has been implemented.

27. You find yourself feeling exhausted after having absorbed and processed the feelings of others.

When someone needs to bend your ear for a prolonged period of time and you find yourself having to be present for someone, and receptive to their emotions, you might feel quite exhausted. Spending the day feeling what others feel and dealing with their problems from their perspective as well as your own is no small feat.

This is why a good deal of empaths choose not to go into fields wherein they have to manage and deal with the emotions of others. It's a talent they have, but if your full-time job is that draining, you're liable to burn out before too long.

Finding a balance when helping people is key. Make sure that you're not giving more than you have to give.

28. Sensory overload is much more easily achieved.

Sensory overload can be a very overwhelming feeling and can require different coping mechanisms to rectify it. If you're out at the grocery store, surrounded by people, you have a lot to pick up on. There are noises all over the place, people having conversations as you pass, and it can reach a "fever pitch."

When things reach that fever pitch, it's not uncommon to have something of a "freak out." The person experiencing it can begin to yell, panic, or just shut down entirely.

When this happens, it's important to try to focus on one specific thing and try to calm the overload. If leaving the area is possible, doing so could help the calming process to continue.

29. You are affected by the general atmosphere of a room or "vibe."

If there are a few angry people in a room and the atmosphere seems affected, that could chase off or at least unsettle an empath. They pick up on that tension and it has a very real effect on how comfortable they can get in that space.

For instance, if you went to a party and the hosts had gotten into an argument before people began to arrive and had no time to resolve it, that could thoroughly ruin your chances of enjoying the party unless something is done to rectify the situation between those two hosts.

30. Beauty moves you deeply, sometimes to tears.

Art, sunsets, architecture, nature, animals, people, and anything else that can have a beauty that inspires an emotional response. If you've consistently found yourself feeling profoundly affected or influenced by something's beauty, that is a trait of a highly sensitive person.

Someone who isn't aware of their abilities as an empath or a highly sensitive person might be alarmed at this trait. They might see it as a sign that something is wrong either with the stimulus or with them.

You can rest assures that, if this is something you've experienced, there is nothing wrong with you. There is nothing wrong with art, music, sunset, architecture, people, etc.

31. You tend to adopt the feelings of others and feel them as though they're your own.

This is a rather basic trait of an empath, but it is also a very essential one. The emotions that are felt by the people around you in your life, will inevitably reflect in your own emotions at some point or another. You will, on some level, feel that which is being felt by the people who are around you.

It can be assumed that this effect will increase depending on the strength of your connection with the person, or your involvement with the things that are currently affecting them emotionally.

For instance, if you don't particularly know someone, but you're right next to them when they get bad news, you might feel that more strongly. If you get into a fender bender and the driver of the other car becomes very upset or stressed, you have a higher chance of feeling that than if you happened to pass that fender bender on the street.

32. Conflict can make you physically ill.

It's possible to be made physically ill by conflict in your immediate vicinity. If you are trying your best to make something work, only for conflict to arise in that situation, you might feel sick to your stomach, develop a headache, or even feel like you can't breathe very well.

There are a good number of circumstances during which this can manifest itself and some of them are rather more mundane than we might anticipate. For instance, someone shouting at you in traffic, someone getting impatient in line behind you at the DMV, a dissatisfied customer in a restaurant who's making a fuss, two drunk guys outside of a club, and much more. Conflict can arise from a good many situations in life, and it's impossible to avoid it categorically.

What one can do, however, is choose to remove oneself from situations once conflicts arise if we cannot be reasonably expected to resolve it before removing ourselves. What is meant by this is that if you stir up a conflict unintentionally or otherwise, it would be rude to simply remove yourself without resolving it.

If the conflict has nothing to do with you and it could be resolved without your investment or involvement, then removing yourself is wise. Since conflict has such a profound effect on empaths, avoiding conflict is a matter of survival and emotional health.

33. You cannot see someone who needs help without desperately wanting to provide it.

In an empath or a highly sensitive person, compassionate empathy is in overdrive. This means that when you see someone in front of you who are having a difficult time with something, or who could use some help, you will feel a compulsion on every level to intervene or help.

This, just like with the conflicts, is not always in your best interest as an empath. Part of what you will need to learn is the management of emotional resources. Don't over-extend, don't give more than you have, and don't overload yourself with so many problems of others than you hardly have the time, energy, or attention for your own.

34. Occasionally, you will feel overwhelming emotions that are seemingly "out of nowhere."

As you go along through your day, you will pass by people who are experiencing emotions. Most people are experiencing emotions as they go through their day. Occasionally, as you're out there, someone else's emotion will find its way in without you being cognizant of it.

When that happens, you might feel an emotion that seems like it's coming from nowhere. This doesn't mean, however, that it's less valid or less of real emotion that you're feeling when this happens.

The biggest thing about this type of thing happening is that it serves as an interruption in your day. It can trip you up, but if you know that you're susceptible to such outbursts or situations, you can get through it as it comes up and then go about your day from there. You won't have to worry about what "set you off" for the rest of the day.

35. It's very hard for people to lie to you.

Because of the small details that you're apt to notice throughout your day and your interactions with others, you tend to pick up on the little things that sound off when someone is trying to lie to you. In addition to this, you pick up on inconsistent details in the story behind the lie.

If you know the person who is trying to lie to you, you're even more likely to be able to spot the things that would tell you if someone is lying to you.

Say, for instance, your significant other untruthfully says, "I'm fine," but you know that isn't true. You know what they sound like when they say they are fine, and they sounded different. You'll notice drops in pitch and tone, you'll notice strange inflections and more that will show you when things don't line up.

36. You have a "big heart," and will often give too much of yourself.

As someone who understands the emotions and the troubles of others on such an intrinsic level, you know how profoundly kindness can affect someone's entire day. You know what it means to impart positivity into someone's day so that the whole tone of their day is shifted into a more positive one.

Doing this, however, is not always to your benefit. It's not always to your detriment, either. You should be judicious about how and when you spend your time and energy helping someone to be positive.

You are not an infinite, inexhaustible fountain of positivity. You are able to create more positivity day by day, but you need to take the time to replenish that energy. You need to recuperate.

As they often say, "You cannot pour from an empty glass. Take care of yourself first."

37. You seem to be a walking target for "energy drainers."

People who tend to need all the positivity they can get will find you and cling to you. People who do this are known as "energy vampires," or "positivity vampires." They will see and be drawn to the light that you provide, but they can very easily drain all of it out of you, needing all the light you have to offer and more.

It's important to bear that in mind, as well as the fact that you can't pour from an empty cup. You can only give what you have to give. You cannot give more than that and you shouldn't even give as much as you have. If you give all that you have, there is nothing left for you to manage your life.

38. You feel that you know, without asking, what is going on around you.

Intuition is a large part of being an empath or a highly sensitive person. You can see the things that are going on in the environment and tell if there was recently an argument between the people in the room you just walked into, or you know who someone was talking to before they got off the phone, and so much more.

A large number of the situations that an empath will deal with are the mundane, day-to-day experiences. We are, after all, just normal people who are getting through our daily lives with a higher sensitivity than most.

39. You're an effective communicator and listener.

Being more empathetic and highly sensitive gives you a better look at how to fully acknowledge and accommodate someone in conversation. You know what people are looking for in their interactions with others, and you know how to simply be present and lessen the burden that someone is dealing with in their emotions.

Effective communication is centered on proper, active listening and appropriate acknowledgments. Since these are all part of what an empath seeks to give others, people will find you to be a very effective communicator and confidante.

40. You have mood swings.

Thanks to the sensitivity that we experience, it's easy for small stimuli to send us into a mood in a deeper way than we might have otherwise expected. Thanks to the large number of stimuli we encounter throughout the day, it can seem like our moods are swinging from one into the other.

If you're on the lookout for these types of things and you're focused on giving yourself a beat to think about and process the things going on before acting out after a mood swing, we can do well at keeping the swings at bay.

41. You have a trustworthy magnetism.

Thanks to your calming demeanor, your automatic understanding, and compassion for others, and to your ability to give emotional peace to others, people will see you as trustworthy. If they can be calm with you and feel that they are safe with you, they feel like they can trust you.

As a result of this, you will find that people will tell you more things that you wouldn't expect someone to tell you. People you've known for a very short time will suddenly come to you and tell you about past traumas, current debacles, family histories, and so much more.

Thanks to your magnetism, people will feel *compelled* to tell you things.

42. You might reach for addictive substances to escape the other traits of an empath.

Being an empath or a highly sensitive person can be exhausting. It can be very taxing if the things that can come up aren't properly managed. Being an empath can be emotionally, physically, and mentally exhausting.

As you're going through all the trials and tribulations of being an empath, it can be tempting to reach for substances to "soften the blow," or ease the strain that it puts on you.

As with any substances used for the purposes of coping or emotional alleviation, it is prudent to use caution. Utilizing substances with no prescription and utilizing multiple of these can carry a good deal of risk. It is best to exercise caution with such things and to exhaust any other avenues of relief before going down that route.

43. You're very creative.

Being in tune with our emotions and to minute details, creative pursuits come much more easily. We find a lot of reward from those pursuits and we take a lot of enjoyment in them as well.

If you find that a good number of the items in this chapter fit you and you haven't gotten into any creative pursuits to date, give it a shot. Try coloring, drawing, or any other creative pursuits that might interest you and see how that does.

A lot of times, those pursuits have a regenerative or recuperative effect on empaths and highly sensitive people.

44. Clutter and a crowded space make you uneasy or stressed.

As small details tend to fill and occupy the mind of an empath and a highly sensitive person, the details of the environment surrounding you will also do so. People who are highly sensitive will often find that clutter in their immediate space will stop them from focusing or keep them from feeling like they can work.

It makes it difficult to sit at ease, it makes it difficult to create artistic work, and it makes it difficult to focus on just about anything of any import.

How many of these traits stick out for you? How many of these things did you read, only to find that it describes something that you do frequently? Did you find anything described in this chapter that explained something you were doing, that you didn't even know you were doing?

How to Differentiate

Someone who is neurotypical experiences mental and emotional processes in the center of those spectrums. Their capacity for sensory overload isn't as high, their understanding of the emotions of people around them is largely contextual, and things are largely considered "normal."

Empaths, however, tend to experience the emotions of the people around them with a severity that can be hard to understand for those who don't experience that. Someone who is invested in something going on in front of them will tend to feel the things going on between the people involved.

Let's say, for instance, that someone is watching two people recite their vows to one another. We'll call this person Peter. Peter knows the bride and groom, he loves them dearly, and he knows how happy they make one another. When he listens to the groom recite his vows, he feels the pride, joy, nervousness, and love that the groom is feeling. He feels it coming from the bride as well. He is invested, and these emotions are very deeply real at that moment.

Now, let's take a situation which is a little less common, and which evokes a slightly less emotional response than a wedding might. Let's say that Irma is watching two people argue. As she's watching those people argue, feel pain, feel anger, feel frustration, it would be difficult for her not to feel those same emotions while watching the argument. Once it's resolved, however, Irma will feel that same catharsis, resolution, and relief as well.

Someone who is highly sensitive or empathic may also feel the pride that another one feels when sharing details of their accomplishments. They may feel grief when someone talks about losing someone, even if the empath has never met them. They may feel jealousy when someone talks about something that makes them feel jealous. They may feel offended when someone else gets a parking ticket for going one minute over the time on their meter.

There aren't any hard lines on what an empath will feel, why they'll feel it, or even the extent to which they'll feel that emotion. One can put money on their emotions having more weight and volume, on their ability to tell how someone is feeling before most, and on their perception of the things that are left unsaid amongst a pair or group. Picking up and dropping hints are actions that seem to have the same severity as shouting how one feels to the advanced empath.

Exercise:

How to Spot an Empath.

With the person from the first exercise in mind, answer these questions honestly.

For each question you answer with, "Yes," give the person one point.

1. Does the person have a tendency to be shy or to seem introverted?
2. Do they tend to prefer to take themselves places than carpool?
3. Do they seem to need a lot of alone time?
4. Are they easily startled?
5. Does the person tend to reach for food in times of stress?
6. Do they tend to avoid multitasking when possible?
7. Would you ever consider them to be socially reclusive?
8. Have they expressed concern about being emotionally smothered?
9. Is nature something that seems to recharge them?
10. Do they prefer small groups to large crowds?
11. Are they sensitive to a lot of noise, smells, or people who talk incessantly?
12. Do they get hurt easily?
13. Are they overly sensitive to medications and/or substances like caffeine and alcohol?
14. Are they commonly overwhelmed?

15. Do they need a recuperation period after being in large crowds?
16. Do they often express concern that they're "not fitting in?"
17. Do they have sensitive skin?
18. Do they seem to take on the emotions of people around them?
19. Does conflict make them ill?
20. Do they prefer small towns to big cities?

1-5: They are empathetic toward people but may not be an empath.

6-10: They have moderate empathic tendencies.

11-15: They have strong empathic tendencies

16-20: They are definitely an empath.

Were you right?

_____

Chapter 4: An In-Depth Look at Empaths and Life

Case Studies

While the scientific evidence of empaths, their abilities, their proclivities, and their traits seem to be the subject of debate in the scientific fields that study them, the evidence does a lot to substantiate the things that empaths know they're dealing with on a consistent basis. Scientists who remain unconvinced say the evidence is indirect, which is not inaccurate. We do have some dots to connect when it comes to that evidence. Those connections tend to seem more obvious to the people who experience those things firsthand.

Mirror neurons are among the most compelling discoveries when it comes to the abilities of one to empathize with another. It is true that the perception we have of the emotions of another are filtered through our perceptions of emotions as we have come to understand them, but the neurons themselves are triggered by outside stimuli before it ever passes through that filter. Those neurons go right to work regardless of how we perceive that input after the fact. This was investigated by Dr. Marco Iacoboni in 2008 in connection with Ahmanson-Lovelace Brain Mapping Center, Department of Psychiatry and Behavioral Sciences, Semel Institute for Neuroscience and Social Behavior, Brain Research

Institute, David Geffen School of Medicine at UCLA in Los Angeles, California.

Another study conducted by Hatfield, Cacioppo, and Rapson in 1994 suggests that the concept of emotional contagion is a large part of how empaths are able to pick up on the things that are felt and thought by the people around them. Emotional contagion is the proclivity for members of a group to synchronize their emotions, attitudes, understandings, speech, and behaviors with and without the use of mutual agreement to do so.

What scientists agree on is that these studies prove is the existence of empathy as a general concept, and some suggestions as to how it's facilitated, created and amplified. What scientists do not agree, is that this substantiates the existence of empaths. This has bred some skepticism as to the existence of empaths, their abilities, and the validity of the claims about these abilities and instances in which they've been used.

Those who have experienced these things firsthand have had difficulty relaying their experiences to the scientific community in a way that validates their claims in any vast or sweeping way. As more and more scientists investigate empaths, however, the more valid the claims seem to be, and the more evidence seems to come up to substantiate the claims. As neuroscientists learn more about the brain and its many functions, more tests and data are coming to light about empaths and what they can do.

There does seem to be an added benefit to finding out what it is that causes empaths to feel the way they do, act the way they do, do the things they do, and what sets them apart from those who would be considered neurotypical. This is that those who would seek to feign empathic abilities in order to generate a following, revenue, or other benefits, are closer to being disproven and revealed to be dishonest. A difficulty that many empaths have is being taken seriously or understood when there are those who would feign these abilities for their own personal gain. As we become more able to weed out those presences, the more valid empaths will be made to feel.

In the experiments that have been done to monitor the mirror neuron networks in the brains of empaths, scientists have seen an increase in brain activity. This being said, there are many variables when it comes to the mind and there are many things that could explain various types of behaviors. More experimentation, documentation, and understanding may be necessary to positively state that empaths exist, their experiences are valid, and their abilities are different than that of a typical person.

In her 2017 book *The Fear Factor*, neuroscientist and psychologist Abigail Marsh described how she went about finding evidence of the difference between the brains of empaths and the brains of people who have what would be considered a typical empathetic response. In her work, she uses the word "altruists," to describe people who tend to act more selflessly and empathetically.

Marsh's motivation in writing this work and in researching altruists was to find out what it is that causes people of this nature to engage in selfless acts when no obvious benefit or positive outcome is immediately apparent, and even when doing so seemed to present a cost to the person engaging in that act. In her efforts to recruit some of the most selfless people she could, Marsh reached out to people who had committed the most selfless act possible with a high risk involved: donating a kidney to complete strangers. Most of these were even done anonymously.

Marsh took to showing her participants pictures of peoples' faces with varied expressions while monitoring brain activity. The brain activity was measured against a control group of people who had not donated their kidneys and the altruistic group tended to be the most sensitive toward facial expressions that indicated fear. When the participants recognized fear in the faces they were seeing, activity spiked in the amygdalae, an area of the brain concerned with the processing of emotion. According to Marsh's findings, the amygdalae in the altruistic group also tended to be an average of about 8% larger than the amygdalae of the control group.

Marsh designated three different types of altruists, based on the motivations behind their behaviors. Those three are kin-based, which is kindness or altruism that is focused specifically on those who are closest to or related to the altruist in question, reciprocity-based, which is altruism that is based on the assumption that similar concessions and actions will be returned when needed in the future, and care-based, which is the improvement of the well-being of another, or the contributions to their well-being based on their need.

Marsh's research appears to favor the care-based form of altruism, and most empaths seem to exhibit this type of behavior on a consistent basis. The motivation for empaths to do the things they do to help others has been found on a fairly consistent basis, to be centered on the well-being of the people they're helping. An empathetic response seems to generally have that goal in mind throughout the many different displays that can be employed.

A study conducted in 2018 suggests that psychopaths and empaths are polar opposites in terms of their abilities to feel and exhibit empathy and altruism. To further illustrate this point, it was found that the brains of psychopaths had amygdalae that were an average of a whopping 18% smaller than that of the control group. This tells us that the brains of empaths and psychopaths are both abnormal and are such in opposing directions.

Examples of Empathic Behavior

Let's take a look at the traits of an empath and go through some examples of what each of those might look like from an outsider's perspective.

1. **Strong emotional content on television has a profound impact on empaths.**

   Watching television with someone who has a very high empathic response can be somewhat alarming if you're not familiar with it. It doesn't seem to take very much for the person to become visibly upset by the things that are taking place on the screen if they're of a strong emotional nature. Let's take a look at a somewhat less common example.

   Let's say that something happens on television that is unjust. In many cases, what's on television might even be a work of fiction that depicts this injustice. An empath might find themselves getting all worked up about what's going on, talking at length about how it isn't fair, or they might even go so far as to turn off the television and do something else because they don't want to deal with it anymore.

Another example could be if the person is watching television and something very sad happens. This person might end up crying, even if you feel just fine when watching that same thing. They might end up crying in anticipation of something sad happening, or they might feel sad for some time after the show or movie has ended.

2. People are always asking empaths for advice.

An empath can act as sort of a beacon for people who need advice on matters of the heart, or even matters of a more practical nature. If you are close with someone who is deeply empathic in nature, you might find that people are always calling just to get that person's perspective on things that have absolutely nothing to do with them in the first place.

The empathic person, no matter how far removed, will often accept the request for help, will listen to what's bothering the person, and offer what solutions or advice they have. This is all without gaining anything or having any personal investment in the situation being discussed.

3. **Intimate relationships can overtake all of the empath's thinking and the energy they get from their significant other flows throughout their entire life.**

If the empath you know has a significant other, you might find that that person is quite the focus of most of their energy. You will particularly notice this when the empath's significant other isn't doing well. In such cases, the empath will have a much stronger response and will have difficulty focusing on or being effective at anything else until that situation is resolved.

Empaths are particularly used to people asking for their advice when they're going through things. When an empath needs to reach out, they may not do so depending on how strong a support network they've had throughout their lives.

If the empath can't seem to focus on anything but the matters of their significant other, it can be difficult to refocus the mind onto something that is more productive.

4. Someone who doesn't know the empath very closely might think them anxious or introverted.

Empaths are often misidentified as having anxiety or as being introverted. In many cases, the empath simply needs to take some time in solitude to recharge a little bit. Solitary tasks that produce small amounts of dopamine in the brain are very beneficial to the empath in general and can serve as a recuperative measure.

Empaths who find themselves making frequent use of this method could be seen as reclusive, introverted, or shy. The reality is generally that those who do these things are quite outgoing and extroverted, but that they need a lot of recharging in order to keep up with the energy they spend on being outgoing and extroverted.

5. Regardless of introversion or extroversion, they withdraw often.

As stated above, withdrawing and taking time to do solitary tasks is basically a survival tactic for the empath. If a friend of yours frequently declines to go on outings with you, to parties, to amusement parks, or to things which require much emotional energy output, it could be that they just need some time to do their own solitary activities for a short while before diving right back into all that fun stuff.

6. When thinking of leadership roles, the empath always assumes that means putting the team first.

If you have ever known an empath who is in any position of authority, you will find that the person will not speak about the position in terms of what that position can do for them or can get them. They take the responsibility they hold for their teams quite seriously and they do everything in their power to ensure that the people working under them are perfectly facilitated.

When their juniors or staff fail to do something, the empath will often take time to reflect on how they failed to properly facilitate their success. In some cases, this may just come across as extreme upset about the lack of success. Incredulity at how it happened and even anger could manifest if the empath felt they were responsible for the failure.

7. They have an imagined world in their mind that is rich and vibrant.

Most empaths have a very active imagination that is always working, growing, improving, intertwining and developing. Telling bedtime stories is sometimes easy for the empath, as they have a wealth of information to pull from that is ready to be told. This is not always the case, but it has been such in enough cases to be considered an attribute of empathic people.

8. Others find the presence of an empath to be quite calming.

Empaths tend to be very easy to be around. Something about their perception of the emotions and feelings of the people around them makes them seem so much easier to be around. It's hard to feel like the person who understands you on a fundamental level is judging you or is in some way, making you uncomfortable.

Empaths will often be paid compliments like, "you're so easy to talk to," "I always feel relaxed around you," and "talking to you is just so refreshing." Something about talking to people who perceive your emotions without you having to work to explain yourself makes empaths so much easier to be around and connect with than people with average or typical responses.

9. **Hunger very quickly turns into anger, sometimes even before hunger.**

You have possibly heard the term "hangry" to refer to people who have not eaten and who are, as a result, quite angry or irritable. Unfortunately, those who have not had enough to eat and who are highly sensitive can tend to fall victim to this uncomfortable set of circumstances much more readily than some others might.

It's best to keep some snacks in your bag if you're going to be out for the day and to avoid crowded or public spaces if you have not had the opportunity to eat enough.

The grocery store is probably the worst place to find yourself when you haven't eaten because you will buy every snack food you can find and you will bite everyone's head off in the process.

10. **They're highly sensitive to wardrobe malfunctions.**

The odd tag sticking out of the back of your shirt, itchy material, slipped sock, or rogue thread might be a minor annoyance to most people. To empaths and people who are highly sensitive, these sensations do not ever let up or calm down. If these issues with their clothing persist, they will continue to be acutely aware of it until it gets resolved.

If you know an empathic person, you might have experienced them swiping away at their arm to remove a rogue hair that has fallen, only to have to go back over the area again and again with increasing frustration every time the hair isn't properly removed or placed.

From an outsider's perspective, this can seem downright silly. To the empath, it is frustrating and can make you feel like screaming until the feeling stops.

11. Criticism is painful beyond reason.

For the empath and the highly sensitive person, criticism can feel like a slap in the face. Rest assured that every empath has worked on seeing it differently, looking at it from a helpful angle and trying to get help from it that there is to get. Some have succeeded, but it's a large hurdle that many have to really try to get over.

Those who offer constructive criticism of our creative pursuits are rarely trying to hurt us with that criticism. We do know this on a cognitive level, but there's always going to be that initial shock and sting from the delivery of that statement.

12. They feel an overwhelming love for pets, animals, or babies.

When an empath sees something cute, the whole world has to know about it and everything must stop until the cuteness is properly acknowledged by everyone within earshot of the empath. It's highly possible that the empath might not be able to get anything done while in the presence of a cute animal or baby because they're so preoccupied with the cute baby in their vicinity.

It's best to wait until after work hours to introduce a baby or an animal into the area where an empath is unless you're okay with absolutely nothing getting done, except for some cooing, playing, cuddling, and picture-taking.

13. They're exceedingly perceptive and minor details don't escape you easily.

The empath is generally the person in your life who can tell from about a mile off if something has gone awry. They're great at checking statements, bills, and Where's Waldo?

Someone who is empathic will often find that they're very perceptive to small changes, little details, things that were meant to fly under the radar, and things that people would rather they don't notice. This is part of what makes lying to an empath so much harder. They pick up on all the little inconsistencies, the changes in stories, and the little tells that people have when they're being dishonest.

14.They're prone to jumping or startling easily.

If you find that sudden loud noises make someone jump more than they should, they could be a highly sensitive person or an empath. Furthermore, if you find that this trait lessons when they're particularly drained, exhausted, tired, or depressed, that jumpiness is rooted more in their higher sensitivity.

It would be nice if being more sensitive to things, being more aware of small or minute details, and being less able to be lied to meant they weren't easily startled. Instead of this, however, they find themselves so completely immersed in the things that they do in every moment that when something comes up to snap them out of it, they can become quite jarred or unsettled.

15. Once startled, they may be shaken for a while or experience "aftershocks."

Have you ever seen a person startled in a really big way, perhaps as a joke by a friend or loved one, only to feel "aftershocks," or shivers afterward? It might seem like they're anticipating it happening again, every part of them tenses up for just a quick moment, then they go back to what they were doing a moment prior.

Being an empath means they're aware of a lot of things. Being aware of so many things comes to be something that they rely on from day to day and when they're suddenly and loudly confronted with something of which they weren't aware, it can catch them off-guard in a big way.

The systems in the body can sometimes seem as though they're trying to overcompensate for that lack of awareness by being hyper-aware after the fact. Cognitively they know that this wasn't the intention of the person who startled us, they know that being hyper-vigilant now won't help, and they know that it won't likely happen again. This does not, however, quash that response.

16. Stimulants are very effective in short measure.

An empath or a highly sensitive person might find that one cup of coffee can do a great deal to "light the fire under them," so to speak. With all the nervous responses being more highly tuned in and with all the sensitivities being raised, it makes sense that a little bit of a stimulant would go a long way.

An empath should be careful of the stimulants they take into their bodies and be sure not to overdo it. Overuse of caffeine and other stimulating substances can cause anxiety and other issues in the mind and body if left unchecked. It is best to try to limit how much they take on and see if they notice any differences.

17. Depressants are very effective in short measure.

Just like with stimulants, depressants will take effect very quickly and will often last. Alcohol might hit a little harder for people who are highly sensitive. In addition to this, certain substances in the body could fail to have the intended effect and just make you feel ill.

It's prudent to be dubious of new substances and take only what is prescribed by a medical professional.

18.It's easy for them to get a feel for where someone is coming from when telling you something.

When someone is explaining something to them, they might have an idea of exactly what the person means within the first few seconds of them talking. This can trip them up from time to time when they're ready to move onto the next phase of the conversation, but the person in front of them is still working on explaining things that they've already grasped.

It's important for an empath to recognize this mechanism at work and to be kind in such an event. Most people don't understand how someone could possibly know the things they know at such a point in the conversation, and cutting off the communication of someone who is trying to work with them is a very fast way to complicate the relationship.

19.They do a lot of introspection and deep thinking.

People might find an empath they know to be "zoning out," or "spacing out" on a semi-regular basis. People who are highly sensitive and who are empaths will often find that there's a good deal of things going on behind the scenes, so to speak. There are a lot of thoughts about the things going on in their lives, the things that are going on with their friends and family, or the scenario in their head could be completely hypothetical.

20. Pain sets in more easily.

Without any medical diagnosis like fibromyalgia, arthritis, dermatitis or anything else, it would seem that things just hurt an empath a little more easily. Some empathic people will find that little more than a soft touch can cause them a sharp pain in some areas of their bodies.

No bruising or otherwise alarming indicators of anything wrong with their bodies, other than pain that occurred very quickly and in a very sharp way. This can complicate things for someone with a more active lifestyle, so be sure to be accommodating if someone tells you they're dealing with this.

Are there any areas of your body that are particularly sensitive?

21. They ask the big questions in life and seek a lot of answers about the status quo.

"Why are things the way they are," is a pretty common big question to ask. It's very broad, it has a lot of answers, and it could keep an empath busy pondering for days on end. However, the questions that an empath will find themselves asking, have to do with life's deeper subjects, as well as some that might be hard to articulate until they've been mulled over for a good long while.

Have you ever wondered about something, but you had no idea how to broach it with someone to discuss it with them? Or thought that you could figure out how to word the question, but you doubted very much that they would be interested or see you normally after you asked it?

22. They find cruelty and violence to be abhorrent.

Being in-tune with the emotions, feelings, and pains of others, it's easy for empaths to put themselves in the shoes of someone being brutalized, without ever meaning to. When they watch the news, they see people going through worse pain than can be imagined, but they're right there alongside them.

Watching someone who is at a severe disadvantage being neglected, harmed, or otherwise sustaining any measure of cruelty will often rattle someone who is highly sensitive. This might be the kind of thing you choose to remove from your television watching, or it might be something you do your best to avoid even in conversation.

When these things happen around an empath, they might find themselves overwhelmingly compelled to jump into the thick of it and do something about it. Compassionate empathy response is quite strong in such an event.

23. They feel ailments or illnesses as someone they love is going through them.

It's possible that you've heard of "sympathy illness," or "sympathy pains." This is when someone with whom you're very in-tune is going through something painful or sickening and you, as someone who's very connected to that person, will feel some of the effects of that as well.

This is something that can happen to just about anyone who happens to be strongly connected to someone who is going through something. For empaths, however, this can happen with just about anyone you've even just met.

Being in a nursing home or hospital might be difficult for you as an empath, because you leave feeling more ill, less vibrant, or just exhausted at the very least.

24. Deadlines and time limits leave you feeling shaken or rattled.

Keeping to deadlines and time constraints isn't necessarily difficult for an empath to do from a work effort standpoint. However, they might find that time limits on things tend to make them feel more harried, pressured, and less effective. It can seem like all the energy they originally had to work on the project is completely occupied by the time limit that's been imposed on them.

Things they should have easily been able to achieve otherwise, seem to be slammed up against that timeline and can only be accomplished with stress, a furrowed brow, and terrible personal care practices.

Don't allow your empathic friends and family to skip meals to get to those deadlines; they need to eat, sleep, bathe, and breathe. They may need your help to remember this

25. Their greatest efforts are expended on not messing up.

Empaths and highly sensitive people have a tendency to be concerned with being a burden on others and with messing up. Because of this, there is a good deal of pressure exerted from within one's own self that tells us not to mess up or that we should concentrate on messing up less.

The Catch-22 here is that when one is hyper-focused on not making mistakes, it opens the door to a lot more mistakes than would have occurred if one had simply been able to relax.

This can be changed, thankfully, but it is quite an exhausting thing to deal with in the interim.

26. Change is jarring or even upsetting.

Empaths perceive change everywhere, on even the tiniest scales. It's up to them to see when things are going differently with the people around them at work and in life, and as previously mentioned in this list, tiny details always seem to snag our attention on their way past.

Thanks to this, large changes that could seem normal to others around them, could seem completely cataclysmic to someone who is an empath or a highly sensitive person.

This doesn't mean that they can't adapt to change and that nothing should ever change around an empath or highly sensitive person. What it does mean, however, is that those around us could stand to give empaths a little warning, or at least give them a minute to get adjusted to how things will be since the change has been implemented.

27. They find themselves feeling exhausted after having absorbed and processed the feelings of others.

When someone needs to bend their ear for a prolonged period of time and they find themselves having to be present for someone, and receptive to their emotions, they might feel quite exhausted. Spending the day feeling what others feel and dealing with their problems from their perspective as well as their own is no small feat.

This is why a good deal of empaths choose not to go into fields wherein they have to manage and deal with the emotions of others. It's a talent they have, but if their full-time job is that draining, they're liable to burn out before too long.

Finding a balance when helping people is key. Make sure that your empathic friends are not giving more than they have to give.

28. Sensory overload is much more easily achieved.

Sensory overload can be a very overwhelming feeling and can require different coping mechanisms to rectify it. If they're out at the grocery store, surrounded by people, they have a lot to pick up on. There are noises all over the place, people having conversations as you pass, and it can reach a "fever pitch."

When things reach that fever pitch, it's not uncommon to have something of a "freak out." The person experiencing it can begin to yell, panic, or just shut down entirely.

When this happens, it's important to try to focus on one specific thing and try to calm the overload. If leaving the area is possible, doing so could help the calming process to continue.

29. They are affected by the general atmosphere of a room or "vibe."

If there are a few angry people in a room and the atmosphere seems affected, that could chase off or at least unsettle an empath. They pick up on that tension and it has a very real effect on how comfortable they can get in that space.

For instance, if you went to a party and the hosts had gotten into an argument before people began to arrive and had no time to resolve it that could thoroughly ruin your chances of enjoying the party unless something is done to rectify the situation between those two hosts.

30. Beauty moves them deeply, sometimes to tears.

Art, sunsets, architecture, nature, animals, people, and anything else that can have a beauty that inspires an emotional response. If they've consistently found themselves feeling profoundly affected or influenced by the beauty of something, that is a trait of a highly sensitive person.

Someone who isn't aware of their abilities as an empath or a highly sensitive person might be alarmed at this trait. They might see it as a sign that something is wrong either with the stimulus or with them.

They can rest assured that, if this is something they've experienced, there is nothing wrong with them. There is nothing wrong with art, music, sunset, architecture, people, etc.

31. They tend to adopt the feelings of others and feel them as though they're their own.

This is a rather basic trait of an empath, but it is also a very essential one. The emotions that are felt by the people around them in their life, will inevitably reflect on their own emotions at some point or another. They will, on some level, feel that which is being felt by the people who are around them.

It can be assumed that this effect will increase depending on the strength of their connection with the person, or their involvement with the things that are currently affecting them emotionally.

For instance, if they don't particularly know someone, but they're right next to them when they get bad news, the empath might feel that more strongly. If they get into a fender bender and the driver of the other car becomes very upset or stressed, they have a higher chance of feeling that than if you happened to pass that fender bender on the street.

32. Conflict can make them physically ill.

It's possible to be made physically ill by conflict in their immediate vicinity. If they are trying their best to make something work, only for conflict to arise in that situation, they might feel sick to their stomach, develop a headache, or even feel like they can't breathe very well.

There are a good number of circumstances during which this can manifest itself and some of them are rather more mundane than we might anticipate. For instance, someone shouting at you in traffic, someone getting impatient in line behind you at the DMV, a dissatisfied customer in a restaurant who's making a fuss, two drunk guys outside of a club, and much more. Conflict can arise from a good many situations in life, and it's impossible to avoid it categorically.

What one can do, however, is choose to remove oneself from situations once conflicts arise if we cannot be reasonably expected to resolve it before removing ourselves. What is meant by this is that if you stir up a conflict unintentionally or otherwise, it would be rude to simply remove yourself without resolving it.

If the conflict has nothing to do with them and it could be resolved without their investment or involvement, then removing themselves is wise. Since conflict has such a profound effect on empaths, avoiding conflict is a matter of survival and emotional health.

33. They cannot see someone who needs help without desperately wanting to provide it.

In an empath or a highly sensitive person, compassionate empathy is in overdrive. This means that when they see someone in front of them who's having a difficult time with something, or who could use some help, they will feel a compulsion on every level to intervene or help.

This, just like with the conflicts, is not always in their best interest as an empath. Part of what they will need to learn is the management of emotional resources. They need to make sure they don't over-extend, don't give more than they have, and don't overload themselves with so many problems of others that they hardly have the time, energy, or attention for their own.

34. Occasionally, they will feel overwhelming emotions that are seemingly "out of nowhere."

As they go along through their day, they will pass by people who are experiencing emotions. Most people are experiencing emotions as they go through their day.

Occasionally, as they're out there, someone else's emotion will find its way in without them being cognizant of it.

When that happens, they might feel an emotion that seems like it's coming from nowhere. This doesn't mean, however, that it's less valid or less of real emotion that they're feeling when this happens.

The biggest thing about this type of thing happening is that it serves as an interruption in their day. It can trip them up, but if they know that they're susceptible to such outbursts or situations, they can get through it as it comes up and then go about their day from there. They won't have to worry about what "set them off" for the rest of the day.

35. It's very hard for people to lie to them.

Because of the small details that they're apt to notice throughout their day and their interactions with others, they tend to pick up on the little things that sound off when someone is trying to lie to them. In addition to this, they pick up on inconsistent details in the story behind the lie.

If they know the person who is trying to lie to them, they're even more likely to be able to spot the things that would tell them if someone is lying to them.

Say, for instance, their significant other untruthfully says, "I'm fine," but they know that isn't true. They know what they sound like when they are fine, and they sounded different than that. They'll notice drops in pitch and tone, they'll notice strange inflections and more that will show them when things don't line up.

36. They have a "big heart," and will often give too much of themselves.

As someone who understands the emotions and the troubles of others on such an intrinsic level, an empath knows how profoundly kindness can affect someone's entire day. They know what it means to impart positivity into someone's day so that the whole tone of their day is shifted into a more positive one.

Doing this, however, is not always to their benefit. It's not always to their detriment, either. They should be judicious about how and when they spend their time and energy helping someone to be positive.

They are not an infinite, inexhaustible fountain of positivity. They are able to create more positivity day by day, but they need to take the time to replenish that energy. They need to recuperate.

As they often say, "You cannot pour from an empty glass. Take care of yourself first."

37. They seem to be a walking target for "energy drainers."

People who tend to need all the positivity they can get will find empaths and cling to them. People who do this are known as "energy vampires," or "positivity vampires." They will see and be drawn to the light that empaths provide, but they can very easily drain all of it out of them, needing all the light they have to offer and more.

You may know an empath who has that one friend who always seems to need something. That person who always needs the empath to go out of their way to give them what they need, only for the empath to be left with no positive energy at the end of it all. Pointing this out to the empath will help them to see what the other person is doing to them and leaving them with. The empath will tend to understand when someone is using them, and they should be made aware that they don't deserve that.

It's important to bear that in mind, as well as the fact that they can't pour from an empty cup. They can only give what they have to give. They cannot give more than that and they shouldn't even give as much as they have. If you give all that they have, there is nothing left for them to manage their lives.

38. They feel that they know, without asking, what is going on around them.

Intuition is a large part of being an empath or a highly sensitive person. they can see the things that are going on in the environment and tell if there was recently an argument between the people in the room they just walked into, or they know who someone was talking to before they got off the phone, and so much more.

You might find that the empath in your life will ask eerily specific questions about the things going on in your life without you telling them anything that would give them that impression. Have you ever known someone who always seemed to know what questions to ask?

39. They're an effective communicator and listener.

Communicating effectively with the people around them is an essential part of picking up on the emotions that are being dealt with by the people around them. Empaths can gauge a lot of what is going on without asking, but being able to communicate with people, get onto their level, understand what they have to say, and to be able to see where they're coming from is one of the things that makes an empath most valuable as a friend and confidante.

It's one of the things that makes people so comfortable around empaths. Being able to communicate with and thus understand someone makes them more approachable.

40. They have mood swings.

The empath has a lot of emotional matter swung into their direction at most times of the day. This does create the unfortunate proclivity for mood swings, especially if the person is around a good deal of other people if the person hasn't had the opportunity to recharge, if they haven't eaten, or if there's just a lot going on in their general vicinity.

This can make living with an empath a little bit more difficult, because you may need to be the person to bring them back down to Earth for a moment and snap them out of the swing. This can be done, however, and the more understanding of their own abilities the empath has, the easier this whole situation will become.

41. They have a trustworthy magnetism.

Thanks to their calming demeanor, their automatic understanding, and compassion for others, and to their ability to give emotional peace to others, people will see the average empath as trustworthy. If someone can be calm with an empath and feel that they are safe with them, they feel like they can trust them.

As a result of this, the empath will find that people will tell them more things that you wouldn't expect someone to tell most people. People they've known for a very short time will suddenly come to them and tell them about past traumas, current debacles, family histories, and so much more.

Thanks to their magnetism, people will feel *compelled* to tell them things.

42. They might reach for addictive substances to escape the other traits of an empath.

Being an empath or a highly sensitive person can be exhausting. It can be very taxing if the things that can come up aren't properly managed. Being an empath can be emotionally, physically, and mentally exhausting.

As they're going through all the trials and tribulations of being an empath, it can be tempting to reach for substances to "soften the blow," or ease the strain that it puts on them.

As with any substances used for the purposes of coping or emotional alleviation, it is prudent to use caution. Utilizing substances with no prescription and utilizing multiple of these can carry a good deal of risk. It is best to exercise caution with such things and to exhaust any other avenues of relief before going down that route.

43. They're very creative.

Being in tune with their emotions and to minute details, creative pursuits come much more easily. Empaths find a lot of reward from those pursuits and they take a lot of enjoyment in them as well.

If you know someone who fits a lot of the descriptions in this section, but they don't have very many creative pursuits, it could be worth a look. It could be something they're interested in starting up with and it could be something they'd be more comfortable exploring with a friend.

If you have a creative hobby that you enjoy, try offering for the empath in your life to join you and see if they get any enjoyment out of spending time with you and out of creating something new.

44. Clutter and a crowded space make the empath uneasy or stressed.

Depending on how the surrounding space is set up, the empath can be overwhelmed by clutter or chaos in their immediate environment. It can make thinking in a straight line more difficult for the person who is overly sensitive to that clutter or mess.

The empath might find shows on things like decluttering, organizing, or cleaning to be a very relaxing background for their days off. Seeing a very disorganized area being put to rights can help to put an empath at ease and can be more entertaining for them than might otherwise make sense.

Exercise:

Help Your Local Empath

If you have found the examples of empaths to describe someone who is close to you, consider reaching out to the person to find out what sorts of things they like to do in their free time. If there are quiet or relaxing activities that they like to do, see if they would like the company someday while they engage in that activity.

Spending time with an empath while being calm, doing something fulfilling, and not being exciting can be a very recuperative exercise for the empath. If they know they can call on you when they're looking to do activities of this type, the empath will generally feel closer to you and more comfortable being themselves with you.

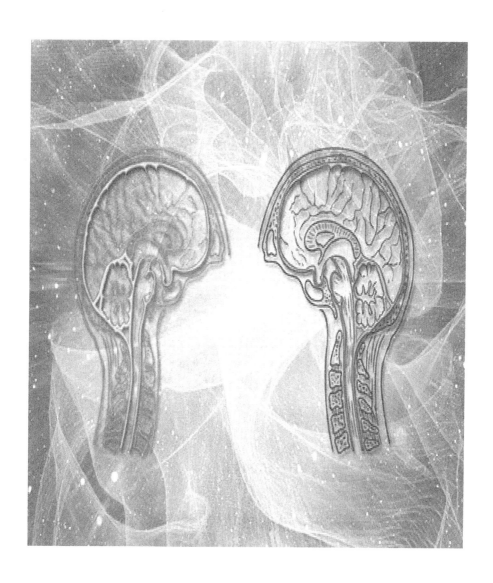

Chapter 5: Are You an Empath?

The Test

Exercise:

Are you an Empath?

Answer these questions honestly.

For each question you answer with "Yes," give yourself one point.

1. Have I been labeled as shy, overly sensitive, or introverted?
2. Would I rather drive myself somewhere, so I have a way to leave before others?
3. Does it take me a long time to recover after spending an extended period of time with an energy vampire?
4. Am I easily startled?
5. Do I eat more than I need to when coping with stress?
6. Do I prefer to do one task at a time, rather than overwhelm myself by multitasking?
7. Am I socially reclusive at times?
8. Am I afraid of being smothered in intimate relationships?

9. Do I find nature to be recuperative or restorative to me?

10. Do I prefer small groups or even one-on-one interactions to large parties or gatherings?

11. Do I get mental overwhelm from people who talk continuously, loud noise, or odors?

12. Do I have a low threshold for pain?

13. Do I have a strong reaction to caffeine or medications?

14. Am I anxious or overwhelmed with any sort of regularity or frequency?

15. Do I need a recuperation period after being in large crowds?

16. Do I often feel like I'm not fitting in properly?

17. Do I have chemical or skin sensitivities that are exacerbated by scratchy clothes?

18. Do I seem to absorb the feelings of others?

19. Do I get sick over conflicts?

20. Do I feel more at ease in small-scale settings or cities than in large ones?

1-5: You are empathetic toward people but may not be an empath.

6-10: You have moderate empathic tendencies.

11-15: You have strong empathic tendencies

16-20: You are definitely an empath.

Understanding You

The first thing to understand, if you've found that you're an empath from the information in the previous chapters, is that there is nothing wrong with you. You have some abilities that aren't considered completely typical, and those can come with their own unique troubles and responsibilities. This does not mean, however, that you're not normal and that you have a responsibility to others to use them.

Being an empath means knowing what's going on with the people around you. What it doesn't mean is that you need to do anything with that information. It doesn't mean you have to get involved in the lives and business of others if it's not prudent for you to do so and it doesn't mean that you have any responsibility to deal with people who don't make you happy.

A large part of managing your empathic abilities and staying happy is making sure that the people with whom you're surrounding yourself are positive, will contribute to your own personal growth and improvement, and who will not attempt to do things that will hamper those things. The world is full of many different types of people and you are, in no way, obligated to entertain or help them all.

You're a human being like everyone around you and you do have needs that should be met. You need to sleep, eat, and have periods of personal fulfillment and enjoyment. You need to spend time doing the things that make you happy, you need to spend time doing things that will make your life better, and you need to spend time with people who don't leave you feeling like a used tissue by the end of your interactions. I know you know what I mean.

People who are empathic can get into a pattern in which they focus only on helping the people around them who are loudest. It is possible to get so carried away dealing with, solving, and mediating the problems of the people around you that your own problems go neglected or even get worse, depending on the scale of the neglect.

Let's take a look at a hypothetical example of someone who is empathic, but who isn't doing the things that they need to do before helping those around them.

Rosalind is an empath who is in a long-term relationship with Barry. Rosalind is an established member of her community who is well-known as the person who solves problems, is a great listener, who wants to help everyone, and who is like the community's surrogate mom.

Thanks to this reputation, Barry has to deal with people calling, coming by the house, or emailing his wife on a semi-regular basis, regardless of what she might be doing at the time. And true to

Rosalind form, regardless of what she may be doing at the time, she will drop whatever she is doing and get right to work on helping the person who has insinuated themselves right into the middle of her day, evening, night, or what have you.

Barry, who noticed Rosalind doing the dishes when the phone rang, is left to stare at the full, soapy sink when Rosalind rushes off to the neighbor's house to deal with their feuding in-laws. On another occasion, Barry promised Rosalind that they would go out to dinner for her birthday, only for Rosalind to be called over to another neighbor's house only moments before they were meant to leave. Rosalind rushed off and wasn't seen again for several hours that night.

Barry has pulled Rosalind aside on numerous occasions to express concern that she's not gotten a full night's sleep in weeks, that her migraines are increasing, the dishes keep getting left in soapy water while Barry minds the whole rest of the house, she's not eating properly, and Barry has scarcely seen her for more than fifteen minutes in the last month. Rosalind, now seeing that someone she cares about deeply is suffering, feels that sadness, that concern, and that worry.

Now, Rosalind is feeling all the emotions of everyone within a 10-mile radius of her house, and her bills aren't getting paid because she's too busy running around solving everyone else's problems to mind her own. How do you think Rosalind is doing emotionally, physically, and mentally? What is your assessment of her current state?

Now that you've gotten a proper picture of what Rosalind is dealing with from all those angles, let's take a look at a much more practical approach to managing one's own mental and emotional health while still helping the people around you when it's possible for you.

The absolute first step is to change your definition of the word *possible*. It is not possible to rush out and help someone with family matters while you're in the middle of dinner. It is not possible to skip breakfast in order to listen to someone else's problems. It is not possible not to shower for several days in a row while you're helping someone with a project for their house.

It is not possible to sacrifice your own well-being in order to save someone else's.

So please stop trying. Take care of yourself, your house, your own needs, before the needs of the people around you.

It is okay to help people around you, and it's okay to jump in and help someone with a crisis if you're the person they trust most for the job. Some criteria need to be met in this event.

1) The person needs to be able and willing to do the same for you if the tables were turned.

2) If you have anything that you really should be doing instead for your own well-being, then you need to say no.

3) If you would be putting your well-being or the well-being of anyone in your family on the line in order to do so, you need to say no.

You can't compromise on these, or you will find yourself snowed under a good deal more problems than you're helping to solve.

How to Stay Emotionally and Mentally Healthy

There are a number of things you can do when you're going through a rough patch with your emotions, with the people around you, or with your sensitivity to the world around you.

First, we will cover some things that are specific to being an empath, then I recommend that you do some looking into general stress release tactics that sound enjoyable to you. You should employ these tactics any time you're taking time for yourself, as a reprieve from the things going on around you.

1. **Remove yourself from a position of responsibility when someone else is hurting.**

It's so important to remember that someone in your immediate environment does not automatically deserve all of your attention and your emotional investment. If you find yourself dealing with someone who has a large emotional pain they're going through, it is not automatically your obligation to help that person.

Helping others can be so gratifying and fulfilling, but it's important not to do this so often that it becomes difficult or draining for us to do so.

In some instances, shedding that responsibility and allowing yourself to disconnect from the feelings of another can be so freeing. It can provide immediate relief and give you the chance to do some immediate recuperating from the stress and emotion you had already taken on from that person.

Many of us don't need to become completely involved in someone's gripe or problem to become aware of and immersed in those feelings ourselves. Sometimes their very presence just pulls us right into it and we're feeling it for them before they come to us about the situation.

Allow yourself to take a break once in a while and allow yourself to feel like that's okay.

2. Let yourself feel the pain or negative emotion, rather than trying to escape from it.

Catharsis is so important. Sometimes, if there is a negative emotion threatening to take hold of our mental space, holding it at bay and avoiding feeling it only makes it worse. It is possible for the things we do instead of processing those emotions to make them worsen as they wait, pent up in yourself, waiting to be processed.

Emotion is not something that ages well, and it's not something that can generally be ignored without significant repercussions or drawbacks. If you find yourself feeling like you "might get mad," but you don't want to be mad and are avoiding dealing with it, I have news for you. You are still mad, and you will stay mad until you deal with that issue.

Take some time for yourself and do the things that you need to do to fully process the emotion that you're avoiding dealing with. Once you do that, you will find that that emotion suddenly carries so much less weight than it did previously. You will also find that you won't be worrying about not feeling that thing anymore.

Emotions can be frightening, but they're quite fluid and change frequently. Do yourself a favor and process those feelings before too long. That way, it's out of the way, and you can move onto the next, more positive emotion.

3. **Realize that, as an empath, you can still exhibit negative traits, and work on them.**

Being an empath and being aware of the emotions of others does not mean that we cannot be mean or display toxic tendencies from time to time. In fact, if we find ourselves loaded down with the emotional energies of other people for so much time out of our lives, then it makes sense that those energies could manifest some behaviors that are not as healthy as we might like.

This is not to say that the empath cannot organically have some negative behaviors or toxic traits. These things can be developed or picked up from a number of places. Humans are, in every way, still human. We are still subject to the failings and missteps of our peers. We may say things we don't mean, be grumpy and snap at someone, or any number of other things that could cause someone to feel bad after speaking with us.

Recognizing that we are capable of having poor, toxic, or rude behaviors is the first step to being able to change them. Knowing how we are making others feel and perceiving the effects that we're having on the people in our environment can be a great measuring tool for knowing when it's time to make some changes.

4. **Allow yourself to see the good in you, and to build self-esteem from them.**

You are a good person and you deserve to feel like you are a good person. Knowing that you've done so much for people should make you feel really great about yourself, and you are more than welcome to remind yourself of the good things about yourself if you ever find yourself feeling badly about it.

As empaths, we tend to be able to pick up on when people are feeling neglected, low self-esteem, low self-worth, etc. We're able to spot those things and then we're able to tell those people what they need to hear in order to get them back up on their feet, doing well, and getting on their way to the next amazing thing they're going to do.

Allow yourself to do this for you. If you are going through a negative patch and you feel like you could use the ego boost, look at the things that you've accomplished and the things that you do on a daily basis from the perspective that you would if you were talking to a friend in your position. Then talk to yourself in the same way that you would talk to that friend.

Taking pride in who you are and what you've done is a great way to heal yourself using your empathic tools.

5. Don't shut people out of your life and your heart.

The people in your life who know you and love you, want to be there for us through thick and thin. We can tend to put our guard up in an effort to shield the innermost parts of ourselves from being touched by the negative emotions or inklings of others. As such, we can tend to go too far and keep people from getting through to us entirely.

It's important to regularly evaluate how thick our shields are, how close our boundaries are, and whether or not we need to lessen them a little bit. Doing so could allow the right people to get closer to us and impart some positive things into our lives.

6. Practice mindfulness.

Being mindful has the potential to be a very freeing exercise. Take your journal and practice mindfulness about your empathic abilities, about your life, about the people around you, and about the things going on in your life.

Doing this along with meditation, yoga, walking, and other physical activities that help you to be focused and mindful can provide a lot of release for people with empathic abilities.

Mindfulness can be achieved in a number of ways, and there isn't really a wrong way in which to be mindful about the things going on around you, or in your life in general. Taking the time to think about things and to be present is a great exercise that can be very grounding.

Take a look into the different types of mindfulness and prompts for mindful journaling that stand out to you. Once you find one, take the opportunity to put it to work in your journaling. See what that does to help heal you from the things you've dealt with.

7. **Seek out other empaths so that you have someone who can relate to what you're going through.**

Something as simple as having someone in your corner who knows what you're going through can serve to alleviate so much pressure on a person. Having empathic abilities can be beyond exhausting and it can be such on a daily basis. If you're trying to talk through the things that you've been dealing with, and the person you're talking to has no earthly idea what you're talking about, it can be hard to see that conversation as productive or helpful.

If you can find someone who understands what it feels like to know what the people around you are feeling, to know what it feels like to be walking through a crowded store and suddenly have the overwhelming urge to flee, and who knows what it can feel like to attract people who seem to be a complete drain on your energy, passion, and emotions, it counts for so much. Not having to explain every part of what you're dealing with saves so much energy and can actually serve to give some of it back.

How to Help the Empaths around You

The empaths in your life might have no idea they're completely loaded down with emotional strife and stress until things come to ahead. Some people have figured out what their natural responses are to stress, how they look, how they feel, and how to counteract them.

Empaths, however, have a tendency to put their own emotions and their own troubles on the back burner if they see someone else's trauma, stress, pain, struggles, or issues as being more important than their own. This is generally when the empath could also be described as a "people pleaser." It is imperative to help this type of person to understand that when attempts are made to please everyone, it is typical for *no one* to end up happy.

The empath is overloaded beyond all reason, those who are closest to the empath are upset that someone they care about is being overloaded, the people they are trying to help have placed all their eggs in the empath's basket, so to speak, and there just isn't much opportunity for happiness and success in such cases. It is best to manage expectations, improve strategy, and distribute work evenly.

If someone is asking you to help them with something, ensure that the person knows this is not something that you're simply going to be doing or resolving for them. Split the work into manageable pieces amongst yourself, the person asking for help, and anyone else who is willing to contribute to this cause. Doing so gets more people involved, inspires a sense of community or group bonds, and gets the job done faster, and no one person is saddled with all the pain or exhaustion at the end of everything.

Having the ability to strategize, work hard, solve problems, understand what needs to be done, and the time to dedicate to the cause does not in any way obligate you to be the sole person on that project or even to work on it at all. You may need to repeat this to yourself as a mantra, but I promise it is true. The more you understand that helping other people to your own detriment isn't help, the better off you will be.

Helping someone when you are able to do so when you have the time when your own obligations permit, and when you have the proper resources is perfectly acceptable and it's admirable in every case. Killing yourself to help others because you know what it's like to be in that position doesn't help you. In most cases, if the person you were helping truly had a perfect understanding of what you were going through to help them, they could stop you immediately. No one wants you to suffer in order to help them. Those who do want you to suffer do not deserve your help.

As you begin to learn this, and as you begin to spot the empaths around you who are doing exactly what is described above, you will all need to work together to keep one another on the right path. This doesn't mean rolling up your sleeves and jumping into the thick of it with one another, but it means offering helpful reminders when they talk to you. "You have your own things to worry about," "So-and-so wouldn't want you killing yourself to make this work," "You need rest," and similar reminders are most welcome and generally quite needed amongst those who are highly sensitive and empathic.

Knowing someone who is empathic can be a responsibility of its own, even if you are not empathic. Helping those people is not impossible, however, and I can assure you they will need it from time to time. One of the things you can do for the empaths close to you suggests that they read the books in this bundle. These books are meant to help empaths to understand why they are the way they are, what they need to do in order to stay healthy, how to understand what it is that's affecting them in life, and how to keep their own needs in their view at all times.

If someone you know is an empath, consider doing any of the following with them to help them to recuperate in between big occurrences in their lives:

1. **Meditation**

    Meditation can be done in groups with a teacher, in groups with no teacher, by yourself, in groups with a guided meditation recording, and a number of other ways. With meditation being such an effective and proven means to help someone to decompress, de-stress, relax, re-center focus, and more, this could be a great activity to do with the empath in your life.

    This is meant to help you recharge your batteries, feel focused, feel refreshed, and can even have long-term benefits on the body, mind, and soul. Consider asking the empath in your life if they would like to take the time to meditate with you on a semi-regular basis.

Doing so can not only provide the benefits above, but it can also strengthen your relationship with one another and can cement your place in their life as a confidante and a healthy friend to have.

2. Spend time in nature

Nature has been found to have a hefty number of benefits for empaths and highly sensitive people. Spending time by a creek, listening to the babbling water and nearby wildlife, hiking on a nearby trail, disconnecting from the electronic buzz of everyday life to watch clouds pass overhead, weeding the garden, going for a swim in the lake, having a day at the beach, picking wildflowers, taking pictures of the woods and the animals in them, going to the zoo and watching all the animals playing... There isn't a limit, as nature is all around you and all of it will serve the empath very well.

3. Aromatherapy

With essential oils, candles, incense, and so many other means, there isn't a shortage of ways to infuse one's environment with smells that will relax, invigorate, inspire, cleanse, and relive you. Do a little research into the different aromatherapy media, the scents, and their benefits. Find one that fits the purposes from which the empath in your life could benefit, and pick up a couple of things. They will love it!

4. Creative hobbies

Sometimes, all the empath in your life needs is a little bit of time alone with a friend, some decoupage glue, and free license to go nuts! Being creative is such an invaluable outlet for someone who has a large creative streak within them. Sometimes the mere mention of the craft store will trigger excitement in the empath that cannot be quelled until crafting supplies have been procured. Go nuts, inspire one another, create together, and make sure to enjoy one another's company as you make beautiful projects together for no other reason than the fact that it's fun and relaxing to do so!

All of the above are great ways to help, inspire, invigorate, and recharge the empath in your life. Don't shy away from asking the empath in your life if they need anything, because, in a lot of cases, they won't want to ask anyone. Even in cases in which an empath knows they need someone else's help, they can feel discouraged from asking for it.

If you create and perpetuate a pattern of offering help, whether you think they need it or not, the person will only get more and more comfortable with the idea of you helping them.

Conclusion

Thank you for making it through to the end of *Empath Discovery: A Survival Guide for Beginners for Understanding the Empathic Brain, Discovering Your Dark Side, Embracing Your Emotional Skills and Getting Stronger Daily. Healing Modalities and Personality Types*! Let's hope it was informative and able to provide you with all of the tools you need to achieve your goals whatever they may be.

If you haven't done so already, your next step is to complete the exercises laid out in each chapter for you. These exercises will help you to understand the mechanisms at work, will help you to find healthy coping strategies, and will help you to heal from past traumas or incidents.

If you have completed these exercises, your next step is to ensure that you've read the other books in this bundle! Those are *Empath Protection: A Psychic Survival Guide for Understanding Narcissistic People, Setting Boundaries Around Dark & Mystic Personalities, Sustaining Your Emotional Energy and Achieving Healing & Empath Learning: A Complete Emotional Healing & Survival Guide for Highly Sensitive People to Reveal the Dark Mystic Secrets, Improve Skills & Habits for Defeating Energy Vampires and Overcoming Psychic Exams.*

The other books in this bundle will serve to aid the empath in healing from the emotional trauma of a narcissistic relationship, how to spot narcissistic people before they become a problem, and how to cultivate meaningful relationships and help them thrive with the power of empathy.

Thank you very much for reading and please share the information you found helpful with friends and family who may also benefit. Finally, if you found this book useful in any way, a review on Amazon is always appreciated!

EMPATH LEARNING

A Complete Emotional Healing and Survival Guide for Highly Sensitive People to Reveal the Dark Mystic Secrets, Improve Skills and Habits for Defeating Energy Vampires and Overcoming Psychic Exams.

By Crystal Gift

Table of Contents

Introduction

Congratulations on downloading Empath Learning: A Complete Emotional Healing and Survival Guide for Highly Sensitive People to Reveal the Dark Mystic Secrets, Improve Skills and Habits for Defeating Energy Vampires and Overcoming Psychic Exams and thank you for doing so.

The following chapters will discuss many aspects of the life of an empath. Someone who as highly sensitive as an empath has a good deal of unique challenges throughout life, and personal relationships. It is the goal of this book to provide practical tools the average empath can use to forge a path ahead in life while protecting themselves from the emotional incursions in their environment.

This is a very popular subject with many published works to offer answers for empaths and those who know them. Thank you for choosing this book out of that vast number. It is our sincere hope that you find the information in these pages to be of use to you and that you can find answers within it.

Happy reading!

Chapter 1: What it Means to be an Empath

What is Empathy?

A standard dictionary will tell us that empathy is the ability to understand what someone is experiencing from their point of view. So, let's take a look at the more involved details of that concept. When we say that someone is empathetic, we mean that they have the ability to put themselves in the shoes of the person in front of them, see things as they see them, experience what it must feel like to be in that position and then act according to what that ability has shown them.

You will often hear the empath say things like, "this must be hard for you," or "I can imagine such a thing being hard on you." They really mean that. Someone who is empathetic has idealistically taken a walk in your shoes, has gotten an idea of how the current or proposed situation may affect you, and is thinking with that when they discuss it with you.

This concept is one that is rather commonly discussed and understood. Less so is that there are three subcategories of empathy that are otherwise focused. This can lead to different results. Let's explore each kind of empathy and what they mean individually.

Cognitive

The cognitive type of empathy gives you an insight that can sometimes seem like mind reading. As it turns out, it is not so much mind *reading* as it is the *prediction* of the thought process. This brand of empathy, so to speak, gives you a clear enough grasp on the way someone ticks that you can put yourself in their shoes enough to plot their next move.

As much as it sounds like something out of Sherlock Holmes novel or a drama television series, it really does work and our thoughts do occur according to a pattern on a regular basis. Like with many things, if you're too close to the pattern, you may never see it. Someone who is empathetic on a cognitive level can effectively plot that mental course and see where you'll end up.

This is, of course, the product of getting to know you and getting a feel for your responses to things. Very few situations are as miraculous as Sherlock Holmes, wherein he can get to know your next move simply by talking with you for thirty seconds and looking at the crumbs on your collar.

One of the many bonuses of cognitive empathy is being able to determine what someone can comfortably handle. This makes it particularly useful in the workplace, from a leadership role. If you can predict what someone's response will be to a specific task or workload. If you want to assign several different projects to someone who you know thrives off of one clear path laid out for them, you might be setting them and yourself up for failure.

However, if you're looking to assign these tasks to someone who you know operates very well on multiple tasks, with very little direction, you're far more likely to see positive results. These positives benefit you, your employees, and your company as a whole. It should be noted that if one of your staff thinks in a way that allows them to accomplish a lot in a very short time, they should be getting paid more than the person who does less in the same time! This concludes my small endorsement for the studious multitasker.

Let's take a look at some examples of what cognitive empathy could look like in a professional setting. Let's say that the director's assistant has cognitive empathy. She is aware of how thought processes will go, and this helps her in her work of anticipating and exceeding the director's needs throughout the day. A lot of what makes her job flow smoothly is knowing what the director needs before he has to ask her for it, so he's never left waiting for her to complete a task. While this could seem very demanding, his job isn't necessarily made any easier if asking his assistant for things doesn't save him any time.

So this assistant, we'll call her Laura, is able to understand what the director (we'll call him Tom) will need based on a history of what he has needed in the past, as well as his thought process about the things that are occurring in his job. If she understands what Tom is dealing with, then Laura is far more likely to be able to say, "He's going to want me to make copies of those documents for him and bring coffee while I'm at it." Now, this is where her acumen as an assistant comes in. She knows that if she waits for him to be done with the documents he needs to be copied, then goes to get the copies and the coffee; he is going to be waiting for her.

Her solution is to go now, get the coffee from the break room, bring the things he will need for his next task, and deliver them at the same time. This way, he is onto the next task while she's off getting copies. Her history with him and her understanding of his preference for the cadence he likes to keep in his work tells her that he would prefer to be busy while she's gone.

It is true that some aspects of this example can be attributed to other learned skills, and which can be explained differently. When considering what empathy is and can do for you, it's important to bear in mind that it's not a superpower. It's not an infallible boon bestowed by the almighty above. It is a sense, like hearing or smell, and it can be honed, weakened, augmented, or otherwise influenced by other factors in a person's life.

Let's take a look at a personal example of how cognitive empathy could affect a situation. Tina comes home from a long day and she's in no mood to deal with any further life responsibilities or chores. The day has taken everything it can take, and she feels that now is the perfect opportunity for her to take some time to do the things that she knows will help her to recuperate from a trying day at work.

Kevin, her significant other, is at home when she arrives. He can see the look on her face and knows that it's a signal of mild distress and slight exhaustion. From this emotional flag, he can put himself in the thought path that he knows she takes in such an event. He knows that when she is sad and tired, she likes to relax, write in her journal, and have a glass of wine. He also knows that she does not like to balance the checkbook, wash her laundry, or scoop the litter box, as had been her intention for the evening before the day she's had.

Kevin, knowing he wants to provide the things Tina needs, greets Tina warmly, directs her to the bedroom to change out of her work clothing, pours a glass of wine and puts her blanket in the dryer for her. Someone with cognitive empathy may not always be this considerate, but Kevin is a gem. Tina takes her place on the sofa with her journal, blanket, and wine, and gets to work unwinding her day. Kevin finishes up dinner and sits contently next to her while doing his own evening activities.

The nature of cognitive empathy is such that it acknowledges the thought path before the emotional path. For some, these two are immediately connected and understood. For others, the cognitive path is quite distinctly separate from the emotional one. In fact, one of the troubles that we will explore more in the fourth chapter of this book is that it is a fairly common problem for people who experience cognitive empathy, to completely miss emotional cues and to respond to them properly.

Based on what you've read here about what cognitive empathy is, can you think of any examples in which cognitive empathy would come in handy? Have you ever found yourself experiencing cognitive empathy? How would someone who is empathetic on a cognitive level respond to some of the things you've experienced in your life?

As we discuss more the different types of empathy, take notes on the aspects that appeal to you and see what type of empathy you employ the most. Do you stick to one category, or do you find that there are aspects from each that describe you accurately? Find out more as we continue to explore empathy.

Emotional

When it comes to empathy, the first thing that people often think of their emotions. This is because emotional empathy *is* an emotion in itself. Emotional empathy is also known as *affective empathy* or *automatic empathy*. This is because the response of tuning into the emotions of others and the capacity to develop sympathy or compassion based on that is a natural urge that many people feel. It's sort of the emotional basis for those two more complex actions.

Let's define compassion and sympathy in order to make a distinction between empathy, sympathy, and compassion.

Empathy – The ability to understand and share the sentiments or feelings of another.

Sympathy – Feelings of pity or sorrow at the misfortunes of another.

Compassion – Leniency and concern for the sufferings of others.

You can see, by these definitions, how these things are interconnected. Can you also see how they are *not* the same response? That will be important as we continue to explore the stages and nature of emotional empathy.

There are three parts to the emotional empathy response that might sound familiar to you:

1. Having a personal emotional response that matches that of the person in front of you.
2. Having personal feelings of distress as a response to the misfortune of the person in front of you.
3. Having a compassionate response to the person in front of you because of their misfortune.

It should be clarified that the distress felt by the empathetic person referenced in item two above are not necessarily the same feelings of distress being felt by the other person. Let's break this down and show an example of what this could look like between a group of people.

Let's say that John and Patricia have been married for several years, but after some incidents that can't be taken back, John decides that it's the best for both of them to end the marriage. John, looking to his friends Alan and Rita for help through this tough time in his life, both of them feel a good measure of empathy for him.

Rita, in particular, is the person that John feels most comfortable talking to about the things that went wrong in his marriage. As he does so, Rita sits with him and hears him out, feeling sad with him for a time. As they begin to talk things through and as she hears more from him about what went wrong, what was and wasn't reciprocated in the relationship, and other things about the relationship, new feelings start to take hold in Rita.

She might feel angry at Patricia for the things that she didn't do properly, or she might feel frustrated that she can't do anything to immediately make John feel better. Whatever feelings begin to surface next; they are *Rita's* unique distress as a response to the misfortune of the person in front of her. From here, she gains an understanding of all that John has been going through and develops a compassionate response toward John.

Can you think of a time when someone needed you and when you were empathetic toward that person? Looking back, do you find that you followed this pattern of empathetic behavior?

Let's explore another situation in which one might exhibit empathy for someone in their life. Let's think of a college professor, Dr. Richter. Dr. Richter has a very strict policy on grading late assignments with a severe penalty. One of his students misses turning in an assignment that is worth 30% of her grade for the class, for the semester.

As such, Dr. Richter is prepared to receive the assignment late, with a severe penalty to the grade. However, the student insists on having a meeting with Dr. Richter during office hours to discuss the grade, the assignment, why it's late, and what they can do to fix it. Dr. Richter is quite certain that there is nothing Emily, the student, can say to change his mind about the way his grading scale works. If the assignment had been important to her, she should have made the time for it.

When Emily comes to visit Dr. Richter, she looks worse for wear. Her skin is pallid, her hair is messy, and her clothes look wrinkly.

For this, as well as for the lateness of her assignment, she apologizes as she takes her seat. This is when she tearfully tells the professor that she had been all set to turn in her assignment at the appropriate time, had blocked out her homework time to allow enough time to complete it when her mother took a nasty spill at home.

She was called immediately after it happened, but before Emily could make any arrangements to get back home, she received the follow-up call that there had been no time for her to come say goodbye. Emily stuck on campus, had her mind and her hands full over the next couple of days, fielding phone calls from friends and family while trying to figure out travel arrangements for the funeral. She had attempted to make contact with all her professors in the shuffle, but she had missed Dr. Richter.

Dr. Richter, not being particularly close to this student, still feels a strong emotional response to her misfortune and the difficulties that she's been having over the last few days. This is his immediate personal emotional response, which matches the person in front of him. She is terribly sad, and he is sad for her as well.

Next, Dr. Richter feels uncomfortable with such a serious subject being discussed with someone he doesn't know, and he feels upset that things played out in such an unfair way for the young lady in front of him. These are the personal feelings of distress that he has in response to the misfortune of the person in front of him.

As they continue to discuss things, Emily begins to feel a little bit better, having someone to talk to, who understands that life is unfair from time to time. While the conversation continues, Dr. Richter hears about the things that she is had to deal within the last couple of days, as a result of her family emergency.

Out of compassion, Dr. Richter tells her that he won't apply the penalty to her assignment if she can get it to him within the next three days. Amazingly, Emily has already completed her assignment, in the hopes that if she brought the completed work with her, that he would be more inclined to be lenient with her, given the circumstances.

She emails her assignment to him while sitting in his office and he agrees that she shall have the fairest grade possible on this assignment with no penalty. This leniency is an act of compassion in response to the misfortune suffered by the person in front of him.

Can you think of a time when you were more lenient or compassionate with someone who was going through a difficult time? What happened? How did it make you feel to make that concession for someone who really needed it?

Compassionate

While compassion is an aspect of emotional empathy, *compassionate empathy* is a sub-category of its own. When one is inclined to feel compassionate empathy, one is often driven to *do* something with the empathy they're feeling. This is the response that tells us to leap into action to remedy the plight or misfortune of the person suffering in front of us. This is the type of empathy that a lot of people try to exhibit. It's seen as selflessness, helpfulness, altruism, and it's held in high regard.

The other two types of empathy have their uses in a good number of situations. In fact, emotional and cognitive empathy are great tools to help you to get ahead in both personal and professional relationships. Compassionate empathy takes elements of both cognitive and emotional empathy and adds action into them. Let's look at some examples.

Nine-year-old Sarah comes to her mother, Mrs. Smith, one day after school and is terribly upset, nearly to the point of tears. Sarah's mother, who is accustomed to seeing her young, spritely daughter in such high spirits, is very concerned about what could be bothering her daughter so much. She asks what's been going on and how she can help.

Sarah tells her that she had brought her favorite stuffed bunny with her to school for show and tell. On her way home from school, a little boy in her class took the bunny from her hands and tossed it out the bus window. Recounting the tale moves Sarah to tears, and her mother is spurred right into the action. She wants the name of the little boy that threw the bunny out the window, the bus driver who let it happen, and she wants to know what was said and done to rectify the situation at the time of the incident.

Sarah tells her that it was Alfie Wilson who threw her bunny out the window. He said that her bunny was "stupid baby stuff," took it from her hands, and chucked it out. She said she stood up and shouted for the bus driver, who shouted for both children to sit down in their seats and keep their hands away from the open windows.

The compassionate empathy response in Sarah's mother is in full force as she calls the school to talk to the office administrator about the incident and informs said administrator that Alfie Wilson's parents will be receiving a phone call shortly to enquire about a replacement bunny. The administrator asks for Mrs Smith not to act rashly and to allow the school office to take care of matters that occurred on the school bus.

Reluctantly, Mrs. Smith agrees and allows the school office to do its work in contacting the Wilson family to mediate the situation. Now, Mrs. Smith might feel a bit stunted in her efforts to resolve the matter and appease this emotional response. However, she has put the right people onto the case, and she will see the resolution as a result. So, here's a small helpful hint in the middle of this example, try to assess what you're actually getting done if you feel like you're not doing enough to help someone!

The next day, Mrs. Smith takes Sarah into the office to meet with the administrator before the first bell and is greeted with a brand-new bunny from the Wilson family and an apology from Alfie. He has been going through some stress at home, and he lashed out at Sarah. His family, however, will address that with him separately.

All has been resolved, and all is good thanks to Mrs. Smith's compassionate empathy response telling her to follow up with the school regarding a most unpleasant interaction on the bus.

Now, because we all expect that a mother would leap in and do what needs to be done for her baby, let's take a look at some compassionate empathy coming from an unexpected source, shall we?

Gerald is a bus driver in the city. He has very strict instructions to stop at stops where riders are waiting, or where riders have requested that he stop. He needs to keep a tight schedule, so he makes it a point not to wait for straggling passengers who might be half a block or more behind the bus stop. This saves him from holding up traffic, and it keeps everyone on schedule.

One day, while he's pulling up to a stop on his bus route, he sees an older gentleman with several paper grocery bags in his arms. He notices the man's pace pick up slightly when he sees the bus. Gerald can tell that at the pace the man is walking and the rate at which he is approaching the stop, there is very little chance that the man will make it to the stop in time.

Nevertheless, Gerald pulls up to the stop, which has been requested, and at which there are a few riders waiting. Once everyone has left the bus and new rides have boarded, Gerald checks his mirror to see the old man, attempting to wave his hand, shout, hold his bags, and run at the same time.

Gerald, seeing the man's sagging clothing, sweating brow, and overloaded appearance, puts the bus in park and decides to wait just a few more moments for the older man to make it to the stop. As he approaches, however, the man loses his footing on the sidewalk and takes a tumble just a few yards short of the bus.

Unable to leave the bus full of passengers, Gerald stands up and asks if there is anyone able-bodied in the crowd who can help and an elderly gentleman who has fallen and needs help. A couple of young gentlemen stand up and disembarks the bus, collecting the man's spilled groceries, and helping the man to his feet.

Before too long, the man, his groceries, and his helpers have boarded the bus, and everyone can be on their way. This was not something that was required of Gerald and was not something that anyone asked him to do. However, with someone who was experiencing compassionate empathy, he could tell that the old man was having a very hard time, desperately needed to catch that bus, and was under more weight than he ought to have been.

As such, Gerald sprang into action getting help from willing strangers and ensured this man he did not know was kept safe, helped to the best of his ability, and taken where he needed to go.

These are the kinds of things the world could use more of, don't you think? If the old man was running toward your bus and fell down, what would you do? Would you risk being late to your next stop, if it meant helping someone in need?

What is an Empath?

An empath is a person who is exceedingly sensitive to the emotions and sentiments of the people in their environment. There are a lot of aspects of being an empath that, when you see them listed out for you, might explain a good deal of the things you have been going through in life without having a name for it.

Having empathy and being an empath are two different things, as you may have gathered from the information in this chapter. Empathy is a natural trait that many people possess. The lack of it characterizes some known mental illnesses, so if you have found a lack of familiarity with the concept from the description and examples above, consider consulting with your doctor.

Being an empath is a fairly involved thing. The highly sensitive person or empath will often know that they are at least somewhat different from others in their abilities, but the abilities can also be honed, refined, understood, and used to one's advantage, just like any natural talent one might possess.

Chapter 2: The Traits of Highly Sensitive People

There is plenty of traits that are shared by people who are highly sensitive. Some of them are about what you would expect from the word "empath," and some of them might strike you as a little bit surprising.

The more you learn about what the traits of highly sensitive people are, the better equipped you can be to thrive with them. Some of these traits can be considered to be a bit of a pitfall, but we will discuss how to overcome this in chapter four of this book.

Getting to know yourself as an empath is a very important part of finding more strength in your abilities. In addition to this, it is an essential part of overcoming the things that can set one back. Knowledge is potential power, so let us take a look at some traits of highly sensitive people and empaths:

45. Strong emotional content on television has a profound impact on you.

    Have you ever been minding your own business, watching television or scrolling through social media, only to find yourself bawling your eyes out in the next moment because of something that happened on the screen? If you're like me, the things that do it the most are people paying surprise visits to loved ones, cute animal videos, and television shows that have a lot of love or death in them. This type of content is definitely meant to evoke an emotional response from the people who watch them, but those who are highly sensitive know what it's like to be sitting there trying to enjoy a television show and suddenly feel overwhelmed with emotion.

46. People are always asking you for advice.

    Having a lot of friends who want to "pick your brain," "bounce things off you," or "get your take," can tell that you're in-tune emotionally and consciously. They can tell that the things you see are things that others cannot see, and they wish to take advantage of your unique vantage point. This is not to say there is anything disingenuous about their interest in your view, but they do want your take on things, and they want to know what you would do in this situation. Being a sensitive person or an empath gives you the reputation of being trustworthy and emotionally intelligent.

47. Intimate relationships can overtake all of your thinking and the energy you get from them flows throughout your entire life.

Some who are empaths or highly sensitive decide to stay single because of this. Personal relationships take a lot of work, maintenance, investment, and communication under the best and most "normal" circumstances. When one of the parties is an empath or a highly sensitive person, it can put a little extra weight on things. You will find that empaths and highly sensitive people will do their best to very quickly address and resolve any emotional conflict in the relationship because, when those come up, they envelop every aspect of that person's life. If this is you, you might find yourself having trouble eating, sleeping, thinking, working, or doing *anything* while there's an unresolved conflict in your relationship. Finding someone who is as ready to resolve conflicts as you are is a very key part of making a relationship work as an empath.

48. Your sensitivity could be mislabeled as anxiety or shyness.

Empaths and highly sensitive people can often—as discussed elsewhere in this list—find themselves being very introspective or can have sudden and seemingly adverse reactions to very mundane or minimal stimuli.

As a result of these factors and some others, it can be possible for doctors, loved ones, friends, or acquaintances to assume that there is something mentally askew or unbalanced. Autism, anxiety, shyness, introversion, and depression are among some of the false suggestions that have been made for those who are highly sensitive to the emotions and sentiments of the people around them.

49. Regardless of introversion or extroversion, you withdraw often.

Being highly sensitive and being an empath can make personal interactions very taxing and exhausting. As a result of this, as well as other factors, the empath will find a great amount of benefit in creating some time in which they can be by themselves and "recharge their batteries." Solitary relaxation activities like coloring, reading, meditating, personal hygiene and care regimens, journaling, listening to music, and games can all be great recharging activities. Because of this semi-frequent need for solitude and seclusion, people may perceive you as reclusive or introverted, in spite of being very interested in talking with others, being outgoing, and making friends when you go out.

50. When thinking of leadership roles, you always assume that means putting the team first.

    As an empath, not putting others first is a pretty foreign concept as a general rule. It is hard for an empath to be centered on themselves and they perceive leaders as the people who are supposed to help the group get to where it needs to be. This means that the leader must ask the team to complete tasks they would not be unwilling or unable to do themselves, in order to achieve a goal that they could not do as individuals. When a leader shows narcissism or self-preservation, it can elicit a disgusted or outraged response from the empath or highly sensitive person. By the estimation of such a person, a leader should be the guardian and custodian of the group they're leading before anything else.

51. The world you've created in your mind is rich and vibrant. Many empaths and highly sensitive people have been thinking, daydreaming, imagining, thinking, positing, and hypothesizing since their childhoods. Because of this, they have unspoken theories and mental models regarding the world around them, they have little stories in their minds, and they may have characters they think about on a regular basis. The imagined ecosystem in the mind of the empath is vibrant, teeming with life that's both new and old, and is always coming up with

something new to throw out in the event of downtime, or just a little too much silence in the room.

52. Others find your very presence to be calming.

Due to the empath's ability to "tap into" the emotional frequency and thought patterns of the people around them, it can tend to have a very calming effect on the people who are near them. If someone is sad, scared, agitated, or experiencing a negative emotion, they will feel alleviation from your being there. This is due in part to the fact that when others who are not highly sensitive experience someone who is feeling a deeply troubling emotion, they have questions. They're curious, scared, put off, or otherwise unaware of what's happening. Someone who is an empath or a highly sensitive person knows exactly what is happening and knows how the person wants to be responded to at that moment. That alone does so much to calm the mind of someone dealing with a strong, negative emotional response.

53. Hunger very quickly turns into anger, sometimes even before hunger.
You've probably heard the term "hangry" before. This is a colloquial term to identify that irrational anger that people can tend to feel when their blood sugar has dipped

a little too low and they need to eat something right away or they will bite someone's head off over something mundane. This is very uncharacteristic behavior for the person, but it is something they seemingly cannot control in traffic or at the grocery store when they have just gone a couple of hours too far without a sandwich. People who are highly sensitive to their own feelings, emotions, and bodily stimuli might find that this happens to them a little more often than they might be comfortable with admitting.

54. You're highly sensitive to wardrobe malfunctions.

This is one that bothered me a lot as a child. Did you ever get to school and notice something like the scratchy tag inside your shirt, itchy wool in your sweater, a popped seam on your sock, or underpants that were just a tiny bit too tight? For most people, things like this will eventually fade into the background of the day when something that's more pressing or important takes the stage. For some empaths and highly sensitive people, this feeling does not ever go away. We can tug at the clothes, re-fold the tag, turn up the music, really throw ourselves into whatever it is we're doing and it will feel like the volume on these issues just gets cranked up another notch as more mental stimuli creep in over the course of the day.

55. Criticism is painful beyond reason.

For the empath and the highly sensitive person, criticism can feel like a slap in the face. Rest assured that every empath has worked on seeing it differently, looking at it from a helpful angle and trying to get the help from it that there is to get. Some have succeeded, but it's a large hurdle that many have to really try to get over. Those who offer constructive criticism of our creative pursuits are rarely trying to hurt us with that criticism. We do know this on a cognitive level, but there's always going to be that initial shock and sting from the delivery of that statement.

56. You feel an overwhelming love for pets, animals, or babies.

You may be familiar with something called "cute aggression," or you might know someone who gets tears in their eyes when looking at something that's "So cute I can't handle it." This is a trait of a highly sensitive person. There is an overwhelming of excitement, happiness, joy, love, and about a million other things that bubble up when you see someone or something that is adorable, and you freak out a little bit. Some people might view this response as a little "extra," but how can you not gush over how cute the little tiny corgi puppy is!

57. You're exceedingly perceptive and minor details don't escape you easily.

    As you go through your day, there will often be small details that stick out to you like a sore thumb. When you bring them up to the people around you, you might say things in response like, "how did you even see that?" To you, however, it might seem like something that you couldn't possibly have missed. Those things that you notice tend to make others see you as a detail-oriented person who has an eye for the minutia or projects. In the workplace, this can be a great advantage and it looks great on a resume.

58. You're prone to jumping or startling easily.

    If you find that sudden loud noises make you jump more than they should, you should be a highly sensitive person. Furthermore, if you find that this trait lessens when you're particularly drained, exhausted, tired, or depressed, that jumpiness is rooted more in your higher sensitivity. It would be nice if being more sensitive to things, being more aware of small or minute details, and being less able to be lied to meant we weren't easily startled. Instead of this, however, we find ourselves so completely immersed in the things that we do in every moment that when something comes up to snap us out of it, we can become quite jarred or unsettled.

59. Once startled, you may be shaken for a while or experience "aftershocks."

Have you ever been startled in a really big way, perhaps as a joke by a friend or loved on, only to feel "aftershocks," or shivers afterward? It might feel like you're anticipating it happening again, every part of you tenses up for just a quick moment, then you can go about what you were doing. Being an empath means you're aware of a lot of things. Being aware of so many things comes to be something that we rely on from day to day and when we're suddenly and loudly confronted with something of which we weren't aware, it can catch us off-guard in a big way. The systems in the body can sometimes seem as though they're trying to overcompensate for that lack of awareness by being hyper-aware after the fact. Cognitively we know that this wasn't the intention of the person who startled us, we know that being hyper-vigilant now won't help, and we know that it won't likely happen again. This does not, however, quash that response.

60. Stimulants are very effective in short measure.

An empath or a highly sensitive person might find that one cup of coffee can do a great deal to "light the fire under them," so to speak. With all the nervous responses being more highly tuned in and with all the sensitivities being raised, it makes sense that a little bit of a stimulant would go a long way. Be careful of the stimulants you take into your body and be sure not to overdo it. Overuse of caffeine and other stimulating substances can cause anxiety and other issues in the mind and body if left unchecked. Try to limit how much you take on and see if you notice any differences.

61. Depressants are very effective in short measure.
Just like with stimulants, depressants will take effect very quickly and will often last. Alcohol might hit a little harder for people who are highly sensitive. In addition to this, certain substances in the body could fail to have the intended effect and just make you feel ill. It's prudent to be dubious of new substances and take only what is prescribed by a medical professional.

62. It's easy for you to get a feel for where someone is coming from when telling you something.
When someone is explaining something to you, you might have an idea of exactly what they mean within the first few seconds of them talking. This can trip you up from time to time when you are ready to move onto the next phase of the conversation, but the person in front of you is still working on explaining things that you have

already grasped. It's important to recognize this mechanism at work and to be kind in such an event. Most people don't understand how you could possibly know the things you know and cutting off the communication of someone who is trying to work with you is a very fast way to complicate the relationship.

63. You do a lot of introspection and deep thinking.
People might find you "zoning out," or "spacing out" on a semi-regular basis. People who are highly sensitive and who are empaths will often find that there's a good deal of things going on behind the scenes, so to speak. There are a lot of thoughts about the things going on in your life, the things that are going on with your friends and family, or the scenario in your head could be completely hypothetical.

64. Pain sets in more easily.
Without any medical diagnosis like fibromyalgia, arthritis, dermatitis or anything else, it would seem that things just hurt you a little more easily. I have met someone whose legs in particular, if touched just a little too hard, she would flinch from pain. No bruising or otherwise alarming indicators of anything wrong with her body, other than pain that occurred very quickly and in a very sharp way. Hip checking a table while walking

past it could thoroughly ruin her afternoon, or at least part of it! Are there any areas of your body that are particularly sensitive?

65. You ask the big questions in life and seek a lot of answers about the status quo.

"Why are things the way they are," is a pretty common big question to ask. It's very broad, it has a lot of answers, and it could keep you busy pondering for days on end. However, the questions that an empath will find themselves asking, have to do with life's deeper subjects, as well as some that might be hard to articulate until they've been mulled over for a good long while. Have you ever wondered about something, but you had no idea how to broach it with someone to discuss it with them? Or thought that you could figure out how to word the question, but you doubted very much that they would be interested or see you normally after you asked it?

66. You find cruelty and violence to be abhorrent.

Being in-tune to the emotions, feelings, and pains of others, it's easy for us to put ourselves in the shoes of someone being brutalized, without ever meaning to. When we watch the news, we see people going through worse pain than can be imagined, but we're right there alongside them. Watching someone who is at a severe disadvantage being neglected, harmed, or otherwise sustaining any measure of cruelty will often rattle someone who is highly sensitive. This might be the kind of thing you choose to remove from your television watching, or it might be something you do your best to avoid even in conversation. When these things happen around you, you might find yourself overwhelmingly compelled to jump into the thick of it and do something about it.

67. You feel ailments or illnesses as someone you love is going through them.

It's possible that you've hears of "sympathy illness," or "sympathy pains." This is when someone with whom you're very in-tune is going through something painful or sickening and you, as someone who's very connected to that person, will feel some of the effects of that as well. This is something that can happen to just about anyone who happens to be strongly connected to someone who is going through something. For empaths, however, this can happen with just about anyone you've even just met. Being in a nursing home or hospital might be difficult for you as an empath, because you leave feeling more ill, less vibrant, or just exhausted at the very least.

68. Deadlines and time limits leave you feeling shaken or rattled.

Keeping to deadlines and time constraints isn't necessarily difficult for you to do from a work effort standpoint. However, you might find that time limits on things tend to make you feel more harried, pressured, and less effective. It can seem like all the energy you originally had to work on your project is completely occupied by the time limit that's been imposed on you. Things you should have easily been able to achieve otherwise, seem to be slammed up against that timeline and can only be accomplished with stress, a furrowed brow, and terrible personal care practices. Don't allow yourself to skip meals to get to those deadlines; you need to eat, sleep, bathe, and breathe. Let yourself do those things.

69. Your greatest efforts are expended on not messing up.

Empaths and highly sensitive people have a tendency to be concerned with being a burden on others and with messing up. Because of this, there is a good deal of pressure exerted from within one's own self that tells us not to mess up or that we should concentrate on messing up less. The Catch-22 here is that when you're hyper-focused on not making mistakes, it opens the door to a lot more mistakes than would have occurred if you had simply been able to relax. This can be changed, thankfully, but it is quite an exhausting thing to deal with in the interim.

70. Change is jarring or even upsetting.

We perceive change everywhere, on even the tiniest scales. It's up to us to see when things are going differently with the people around us at work and in life, and as previously mentioned in this list, tiny details always seem to snag our attention on their way past. Thanks to this, large changes that could seem normal to others around us, could seem completely cataclysmic to someone who is an empath or a highly sensitive person. This doesn't mean that we can't adapt to change and that nothing should ever change around an empath or highly sensitive person. What it does mean, however, is that those around us could stand to give us a little warning, or at least give us a minute to get adjusted to how things will be since the change has been implemented.

71. You find yourself feeling exhausted after having absorbed and processed the feelings of others.

When someone needs to bend your ear for a prolonged period of time and you find yourself having to be present for someone, and receptive to their emotions, you might feel quite exhausted. Spending the day feeling what others feel and dealing with their problems from their perspective as well as your own is no small feat. This is why a good deal of empaths choose not to go into fields wherein they have to manage and deal with the emotions of others. It's a talent they have, but if your full-time job is that draining, you're liable to burn out before too long. Finding a balance when helping people is key. Make sure that you're not giving more than you have to give.

72. Sensory overload is much more easily achieved.
Sensory overload can be a very overwhelming feeling and can require different coping mechanisms to rectify it. If you're out at the grocery store, surrounded by people, you have a lot to pick up on. There are noises all over the place, people having conversations as you pass, and it can reach a "fever pitch." When things reach that fever pitch, it's not uncommon to have something of a "freak out." The person experiencing it can begin to yell, panic, or just shut down entirely. When this happens, it's important to try to focus on one specific thing and try to calm the overload. If leaving the area is possible, doing so could help the calming process to continue.

73. You are affected by the general atmosphere of a room or "vibe."

If there are a few angry people in a room and the atmosphere seems affected, that could chase off or at least unsettle an empath. They pick up on that tension and it has a very real effect on how comfortable they can get in that space. For instance, if you went to a party and the hosts had gotten into an argument before people began to arrive and had no time to resolve it, that could thoroughly ruin your chances of enjoying the party unless something is done to rectify the situation between those two hosts.

74. Beauty moves you deeply, sometimes to tears.

Art, sunsets, architecture, nature, animals, people, and anything else that can have a beauty that inspires an emotional response. If you've ever found yourself feeling profoundly affected or influenced by the beauty of something, that is a trait of the highly sensitive person. Someone who isn't aware of their abilities as an empath or a highly sensitive person might be alarmed at this trait. They might see it as a sign that something is wrong either with the stimulus or with them. You can rest assures that, if this is something you've experienced, there is nothing wrong with you. There is nothing wrong with art, music, sunset, architecture, people, etc.

75. You tend to adopt the feelings of others and feel them as though they're your own.

    This is a rather basic trait of an empath, but it is also a very essential one. The emotions that are felt by the people around you in your life, will inevitably reflect in your own emotions at some point or another. You will, on some level, feel that which is being felt by the people who are around you. It can be assumed that this effect will increase depending on the strength of your connection with the person, or your involvement with the things that are currently affecting them emotionally. For instance, if you don't particularly know someone, but you're right next to them when they get bad news, you might feel that more strongly. If you get into a fender bender and the driver of the other car becomes very upset or stressed, you have a higher chance of feeling that than if you happened to pass that fender bender on the street.

76. Conflict can make you physically ill.

    It's possible to be made physically ill by conflict in your immediate vicinity. If you are trying your best to make something work, only for conflict to arise in that situation, you might feel sick to your stomach, develop a headache, or even feel like you can't breathe very well. There are a good number of circumstances during which this can manifest itself and some of them are rather more mundane than we might anticipate. For instance, someone shouting at you in traffic, someone getting impatient in line behind you at the DMV, a dissatisfied customer in a restaurant who's making a fuss, two drunk guys outside of a club, and much more. Conflict can arise from a good many situations in life, and it's impossible to avoid it categorically. What one can do, however, is choose to remove oneself from situations once conflicts arise if we cannot be reasonably expected to resolve it before removing ourselves. What is meant by this is that if you stir up a conflict unintentionally or otherwise, it would be rude to simply remove yourself without resolving it. If the conflict has nothing to do with you and it could be resolved without your investment or involvement, then removing yourself is wise. Since conflict has such a profound effect on empaths, avoiding conflict is a matter of survival and emotional health.

77. You cannot see someone who needs help without desperately wanting to provide it.
    In an empath or a highly sensitive person, compassionate empathy is in overdrive. This means that when you see someone in front of you who are having a difficult time with something, or who could use some help, you will feel a compulsion on every level to intervene or help.

This, just like with the conflicts, is not always in your best interest as an empath. Part of what you will need to learn is the management of emotional resources. Don't over-extend, don't give more than you have, and don't overload yourself with so many problems of others than you hardly have the time, energy, or attention for your own.

78. Occasionally, you will feel overwhelming emotions that are seeming "out of nowhere."

As you go along through your day, you will pass by people who are experiencing emotions. Most people are experiencing emotions as they go through their day. Occasionally, as you're out there, someone else's emotion will find its way in without you being cognizant of it. When that happens, you might feel an emotion that seems like it's coming from nowhere. This does not mean, however, that it is less valid or less of real emotion that you are feeling when this happens. The biggest thing about this type of thing happening is that it serves as an interruption in your day. It can trip you up, but if you know that you are susceptible to such outbursts or situations, you can get through it as it comes up and then goes about your day from there. You will not have to worry about what "set you off" for the rest of the day.

79. It's very hard for people to lie to you.

Because of the small details that you're apt to notice throughout your day and your interactions with others, you tend to pick up on the little things that sound off when someone is trying to lie to you. In addition to this, you pick up on inconsistent details in the story behind the lie. If you know the person who is trying to lie to you, you're even more likely to be able to spot the things that would tell you if someone is lying to you. Say, for instance, your significant other untruthfully says, "I'm fine," but you know that isn't true. You know what they sound like when they say they are fine, and they sounded different. You will notice drops in pitch and tone, you will notice strange inflections and more that will show you when things do not line up.

80. You have a "big heart," and will often give too much of yourself.

As someone who understands the emotions and the troubles of others on such an intrinsic level, you know how profoundly kindness can affect someone's entire day. You know what it means to impart positivity into someone's day so that the whole tone of their day is shifted into a more positive one. Doing this, however, is not always to your benefit. It's not always to your detriment, either. You should be judicious about how and when you spend your time and energy helping someone to be positive. You are not an infinite, inexhaustible fountain of positivity. You are able to create more positivity day by day, but you need to take the time to replenish that energy. You need to recuperate. As they often say, "You cannot pour from an empty glass. Take care of yourself first."

81. You seem to be a walking target for "energy drainers."
People who tend to need all the positivity they can get will find you and cling to you. People who do this are known as "energy vampires," or "positivity vampires." They will see and be drawn to the light that you provide, but they can very easily drain all of it out of you, needing all the light you have to offer and more. It's important to bear that in mind, as well as the fact that you can't pour from an empty cup. You can only give what you have to give. You cannot give more than that and you shouldn't even give as much as you have. If you give all that you have, there is nothing left for you to manage your life.

82. You feel that you know, without asking, what is going on around you.
Intuition is a large part of being an empath or a highly sensitive person. You can see the things that are going on in the environment and tell if there was recently an

argument between the people in the room you just walked into, or you know who someone was talking to before they got off the phone, and so much more. A large number of the situations that an empath will deal with are the mundane, day-to-day experiences. We are, after all, just normal people who are getting through our daily lives with a higher sensitivity than most.

83. You're an effective communicator and listener.

Being more empathetic and highly sensitive gives you a better look at how to fully acknowledge and accommodate someone in conversation. You know what people are looking for in their interactions with others, and you know how to simply be present and lessen the burden that someone is dealing with in their emotions. Effective communication is centered on proper, active listening and appropriate acknowledgments. Since these are all part of what an empath seeks to give others, people will find you to be a very effective communicator and confidante.

84. You have mood swings.

Thanks to the sensitivity that we experience, it's easy for small stimuli to send us into a mood in a deeper way than we might have otherwise expected. Thanks to a large number of stimuli we encounter throughout the day, it can seem like our moods are swinging from one into the other. If you're on the lookout for these types of things and you're focused on giving yourself a beat to think about and process the things going on before acting out after a mood swing, we can do well at keeping the swings at bay.

85. You have a trustworthy magnetism.

Thanks to your calming demeanor, your automatic understanding, and compassion for others, and to your ability to give emotional peace to others, people will see you as trustworthy. If they can be calm with you and feel that they are safe with you, they feel like they can trust you. As a result of this, you will find that people will tell you more things that you wouldn't expect someone to tell you. People you've known for a very short time will suddenly come to you and tell you about past traumas, current debacles, family histories, and so much more. Thanks to your magnetism, people will feel *compelled* to tell you things.

86. You might reach for addictive substances to escape the other traits of an empath.

Being an empath or a highly sensitive person can be exhausting. It can be very taxing if the things that can come up aren't properly managed. Being an empath can be emotionally, physically, and mentally exhausting. As you're going through all the trials and tribulations of being an empath, it can be tempting to reach for substances to "soften the blow," or ease the strain that it puts on you. As with any substances used for the purposes of coping or emotional alleviation, it is prudent to use caution. Utilizing substances with no prescription and utilizing multiple of these can carry a good deal of risk. It is best to exercise caution with such things and to exhaust any other avenues of relief before going down that route.

87. You're very creative.

Being in tune with our emotions and to minute details, creative pursuits come much more easily. We find a lot of reward from those pursuits and we take a lot of enjoyment in them as well. If you find that a good number of the items in this chapter fit you and you haven't gotten into any creative pursuits to date, give it a shot. Try coloring, drawing, or any other creative pursuits that might interest you and see how that does. A lot of times, those pursuits have a regenerative or recuperative effect on empaths and highly sensitive people.

88. Clutter and a crowded space make you uneasy or stressed.

As small details tend to fill and occupy the mind of an empath and a highly sensitive person, the details of the environment surrounding you will also do so. People who are highly sensitive will often find that clutter in their immediate space will stop them from focusing or keep them from feeling like they can work. It makes it difficult to sit at ease, it makes it difficult to create artistic work, it makes it difficult to focus on just about anything of any import.

How many of these traits stick out for you? How many of these things did you read, only to find that it describes something that you do frequently? Did you find anything described in this chapter that explained something you were doing, that you did not even know you were doing?

Exercise:

Are you an Empath?

Answer these questions honestly.

For each question, you answer with "Yes," give yourself one point.

21. Have I been labeled as shy, overly sensitive, or introverted?

22. Would I rather drive myself somewhere, so I have a way to leave before others?

23. Does it take me a long time to recover after spending an extended period of time with an energy vampire?

24. Am I easily startled?

25. Do I eat more than I need to when coping with stress?

26. Do I prefer to do one task at a time, rather than overwhelm myself by multitasking?

27. Am I socially reclusive at times?

28. Am I afraid of being smothered in intimate relationships?

29. Do I find nature to be recuperative or restorative to me?

30. Do I prefer small groups or even one-on-one interactions with large parties or gatherings?

31. Do I get mental overwhelm from people who talk continuously, loud noise, or odors?

32. Do I have a low threshold for pain?

33. Do I have a strong reaction to caffeine or medications?

34. Am I anxious or overwhelmed with any sort of regularity or frequency?

35. Do I need a recuperation period after being in large crowds?

36. Do I often feel like I'm not fitting in properly?

37. Do I have chemical or skin sensitivities that are exacerbated by scratchy clothes?

38. Do I seem to absorb the feelings of others?

39. Do I get sick over conflicts?

40. Do I feel more at ease in small-scale settings or cities than in large ones?

1-5: You are empathetic toward people but may not be an empath.

6-10: You have moderate empathic tendencies.

11-15: You have strong empathic tendencies

16-20: You are definitely an empath.

Chapter 3: How to Reject Negativity and Heal with Empathy

How to Say No

One of the biggest things an empath will struggle with is feeling like they can't say no when someone asks for something. How, when you know how much people need you, are you supposed to say no? If someone is asking for your help, how do you say no?

The first thing to realize is that you are not a bad person for being unable to help someone when you need it. You are not required to offer your support to someone, simply because they need it. You might be the best-suited person to resolve someone's problems; that does not mean you have to or that it is your responsibility.

In large measure, you will find that if you are unable to provide your help to someone without putting yourself in jeopardy or compromising your daily life, people will understand. Communication, which you have used to your advantage in many circumstances, is the key to saying no. Say it nicely, say it clearly, and say it definitively.

Let's go over some ways to keep yourself from over-extending.

1. Don't agree to anything on the spot.

   When someone asks you to agree to something, you could feel like it is a fine idea at that moment. However, when you return to your own routine, later on, you may find circumstances that preclude you from honoring your agreement, or you might just suddenly feel like it is not something you can do.

   In these situations, you might find that it's better to say, "I'll need a little time to think about that. I'll reach out in the next day or so to let you know." Also acceptable is, "I just need to line a few things up to make sure I can do that for you. I'll be in touch soon."

   You do not need to put a massive amount of time between being asked and giving your answer, but you should give yourself enough time to be properly aware of the things in your life that could more urgently require your attention.

2. Practice the different ways to phrase "No."

There are a lot of ways to say you either don't want to or can't do something. You would do well to practice a good number of them, so you're familiar enough with how to say the ones you like the most.

The more naturally those phrases come to mind, the more naturally you'll be able to respond with them to people who are asking you for things. Of course, we know that it won't be everyone who asks you for something that will need a negative response. We also know that there are obligations that all of us have in life.

However, being asked by a friend to help with some relationship advice or being asked to be someone's ride from the airport aren't things that are compulsory. Being there for your friends is great if you have the time and emotional availability, but that needs to be your first concern.

We'll list some phrases you can practice:

- "I'd like to help, but I'll be unavailable for this one. I hope it goes well for you."
- "Thank you for thinking of me. Unfortunately, my schedule is looking full these days."
- "I don't have the availability for that right now; can we set up another time?"

3. Curtail your availability.

Modern technology has given us the ability to be in about a million places at once. The drawback for this is that you are at the beck and call of anyone who would like to speak with you. Between social media, messenger apps, phones, and everything that keeps us connected to one another, there isn't any communication you can send to someone these days that you can't reasonably assume they'll see within 24 hours.

Because this technology removes all the barriers between yourself and people who need something from you, the responsibility falls to you to put that barrier back into place.

Establishing barriers is probably the most essential tool in being able to say no to things. If you have a very rigid set of rules that you live by, you can rely on those to tell you when you're overextending.

The boundary on immediate communications can be maintained by setting your notifications to be muted past some time in the evening so you can have time for yourself. This could be time to do chores and personal responsibilities, resting, relaxing, emotional exercises, prayer, meditation or anything you prefer to put into your evening.

4. Be firm, yet courteous.

Being assertive doesn't mean needing to be rude. This is a very good thing since telling an empath to be rude to others as a general rule would be like asking a squirrel to ride a bike.

It's important for the average empath to know that you are not being rude by being assertive in refusing to help them. You can tell someone, "I wish I could help you move this weekend, but I don't have the availability," and still be friends with them. You can tell them this and come to the housewarming with a lovely plant to wish them well in their new digs!

People who don't have the gift of being an empath do have the natural benefit of not worrying that their refusal will have negative repercussions with the person they care about. It appears to be a very empathetic response that tells us our use to people is directly proportional to their love for us.

I am happy to assure you, however, that this is not the case in a large number of relationships. Relationships that are predicated on exploiting your usefulness rather than on your feelings of mutual respect, affection, and familiarity are not as healthy and should, if at all possible, be avoided. You are person, not a tool; as such, your worth as a friend should be based on more than your "uses."

5. Understand tactics that are meant to get you to say yes.

There are a number of tactics in use by salespeople, organizations, and people to get you to say yes. It's important, as someone who has a hard time saying no, to be able to spot these. The more you know about the manipulation you face, the better chance you have of avoiding it entirely.

Here are some tactics that you might run into in your travels:

- Give Before Taking

  A technique that is common is to give you a little boost, a shot in the arm so to speak, before asking someone for something they actually want. So, this could look like someone coming to you and paying you a lot of compliments on your abilities and your proficiencies in life.

From there, they see that you're flattered, and they might even ask you some questions about how you're able to do some of the things that you're able to do. Once you begin to explain some of the things you know how to do, the person can use that to appeal to you.

Using your own language and phrasing, they can make a strong case for why they need for you to be the person to help them with what they need. They can make their request sound like exactly the type of thing that you excel at doing. Once they've done that, it will likely feel to you like you're the only person who can help them with the thing that they need. Who can say no to that? You can.

With everything that's been laid out in this list, you can say no to anything that does not benefit you.

- Foot in the Door

This technique employs the technique of getting you to say yes to something that seems benign and easily doable. Once they have your commitment to that aspect of what they need, they will expand the scope of what they're asking you to do.

Of course, you have the option to change your answer and say no at any time, as you haven't signed any legally binding contracts and you're not under any obligation to do the things this person wants you to do.

The reason this is effective is that it very intentionally rests on your distaste for going back on your word, or for backing out of a commitment once you gave your agreement to it. This is unfair, but it's a tactic that is commonly used.

It's advised that if someone begins to add conditions onto an agreement after you've already agreed to it, that you should just stop the conversation there, say "This is more involved than I had initially anticipated, and I don't think it's a good fit for me at this time. Thank you for thinking of me."

Cutting this off and not allowing it to grow into something more will save you a good deal of stress in the long run.

- The Advantage of Authority or Familiarity

Another tactic that people use is to get someone that you know or respect to tell you that they think it's a good idea. In some cases, they only steer the conversation so you think that the person you admire, or respect would tell you that it's a good idea.

This is a rather manipulative tactic and it can be used by family, friends, salespeople, or people who simply would like for you to do something.

In the event that someone is using this tactic with you, you can ask yourself how that person that you know and respect would respond if you told them, "That wasn't something I could comfortably or reasonably do, so I didn't agree." I find that this helps to alleviate the hypothetical pressure that this would impose on the situation and will allow you to confidently tell the person in front of you that you're unable or not interested.

- Give a Time Constraint

Putting a time constraint on an agreement is a way that some people use to add pressure to the decision-making process. As noted in the previous chapter, you saw that a time limit adds a considerable amount of pressure to any process for someone who is sensitive.

Whether the person adding the time constraint knows this or not is unclear. The aim of this tactic is to get you to see the "buy now" response in your head, telling you to jump on the opportunity.

It's bold of someone to assume that you want to jump in on the chance to do something for someone else, but believe me, stranger things have happened.

With this tactic, you can simply say, "Thank you, I'll think about it and let you know." In most cases, the person will take this to mean that they won't hear from you in the future, but if you decide it's something you would like to do, you know that you're making the decision on your own terms.

6. If you must say yes or would like to, give a conditional answer.

A great way to exert control over a situation in which you are giving your help to someone is to dictate some terms for the arrangement. This tactic is particularly effective in situations in the workplace. If there is someone who is shirking work tasks and looking for someone else to do them, this can help you.

If someone is looking for you to complete come tasks for them in the immediate term, you could tell them that, while you're willing to complete the tasks given, you will need some extra time.

Alternatively, you can tell them that you will do *some* of the tasks requested in the time they requested. This encourages people to look elsewhere for the help they need and establishes a boundary around you and your work.

7. Overestimate how much you need for yourself.

   When someone comes to us looking for help and support, the assessment we have to make is of the time, emotional resources, and the energy that we have available. From there, we need to assess how much of those resources we need for ourselves and our tasks, what we have left, and if we're able and willing to spend them on the task being proposed to us.

   When you're making this assessment, it's important to overestimate how much of those resources that you need for yourself. You need to make sure that you have more than enough of those resources to help you through your own life and overestimating what you need will keep you from overselling what you have to give and with burning yourself out.

8. Do not confuse importance with urgency.

   Someone running up to you with something that is urgent and needs to be addressed right away does not necessarily mean that it's important to you. The person who is having trouble could be important to you, but if you're unable to help, that doesn't make that person any less important to you.

   Making these distinctions and holding to them will save you a good amount of trouble in your life and your relationships with the people in your life.

Exercise:

How to Create Boundaries

1. Write a list of everything in your life that makes you feel resentful. Take items from work, your social life, chores, relationships, finances—everything.
2. Think about which of those items you can eliminate by setting a boundary or by saying no.
3. Renegotiate your commitments to make more room for what you need in your life.

Exercise:

Practice Saying No

1. With a pen and paper, make a list of five scenarios in which someone is coming to you for some help, or your involvement that would not be workable, desirable, or helpful to you.

2. For each of those five scenarios, think of three responses that tell the person that you are not interested, able, or willing to be involved. Be as courteous as you'd like but remember to be firm.

3. Pick your three favorite responses from the ones you came up with and practice them out loud. If you have someone who can run through the scenarios you wrote in item one, so you can practice your favorite responses, doing so would greatly benefit you.

Identifying the Negative Energies Present in your Life

The energies that are imparted into your life by the people around you can't be discounted or diminished in their effect on you if you are an empath or highly sensitive person. Those things do have an effect on your quality of life and should be treated as such.

Due to the nature of the relationship you have with the emotions of others, it is imperative to be able to identify the nature of them. Emotions being brought into your environment have a profound effect on your physical, emotional, and mental health. Because of this, allowing people who are emotionally taxing or draining to stay in your life is a danger to you and your health.

As empaths, it can be difficult for us to be firm enough with someone to say that we do not want them in our lives anymore or to simply cut them out of our lives. The best way to go about going something like this is to convince yourself of the value of such an act, so regret does not set in at any point.

Let us take a look at some of the indicators that it could be time to remove someone from your life because of their negative or toxic energy.

1. Their responses to most things are negative.

   It doesn't seem to matter what type of things you bring up to this person, they seem to find a way to make a negative comment or to put things in a negative light. People who do this can make it exceedingly difficult to introduce a productive or positive line of thinking, which can make it hard to want to be around them for extended periods of time. Even from a jocular perspective, if the only comments you can seem to get from this person are negative, positivity isn't even an option.

2. You can trace some bad behaviors of yours back to them. People that you bring into your life should be those who help and inspire you to do well, thrive, and be better. If you have found that you have bad behaviors that have been inspired or encouraged by someone in your life, there is a possibility that the person is negative or toxic. Take a look at some of the bad behaviors you have and ask yourself when you first started seeing that type of behavior in yourself. If you can trace that behavior back to before that person was in your life, you have a behavior you need to work on. If you can trace that behavior back to the person you suspect to be toxic, it could indicate toxicity.

3. You don't trust them.

Highly sensitive people should surround themselves with trustworthy people. As people who are more sensitive, it helps to have people around you who won't take advantage of that or do things that could cause you difficulty. Trustworthy people are an essential part of a secure personal sphere. People you can't trust who are within your innermost circles of friends can cause a good deal of anxiety. It leaves you with the feeling that you need to keep looking over your shoulder so-to-speak and wondering if you need to worry about something that that person is saying or doing while you're not looking.

4. You find yourself talking or complaining about them a lot.

We tend to talk or complain a good deal about the people who cause us a lot of stress in life. The stress that those people cause for us, can keep them centered right in front of our minds at all times. This is because that stress is unresolved and your mind wants to talk about it, complain about it, and work it out. However, as long as you're still connected to that person who is causing you stress, and as long as the things about them that cause you stress remain unresolved, you will continue to feel stressed about them. If you can't get through a party or a glass of wine without this person coming up, you may have some things you need to address with this person, or you may need to remove this person from your life.

5. You feel bad around them more often than you feel good. People that you allow into your circles should bring you joy. You should be able to have happy moments or interactions with them that instill you with a feeling of happiness or comfort. If you find that you can't be at ease with this person or that you can't seem to keep a good vibe going in their presence, there's a good chance their energy is toxic to you, or at least quite negative. It should be a red flag for you if every time you get your mood going on an upward incline, you come plummeting back down when this person starts talking.

6. They find ways to make you feel bad about yourself. There are some people who don't allow you to talk about the things that make you happy, who don't allow you to get any wind in your sails, or who don't allow for you to feel secure in your sense of self for any length of time. These people should largely be avoided at all costs. It is not typical or acceptable for someone in your circles to actively keep you from feeling like a good, valid, or worthy person. You are entitled to be happy about the things that make you happy, you are allowed to feel good

about your accomplishments, and you deserve to feel positive.

7. They're not supportive of you or the things you're doing in your life.

   Friends and loved ones are often the people that we look to for support and guidance in the most sensitive areas of our lives. People that we cannot rely on to support us in any aspects of our lives are not friends that we can keep very close to us. Imagine going to the doctor and getting some troubling news and being told to wait for a few days to get some test results back. Imagine the person who is closest to you in the world telling you that you should just stop worrying about it, get over it, and listen to this story about what happened to them at the grocery store earlier that day. That person is not supportive, and you have no one to lean on in what could be a very scary time for you in your life. This is not the type of behavior one expects from those who are closest to one.

8. Other relationships in your life take a hit.

   People in your life who exhibit toxic behaviors will not often garner complete approval from the rest of the people in your circles. They may tend to bump heads with, wear on, or get on the nerves of the other people in your circles. The empath, in a display of compassionate empathy, will often jump to the defense of this person, hoping to calm the waters and soothe the bonds between all the parties involved. People-pleasing is a trademark of the empath. When this effort goes to waste, you will find that the people in your life who are not toxic will begin to take their leave from you if the toxic person insists on being present. It will be hard for the people who are positive in nature to be around the negative energy for prolonged periods of time, and you may notice a growing distance between you. often

9. You use the stress created by them to indulge in unhealthy coping habits.

   Coping mechanisms and habits are things we can pick up along the way when dealing with a good deal of stress or emotional effort. Things like gambling, drinking, smoking, retail therapy, and more can seem like the perfect thing to soothe what ails us. Because of this, we can find the stress that we get from the more negative people in our lives as carte blanche to reach for the coping habits that make us feel the best, or which give us the most relief per use. If you find yourself thinking of someone in your life, then using the stress you feel about them as a good reason to indulge in some unhealthy coping mechanism, then you should seriously consider removing that person from your personal circles.

10. Over time, your self-esteem starts to dwindle.

    If someone close to you has been causing you a good deal of stress or has been keeping you from taking a win or feeling good about yourself, you could find that your self-esteem will drain steadily over time. Someone who has your best interests in mind and who does their best to build you up is a true friend. Someone who does the opposite of these things should likely be removed from your personal circles as expediently as possible. It is okay if someone doesn't make you feel warm and fuzzy or completely inspired every single time you speak with them. However, if you find that over the course of your knowing someone, you can't even see yourself as half the person you used to, it should serve as a red flag for you.

11. The person prioritizes many other things over your feelings.

    We all have a friend who would like to "drag" us along to things or who would like to push us out beyond our comfort zones to expand our horizons. A toxic behavior that is different than this is consistently doing things that they know will make you feel bad, in spite of any protestations or requests from you. Your feelings should matter to the people you surround yourself with, and you should be able to ask someone to respect your boundaries. If you find that you can't do this with the people closest to you, an evaluation should be made about the intention and nature of those people.

12. The person tries to manipulate you.

People that you love and care about should not be trying to manipulate you. Personal relationships are predicated on communication and respect and, if someone is trying to manipulate you, they're not using either aspect effectively. Someone who is trying to manipulate you will often have ulterior motives in mind that are not to your benefit, and they'll often see you as more of a pawn or bargaining chip than a human being. If you suspect that someone close to you is trying to manipulate you and get you to do things without being direct about it, ask them about it. Ask why this person would rather goad you into doing something with the pretense that it was your own idea, rather than just asking you to do something. Affirm that this manipulation is not some misguided effort at helping you to choose to do what is best for yourself before deciding if this person should be removed from your life as personal liability.

13. The person has a habit of talking badly about others.

There is an old adage that says, "If they talk trash *to* you, they will talk trash *about* you." While this is not categorically true, there is some credence to it. While talking trash isn't a very becoming trait in someone, it's not exactly the most damning either. People get stressed out, people do silly things, and people like to vent about the people and things in their lives that are causing them the most stress. For a good deal of people, this can manifest as talking badly about those people who are causing them stress. If you find that someone you know rarely has anything nice to say about *anyone*, then you might be dealing with a highly negative or toxic person.

14. The idea of spending time with them is exhausting.
    When you have a dinner or coffee date scheduled with this friend, how do you talk about it? Do you say, "I'm meeting Lexi for coffee downtown tomorrow," or do you sigh heavily and say, "I have to go meet Lexi downtown for coffee tomorrow?" There is a pretty significant tonal difference between these two things and there is a significant emotional difference behind them as well. If you find that spending time with your friend is more of a labor than a release, it is because this person is causing you to expend emotional effort. If someone is causing you to spend a lot of emotional effort just to be around them, something might be wrong.

15. They make excuses rather than efforts to improve

How does this person respond when you come to them with something, they've been doing that bothers you? Do they apologize? Do they make an effort to do better the next time such a situation presents itself? Or do they try to redirect the conversation toward something that caused them to react that way? Do their excuses for their bad behavior ever flip the problem back onto you, making it seem like they only behaved badly because of something *you* did? This kind of misdirection is a type of manipulation, and it's meant to make you feel guilty for the things they're doing. This is a common trait amongst toxic people, so be on the lookout for it. Being defensive doesn't mean the person is completely toxic, but in tandem with some of these other items, it can make for a personality that isn't good for you.

16. They do not take responsibility for their actions or the effects they create.

Just like in the item above, they will make excuses for the things that they do. If they can misdirect your attention to some other cause, some other person, or something else to blame for their behavior, that will make them look better in your eyes. They're looking for ways to avoid being seen as toxic, and they're looking for ways to keep you from seeing the things that they're actively doing to damager their relationship with you, so they don't need to face any consequences.

17. They make it difficult to set healthy boundaries.

    Have you ever tried to tell someone that you don't have the time to talk, only for them to continue talking to you? Have you ever told someone that you can't hang out with them that day, only for them to show up because they need to see you? People who find reasons to be in your space every time you declare that you need some time and space for yourself are doing so on purpose. If they're not, they will be mortified when it's pointed out to them that they've been doing it. It's very important to take the time to ask the people around you, "Is this something you're doing on purpose, or can we make some adjustments?" The way the person responds to this line of questioning will ultimately tell you how important your comfort and health are to the person.

18. You don't get anything back for what you give.

    Having toxic or highly negative people in your life is a *lot* of work and it's exhausting. Over time, after you've been putting in a great deal of effort with someone, you will often find that it won't be long before they need you to hop right back in and be right there with them again. If this is the case, it can begin to feel like the person has very little interest in reciprocating the type of care, attention, and work that you've been putting into your relationship with that person. This is where it becomes crucial to broach the subject with the person. It could be beneficial to come to them as a friend, telling them that you need their support for the emotional drainage you're experiencing. Tell them that you need an evening off and ask if they would just spend the evening being with you so you can recuperate a little bit and recharge your batteries, so to speak. Their response should tell you how they really feel about being there for you as a friend, as well as being asked to give even a portion of what they take from you as a friend.

19. You tend to lose your temper in situations involving that person.

Whether it's while you're doing something for that person that you don't want to be doing in the first place, or talking about how much that person is stressing you out, or something else that could even be tangentially related to the person, you might find that you lose your cool a little sooner than you might otherwise. If you find that this is the case more often than not, you might want to reassess the things that you're willing to do for that person, as well as your friendship with them in general. Having friends that instill us with anger, or friends who tend to shorten our fuse is not healthy. This is true in the emotional sense, as well as in the physical sense. Losing one's temper on a regular basis can have negative effects on the heart, brain, and other very important parts of you and your life. Try looking at the things about the person that tends to "set you off" and determine what it is about those things that do it. If you find that the reasons are connected more to you than to the person, you might want to look into some anger management tactics. If you find that they are connected more to that person and the things that they're doing, it could be time to talk with them or remove them.

20. You can't seem to avoid arguments with them.

While every disagreement you have shouldn't cause a full-blown argument that gets out of hand, it's not uncommon to argue with friends from time to time. There is quite a marked difference between the occasional disagreement, however, and being completely unable to avoid getting into an argument with someone every time you see them. If you find that you cannot agree on even the simplest things, there could be some unresolved conflict between the two of you that has gone unaddressed for some time. Talking it out could be the best option for you to get things into the open, air out the grievances, hear each other out, and decide what the best step is for you to move forward with your lives. However, if the person seems unreceptive to such a practice, it could be hard to reach this type of civil discussion. If this is the case, then it appears that talking with them will only lead to further arguments and difficulty. In events such as these, it can be toxic for the relationship to persist between you both. If the person is *picking* fights when you're actively trying to avoid them, this is a toxic and negative behavior. Finding out if the person realizes they're picking fights is a good initial step before determining whether or not there is any potential or viability to the relationship.

21. Being yourself around them causes problems.
    Being yourself with your friends is one of the most freeing things in the world. It is so comfortable, freeing, relaxing, and you do not have to worry about being seen by someone who might judge you for the things you do or say at that moment. However, if this is not the case and you find that being yourself around someone that you're close to causes issues, this could be a sign of toxicity. Your friends should celebrate who you are and vice versa. If this cannot be achieved on both sides simultaneously, the relationship could possibly be non-viable.

22. You find negative traits of theirs rubbing off on you.

Spending time with people will commonly lead to shared traits between them. However, if you find that the traits you pick up from one of your friends tend to be more negative than positive, you might need to do some damage control. Picking up bad habits can be rectified and it's not an automatic indication of a toxic person. However, if the only traits the person has to offer for you to pick up are negative, the person could themselves be negative. Assess how the person behaves in general, what they're like, how you would describe them to someone who doesn't know them and get a feel for what your general conception of the person is. If you're an empath or a highly sensitive person, the chances are that your assessment of this person is right on the money. Don't allow guilt or sadness keep you from being honest with yourself about the type of person your friend truly is.

Exercise:

Critical Thinking

1. Which of these people is toxic?

Ethan –

His connection to Helena has been known to be a rocky one amongst their friends. They often make playfully cutting remarks to one another, but it doesn't seem to bother them. They can tend to be rowdy when they are spending time together, but when it comes down to it, Ethan would be there for Helena if she ever needed it and vice versa.

He has been having difficulty finding anything positive to say about Helena's new significant other, Shiloh. Whenever Helena and Shiloh are together, Ethan will find something negative to say. Helena cannot tell if it is intentional, but it is a consistent problem that has come up since she began seeing Shiloh.

Helena approaches Ethan to ask him what is wrong and why he has been behaving in such a way toward someone that means so much to her. When pushed on the subject, Ethan apologizes to Helena, admitting that it was not fair to put her in the position he put her in by behaving the way he did. He admits that he does not particularly, like Shiloh because of something that was said when they first met. He is open to resolution.

Diana –

Diana's friend Callie has known her since middle school. They've been friends in the 15 years since, and they tend to put up with a lot from one another as a result of that. Diana is known in their circles as the snarky one who always has something to say about what is going on.

The thing is, Diana never has anything *positive* to say about what is going on. Callie approaches her one day to ask what it is that keeps her feeling negative, or like she needs to constantly share negative thoughts with the group.

Diana's response seems defensive and cites the people around her as the reason she acts the way she does. She claims that there is so much negativity being sent her way from people in the group, that she cannot rise above it and say anything that is positive.

Callie, concerned that something is deeply wrong between Diana and the rest of their friends, prods further, hoping to get some specifics about who has been being negative with her. If Diana tells Callie who is causing problems for her, Callie would be more than happy to help her resolve them. However, when asked this question, Diana continues on with defensive responses.

She refuses to acknowledge that she's done anything wrong, but still won't be specific about what it is that has been causing her to act the way she has been. It is at this point that Diana begins to cry. This causes Callie to feel guilty for bringing it up in the first place.

How to Remove Negative Energy from your Life Without Guilt

1. Don't expect that they'll suddenly change for you

   If someone is truly toxic, they're going to continue on with their behaviors and they're going to blame others for them. That's the nature of that personality type, and there is very little benefit to sticking around to see if things will change for that person.

   Toxic people can tend to rope us in with a tearful admission of guilt and promises to do better in the future. However, that promise needs to be immediately and consistently followed by action, or that promise just becomes another manipulation.

   There is also the fact that, in order to truly move on past a toxic relationship, is acceptance. Acceptance that that is who they are and what you do not need them in your life if what they impart in your life is not positive in any way.

The same goes for if the negative that they impart into your life is outweighed in large measure by the negative that they impart into your life.

2. Establish your boundaries and stick to them like your life depends on it.

When you make the effort to remove someone who is toxic from your life, it is essential to set boundaries that cannot be breached under any circumstances. These boundaries will keep you from the "what if" questions and the weak moments when things start to look like maybe letting them back into your life wouldn't be such a bad thing. Your boundaries will keep these things from happening.

People who are manipulative or toxic will tend to drain your emotional resources, and they will find ways to make you feel like they deserve another chance. This perpetuates the cycle of them getting back onto your good side, taking all they can and more from you, and then getting kicked back to the curb. This cycle would repeat until the end of time if you let it.

Setting boundaries around ourselves that toxic people cannot cross is a survival tactic and should be seen this way in all regards. Cutting toxic people out of your life is not "cold," it's not "cruel," and it's not "harsh." If someone is truly toxic, they are unhealthy additions to your life and should not be permitted to persist in your environment.

You deserve peace!

3. Don't get sucked back in by crises.

One of the manipulative tactics that can be employed by toxic people is the sudden emergence of a crisis. They may suddenly tell you that no matter what they said before, or what has happened previously, the current crisis demands your attention and, if you intervene in this crisis, they will do whatever you want, give you want you asked for all throughout the relationship, etc.

There will always be a crisis that occurs when you try to remove yourself from the life of a toxic person. There will always be something that happens to come up right at the right moment to keep you in their life. You don't have to play by those rules, and you don't have to be the one to resolve that crisis for the person. Doing so will almost always be to your detriment.

4. Focus on the solution.

Toxic people bring a lot of unrest and negative emotions into your life. As they do so, it gives you a lot of things that can occupy your focus. Focusing on all the negative things that the toxic person gave you to think about does two things to count against you. The first thing is that they've taken control of your thought process. They have introduced the emotions that are dominating all of your thought processes and keeping you tangled up in that person. The second thing is that it can keep your perspective firmly rooted in the things that are negative.

Being primarily focused on the things that are negative will only serve to give you a negative outlook and make it more difficult to see the positive things that are coming or have the potential to come your way.

The healthy thing to do is focus on the things that have changed for the better and to focus on the positive things that could be. This centers your mind on the possibilities that you now face without the impediment of a negative presence in your life, and it keeps you looking forward with hopeful intent.

5. Know yourself.

One of the things that a toxic person will do when confronted with the possibility of losing someone is exploiting their weaknesses in an attempt to bring them closer together. This is where it's important to be as brutally honest with yourself as you can possibly be. You need to know what your weak points are, what buttons they can push to get the most out of you, and how to keep them from getting a firm grasp on those insecurities, weak points, etc.

The more you focus on strengthening those points and on building upon the strengths you already have, the more you'll grow as a person. The more you do this, the less of a hold the toxic person will have over you, and the less of a chance they will have of getting that hold back.

6. Become familiar with projection.

Projection is a principle discussed in psychology that discusses mechanisms behind people lashing out at others. Sometimes it's not us that the person is lashing out at, but something that they're projecting onto you. Generally, that will be a part of themselves that they're projecting on to you. When they see that part of themselves more or less magnified and reflected, they go for the attack.

Understanding this can be a crucial step in the process of explaining why they acted the way they did. As someone who is more or less a victim of behavior, it can help to have that explanation as a point of resolution or at least as a beginning point for healing.

7. Expect a backlash.

Toxic people spend a lot of time putting themselves into the spotlight in the lives of the people around them. As they do so, they thrive on the focus from others, and they thrive on being at the center of things. When they notice that you're making your exit and you're putting them out of your field of focus, they might show some signs of resistance or disagreement with this. They may tell you that you can't just cut them out without giving them a chance to refute it, or some other such objection.

The truth of the matter is that you don't need anyone's permission to cut anyone from your life and you don't need to keep anyone in your life who won't enrich it. Do not give in to the toxic person when their behavior starts to kick up and get more intense. Use that intensity as a reminder of why that person isn't in your life anymore. Understand that you are showing this person that these behaviors are not viable, and that they need to grow or be forgotten.

8. Make a conscious decision to avoid certain conflicts.

Choosing your battles when you're dealing with toxic people is essential. As someone who is highly sensitive, you need to keep your interactions with toxic people to a minimum for your own health. Engaging in the fights that a toxic person attempts to start with you should be the furthest thing from your mind when you're attempting to put distance between yourself and the toxic person in question.

There may be some situations during the process of removing toxic people from your life, that you simply cannot avoid. You may need to tell the person to their face at least once that they're no longer welcome in your life.

This does not mean that you need to open the door when they come over, or that you need to answer the phone when they call, and you don't need to reply to them on social media, no matter how frequently they might message, tag comment, etc. To give them that opening tears down a barrier that gives them nearly unfettered access to you at all times.

Blocking on social media is a great step to take to remove the traces of toxic people from your life, and it may serve you well to tell mutual friends that you've had a falling out, that you won't be attending events where they will be any more, and then establish the conditions for your friendship with that mutual friend if that's something you wish to do.

9. Enrich your life with more, healthier relationships.

Moving on from toxic people is a huge relief. Amplify that relief by surrounding yourself with the best, most empathetic, trustworthy, outgoing, nurturing, and honest people. Doing so will help you continue to grow, will surround you with positive energies that you can use to thrive, and will give you lots of positive emotions to pick up on and share with your new circle.

Exercise:

Identify and Separate from the Negative Energy

1. Go through the list above and determine if there is anyone in your life who fits the majority of those traits. If there isn't someone in your life who does, think of a character you've seen in fictional works who does.

2. Consider how you would go about removing that person from your life and what would be the most effective way to ethically shut down that connection with the person.

How to Achieve Healing Through Empathy

It has is important to note when looking for the strength in your empathy, that being highly empathetic does not make you a week or soft. It also does not lessen the judgment that you have, which tells you when it is safe to be empathetic or vulnerable with someone.

What empathy does do is give you the ability to keep an open mind and heart about the people in front of you. This allows you to hear things from their perspective, understand what is really going on or being done, then come to an understanding about it.

Using your empathic abilities, you can help to bring others to an understanding of others, or even themselves. Knowing everything that you know about your abilities from the chapters in this book, it is possible to use your empathic abilities as your greatest asset in healing from the things that have happened in your life and to use them as a tool to remove the vulnerability, while strengthening the things that make you unique.

Let's take a look at some specific ways in which you can use your empathic abilities and tendencies to heal from the things that can cause you issues in life.

8. Remove yourself from a position of responsibility when someone else is hurting.

It's so important to remember that someone in your immediate environment does not automatically deserve all of your attention and your emotional investment. If you find yourself dealing with someone who has a large emotional pain they're going through, it is not automatically your obligation to help that person.

Helping others can be so gratifying and fulfilling, but it's important not to do this so often that it becomes difficult or draining for us to do so.

In some instances, shedding that responsibility and allowing yourself to disconnect from the feelings of another can be so freeing. It can provide immediate relief and give you the chance to do some immediate recuperating from the stress and emotion you had already taken on from that person.

Many of us don't need to become completely involved in someone's gripe or problem to become aware of and immersed in those feelings ourselves. Sometimes their very presence just pulls us right into it and we're feeling it for them before they come to us about the situation.

Allow yourself to take a break once in a while and allow yourself to feel like that's okay.

9. Let yourself feel the pain or negative emotion, rather than trying to escape from it.

Catharsis is so important. Sometimes, if there is a negative emotion threatening to take hold of our mental space, holding it at bay and avoiding feeling it only makes it worse. It is possible for the things we do instead of processing those emotions to make them worsen as they wait, pent up in yourself, waiting to be processed.

Emotion is not something that ages well, and it's not something that can generally be ignored without significant repercussions or drawbacks. If you find yourself feeling like you "might get mad," but you don't want to be mad and are avoiding dealing it, I have news for you. You are still mad, and you will stay mad until you deal with that issue.

Take some time for yourself and do the things that you need to do to fully process the emotion that you're avoiding dealing with. Once you do that, you will find that that emotion suddenly carries so much less weight than it did previously. You will also find that you won't be worrying about not feeling that thing anymore.

Emotions can be frightening, but they're quite fluid and change frequently. Do yourself a favor and process those feelings before too long. That way, it's out of the way, and you can move onto the next, more positive emotion.

10. Realize that, as an empath, you can still exhibit negative traits, and work on them.

Being an empath and being aware of the emotions of others does not mean that we cannot be mean or display toxic tendencies from time to time. In fact, if we find ourselves loaded down with the emotional energies of other people for so much time out of our lives, then it makes sense that those energies could manifest some behaviors that are not as healthy as we might like.

This is not to say that the empath can not organically have some negative behaviors or toxic traits. These things can be developed or picked up from a number of places. Humans are, in every way, still human. We are still subject to the failings and missteps of our peers. We may say things we do not mean, be grumpy and snap at someone, or any number of other things that could cause someone to feel bad after speaking with us.

Recognizing that we are capable of having poor, toxic, or rude behaviors is the first step to being able to change them. Knowing how we are making others feel and perceiving the effects that we're having on the people in our environment can be a great measuring tool for knowing when it's time to make some changes.

11. Allow yourself to see the good in you, and to build self-esteem from them.

You are a good person and you deserve to feel like you are a good person. Knowing that you have done so much for people should make you feel really great about yourself, and you are more than welcome to remind yourself of the good things about yourself if you ever find yourself feeling bad about it.

As empaths, we tend to be able to pick up on when people are feeling neglected, low self-esteem, low self-worth, etc. We're able to spot those things and then we're able to tell those people what they need to hear in order to get them back up on their feet, doing well, and getting on their way to the next amazing thing they're going to do.

Allow yourself to do this for you. If you are going through a negative patch and you feel like you could use the ego boost, look at the things that you've accomplished and the things that you do on a daily basis from the perspective that you would if you were talking to a friend in your position. Then talk to yourself in the same way that you would talk to that friend.

Taking pride in who you are and what you have done is a great way to heal yourself using your empathic tools.

12. Don't shut people out of your life and your heart.

The people in your life who know you and love you, want to be there for us through thick and thin. We can tend to put our guard up in an effort to shield the innermost parts of ourselves from being touched by the negative emotions or inklings of others. As such, we can tend to go too far and keep people from getting through to us entirely.

It's important to regularly evaluate how thick our shields are, how close our boundaries are, and whether or not we need to lessen them a little bit. Doing so could allow the right people to get closer to us and impart some positive things into our lives.

13. Practice mindfulness.

Being mindful has the potential to be a very freeing exercise. Take your journal and practice mindfulness about your empathic abilities, about your life, about the people around you, and about the things going on in your life.

Doing this along with meditation, yoga, walking, and other physical activities that help you to be focused and mindful can provide a lot of release for people with empathic abilities.

Mindfulness can be achieved in a number of ways, and there isn't really a wrong way in which to be mindful about the things going on around you, or in your life in general. Taking the time to think about things and to be present is a great exercise that can be very grounding.

Take a look into the different types of mindfulness and prompts for mindful journaling that stands out to you. Once you find one, take the opportunity to put it to work in your journaling. See what that does to help heal you from the things you've dealt with.

14. Seek out other empaths so that you have someone who can relate to what you're going through.

Something so simple as having someone in your corner who knows what you're going through can serve to alleviate so much pressure on a person. Having empathic abilities can be beyond exhausting and it can be such on a daily basis. If you're trying to talk through the things that you've been dealing with, and the person you're talking to has no earthly idea what you're talking about, it can be hard to see that conversation as productive or helpful.

If you can find someone who understands what it feels like to know what the people around you are feeling, to know what it feels like to be walking through a crowded store and suddenly have the overwhelming urge to flee, and who knows what it can feel like to attract people who seem to be a complete drain on your energy, passion, and emotions, it counts for so much. Not having to explain every part of what you're dealing with saves so much energy and can actually serve to give some of it back.

Chapter 4: The Pitfalls and the Advantages

Just like with anything in life, there are positives and negatives. There are things that will act as a boon for you, and there are things that will set you back a little further than you may have initially anticipated.

If you are aware of the things that could set you back, you have a better chance of offsetting them and diminishing their effect on you over time. Some of these, you may never encounter at all. Everyone is different, but these are among the most common pros and cons that empaths have listed. Let us take a look.

Pitfalls

1. Your threshold for overwhelm is lower than others'.
    Because you're highly sensitive to the things in your environment, it doesn't take as long for those things to reach a fever pitch and cause you to feel overwhelmed. Feeling overwhelmed is the indication that we've taken on too much, that we need to take a moment and reassess our commitments and the things we have on our plate and give

ourselves some time to recuperate.Taking time for ourselves, as empaths, is incredibly important. We need to take the time to fill our cups, so to speak, in between our obligations. The better care we take of ourselves in our downtime, the more we will have to give and the more power we will have when it comes down to it.

2. Engaging in things you don't enjoy seems impossible.

    Thanks to the amplification of emotions within you, it can be nearly impossible to wax enthusiastic about the things that bring us no joy. While we do take joy in simple things and we do find happiness in the people around us, it can be hard for us to introduce or create joy in things to override boredom or lack of interest that we already feel. Someone who is highly sensitive will find themselves having a good deal of trouble becoming invested in or excelling in activities they don't enjoy, or which bore them. This has been mislabeled, as Attention Deficit Disorder in some cases, to it is prudent to look for this is highly sensitive children.

3. Reclusiveness.

    Due to the toll that the emotions of others can take on us, it can be difficult to want to stay around people. Feeling things from a lot of sources at once, having a lot of capacity for overwhelming or for sensory overload can drive us into our rooms and keep us there. When those around us see this behavior, particularly in people who are generally very outgoing or vivacious, they can become alarmed. Because of the behaviors, they are used to seeing on a regular basis; the people around us tend to see this behavior as a red flag, or as an indication that something is wrong. Be sure the people closest to you know that you're going through something routine, and that time to yourself is a necessity.

4. If compassionate empathy is used without Emotional Intelligence, you could end up stirring the pot.
    Rushing into a situation with the need to do something about it can cause some troubles for the people around you if you don't go into it with a degree of emotional intelligence at your side. Rushing into things without understanding all of what someone is dealing with can stir up more problems than it could potentially solve. This is only a pitfall if you go into things without an idea of what you will need to do to rectify the situation in front of you, or if you don't know that the person or people involved would like you to continue to be involved or help.

5. When compassionate empathy is used, it can cause you to overstep your bounds into something that others may not want you involved in.

Similar to the situation above, our intuition on the emotions and troubles of the people around us can tend to spring us into action. This is a mechanism of compassionate empathy, and it's a logical response for someone who is highly sensitive to feel as though it's their duty to step into a situation. Understanding a situation does not make it your job to fix it. The people who are having troubles might be looking to resolve the problem between themselves, or just might not want you involved, which is their prerogative. Make sure you're not invading any personal boundaries by trying to help with your gift!

6. It's easy to get exhausted by feeling and dealing with as much as you do.

    There is a lot of emotional and physical energy is expended when you are taking on, feeling, processing, and dealing with all the feelings, emotions, inclinations, and other inner machinations of others around you. Because of this and because of how hard your body is working to process your own emotions that are always running high, you can become exhausted quite a lot more easily than the people around you. It's prudent to make sure you're getting a good amount of sleep each night, as well as taking recuperative measures in your free time. You will find that doing so will help you to stave off exhaustion here and there.

7. You are easily startled.

    If you find that sudden loud noises make you jump more than they should, you should be a highly sensitive person. Furthermore, if you find that this trait lessons when you're particularly drained, exhausted, tired, or depressed, that jumpiness is rooted more in your higher sensitivity. It would be nice if being more sensitive to things, being more aware of small or minute details, and being less able to be lied to meant we weren't easily startled. Instead of this, however, we find ourselves so completely immersed in the things that we do in every moment that when something comes up to snap us out of it, we can become quite jarred or unsettled.

8. Getting sick when others are sick is much more probable. Your immune system could be strong as a horse, and you could still grapple with this from time to time. People who are empathic or who are highly sensitive tend to have sympathy symptoms, which can blossom into full-blown illnesses. This can be a rather irritating drawback of your abilities, so it's important to do everything you can to keep yourself healthy. Keep your hands clean, get your vitamins, listen to the doctor about what measures to take to stave off illness, and keep yourself physically and mentally rested. When you are around someone who is

ill, remind yourself that it is not your illness and that you do not need to pick it up. This has been a helpful sort of mantra for me in the past, and I like to recommend it to others. If nothing else, it puts me in the right frame of mind to focus on the person who is ailing without trying to assume their position in any of it.

9. Withdrawing your help as an empath can make you seem like the bad guy.

    Once people start to get wind of the types of things that you can do and the types of talents that you have with problem-solving and emotional intelligence, they can come to rely on you for your expertise and your understanding. Because of how easy it is to become exhausted when taking on the troubles and the emotions of the people around you, it is often prudent to tell the people around you that you cannot help them with their latest argument, misunderstanding, or issue. This being said, it is a rare empath who can actually tell their friends they won't help them to preserve their own health. Empaths are as selfless as they are intuitive. When you do muster up the energy to tell people that you cannot get involved in their problem and help them with it, you might experience a little bit of resentment. You might find that the person in front of you knows you can help and wants to know why you can't just "take five minutes and help me with this."

You and I both know that it's not just five minutes and that the toll it will take on you makes it prudent to say no. You will get better with this as time goes on and as you get a feel for what your thresholds are.

10. The atmosphere in public places can be overwhelming.

It can be frustrating when you're trying to do something simple like pick up your dry cleaning, and sensory overload sets in. It can stop you in your tracks, or it can simply elevate your stress levels and make you testy. Being out in the outside world opens you up to a host of stimuli that you can't anticipate. Because of the sensitivity empaths tend to feel, it can take just the right combination to noises, people talking, vibrations, light, and movement to make it feel like the whole world is bearing down on you. Daily errands are not impossible, but they are less comfortable.

11. Wearing other peoples' emotions can be exhausting and confusing.

We've covered this in a lot of places in this book, but it really is a pretty big drawback, so I wanted to feature it here. Exhaustion can stop you dead, completely railroad all the things that you wanted to get done that day, and it can knock you down at the precise wrong time. Feeling the emotions and considerations of the people around us means that our bodies are expending the energy to feel something about all the things going on in our lives and the things going on around us *plus* all those of the person sitting next to us.

12. In times of stress, you can become consumed and neglect essential things like self-care and hygiene.
Taking care of yourself is so much more important than you may even realize. Doing the basic things to ensure that you're staying fed, rested, healthy, and clean are not luxuries as we can sometimes feel they are. When you're dealing with a lot of things all at once, it can be easy to get so caught up in them that we don't even know where to begin with taking care of ourselves. We spend our time doing the things that we know will help the people around us because we are intent on being helpful. If we do self-care, we are only helping ourselves, and we often have a hard time rectifying that within ourselves.

13. Easily bored if the mental stimulation hits a sudden lull.
Because empathic people act as human litmus paper for the emotions around them, if there is suddenly nothing going on, we are liable to become quite bored all at once.

Imagine being in a house where the air conditioner, a hairdryer, a leaf blower, a television, a radio, and a vacuum cleaner were all running. Imagine next that the power suddenly went out and everything stopped all at once. Your ears would be ringing from the silence that now surrounds you. This is similar to what goes on for someone whose mind is almost always completely a-flutter.

14. You get so stuck on not messing up, that you mess up worse.

Trying really hard not to make mistakes in any setting is pretty much the perfect formula for making a mistake. It's almost as though the focus on the act of not causing a problem creates those problems for you. Being worried that you will make a mistake will nearly always result in your making a mistake, messing up, goofing, tripping, slipping, or any number of other things that you're trying to avoid. Thanks to this, and the nervousness that can be instilled by your empathic tendencies, it can result in insurmountable, overwhelming anxiety that causes you to lose your balance or your composure.

15. You have the capacity to seem aloof, apathetic, or disconnected from those around you.

Much like the reclusion that you can feel as a response to the things you need to deal with on a daily basis, you can emotionally withdraw. This is a defense tactic that a lot of empaths will employ to keep themselves from being too vulnerable or from emotional bombardment. Thanks to this, it can seem like we're not as invested or connected. That removal can be instrumental in keeping yourself safe and healthy, but it can also put a damper on personal relationships. Be careful who you keep at a distance!

16. Digestive disorders and lower back problems are more common.

    Stress can have a lot of negative effects on the body. Part of this is digestive issues. Stress can cause the hormones and enzymes and processes to slow or overproduce in ways that can cause issues for the body. This is also why stress can cause us to gain unwanted weight. There is also some information that points to the chakra in this part of the body being impeded by a lot of stress, emotional duress or overwhelms. When that chakra is impeded, it can cause pain that area of the body where the lower back and digestive tract sit.

17. Ulcers are more common.

Stress can cause ulcers in the stomach. These are painful internal lacerations that are exacerbated by stress, acid, spicy foods, and greasy foods. When we get these holes or lacerations in our stomachs, they can cause very sharp pains, trouble digesting, sleepless nights, skin issues, and more. If you find that you have stress-related ulcers, you should consult with a physician, avoid greasy and spicy foods, avoid ibuprofen, acidic foods, and get plenty of rest and water.In addition to this, consider utilizing stress-relief techniques to reduce the effects that stress has on you. Taking time to relax and spend time on you.

18. You will feel like a walking receptacle for the problems that others are facing.

    People will tend to pick up on the things that you can do. They will pick up on the things that you have been able to do for yourself and for others. Because of this and because of the tendency that people have to come to you for advice on their problems, you will find that people will want to throw things your way any time they can. You will start to feel like you can't know someone for very long before they trust you enough to tell you all the things that are going on in their life. They will be doing so in the hopes that you can help them to resolve these problems.

19. Cognitive empathy may not connect emotion to the conclusions that you form, so you may come across as cold or unfeeling.

Those who are more cognitive empaths, or whose focus is mainly on the intellectual side of things, may not realize how emotional the conclusions are that they are picking upon. As such, cognitive empaths may find themselves stepping on some toes of being less warm of understanding that the people around them might need them to be. It's not through malice that this can happen; they simply don't realize that the person in front of them is feeling a lot of things connected with those thoughts that the empath is seeing. Be watchful for the emotions of others if you tend to be focused or more in-tune to the cognitive side of the people around you.

20. Fatigue is no stranger.

When someone needs to bend your ear for a prolonged period of time and you find yourself having to be present for someone, and receptive to their emotions, you might feel quite exhausted. Spending the day feeling what others feel and dealing with their problems from their perspective as well as your own is no small feat. This is why a good deal of empaths choose not to go into fields wherein they have to manage and deal with the emotions of others. It's a talent they have, but if your full-time job is that draining, you're liable to burn out before too long. Finding a balance when helping people is key. Make sure that you're not giving more than you have to give.

21. Knowing that something is wrong when no one wants to listen.

    As someone who has an internal monitor that tells them when there is a danger, ill intent, a lie, or a problem, you can often be the first person to know there is something wrong. This can sometimes mean that you know that there is something amiss with someone that you know, and the people around you might not want to hear that. There are more than just a few people in this world who have intentions that are nefarious. Sometimes people of this sort will do their best to ingratiate themselves to a group of people, only to begin exhibiting toxic behaviors once people have become attached to them. It is this sort of behavior that the empath can usually detect. In situations such as this, you will need to work very hard to get your friends to understand what it is that you see in the person, or you will need to simply disagree to be around them for group interactions.

22. Addictions are much more common.

    Being an empath or a highly sensitive person can be exhausting. It can be very taxing if the things that can come up aren't properly managed. Being an empath can be emotionally, physically, and mentally exhausting. As you're going through all the trials and tribulations of being an empath, it can be tempting to reach for substances to "soften the blow," or ease the strain that it puts on you. As with any substances used for the purposes of coping or emotional alleviation, it is prudent to use caution. Utilizing substances with no prescription and utilizing multiple of these can carry a good deal of risk. It is best to exercise caution with such things and to exhaust any other avenues of relief before going down that route.

23. You're a magnet for energy vampires.

People who tend to need all the positivity they can get will find you and cling to you. People who do this are known as "energy vampires," or "positivity vampires." They will see and be drawn to the light that you provide, but they can very easily drain all of it out of you, needing all the light you have to offer and more. It's important to bear that in mind, as well as the fact that you can't pour from an empty cup. You can only give what you have to give. You cannot give more than that and you shouldn't even give as much as you have. If you give all that you have, there is nothing left for you to manage your life.

24. Deadlines and time limits can really affect you adversely.

Keeping to deadlines and time constraints isn't necessarily difficult for you to do from a work effort standpoint. However, you might find that time limits on things tend to make you feel more harried, pressured, and less effective. It can seem like all the energy you originally had to work on your project is completely occupied by the time limit that's been imposed on you. Things you should have easily been able to achieve otherwise, seem to be slammed up against that timeline and can only be accomplished with stress, a furrowed brow, and terrible personal care practices. Don't allow yourself to skip meals to get to those deadlines; you need to eat, sleep, bathe, and breathe. Let yourself do those things.

25. Clutter makes you cringe.

    As small details tend to fill and occupy the mind of an empath and a highly sensitive person, the details of the environment surrounding you will also do so. People who are highly sensitive will often find that clutter in their immediate space will stop them from focusing or keep them from feeling like they can work. It makes it difficult to sit at ease, it makes it difficult to create artistic work, it makes it difficult to focus on just about anything of any import.

Advantages

1. Knowing and being yourself comes more easily to you than others.

    Because of your emotional attunement, you are more able to see and understand the things that are passing through your mind. A lot of people will feel and experience these things without knowing what they are, what they mean, or how to process them. As someone who knows what emotions they're looking at when they're looking at them, and who knows what to do to process them, you have a much stronger advantage for dealing with them and knowing who you are. Others can tend to struggle for years and have no idea who they are; they can have no sense of direction in life because they do not know who they really are or what they want from life.

2. You have the ability to detect a conflict before it grows and meditate or calm it down.

    Being able to resolve conflicts between others can give you a sense of peace that others might miss out on. When you see two people who are simply missing the mark on working something out, you can tell them where that missed connection is. You can show them the points of view that will get either of them onto the same page, level the playing field, and help things to work out the way they ought to. There is something that is deeply gratifying about helping two people to come to an amicable resolution and to bypass the things that can come from a long-running dispute.

3. You can anticipate how certain actions will be met or responded to, making for more optimal interactions.

    If you're talking with someone who is a bit of a flight risk, or who is acting unpredictably, you can know some things before you even speak to them. You can know the types of things to say that will cause them to react negatively. Using this ability, you can say the things that will help them to calm down, you can say the things that will help the interaction to go the way that you need it to go. Knowing how people will generally respond to certain things, you can be sure you're only giving things that will get a positive or productive response!

4. You have an overabundance of energy.

    If you find yourself doing less than you typically do for a few days, you might find that you gain a sizable reserve of energy that you will want to use sooner rather than later. The minor drawback of having a lot of energy built up is that is doesn't keep very well. It's something that you will feel compelled to expend and use as quickly as it can. Think of it like money in your wallet, only the money is on fire and your wallet is made of paper. You have to spend it quickly to protect your wallet!

5. You can tell when something just isn't right.

    Your perception of the vibe or energy around you is usually very astute and you usually perceive things before the people around you. The thing is, this ability isn't only for things like the end of the world, catastrophes, or things out of movies or comic books. You can perceive when someone has ill intentions, you can tell when things might not go your way, you can tell when people are in the middle of an argument that you haven't seen, and you can tell when peoples' vibes aren't calm. These are the things that you can help to aid in small ways. If you walk into your office and you can tell that the person who sits behind you is just having a rough morning, you don't have to say anything at all. You can be there and be calm. You can bring them a donut from the break room without them asking, and you can tell them a little joke to make them smile. Making a difference doesn't need to mean asking their business or getting heavily involved in their struggles.

6. You can often gauge the interests of someone and know what kinds of activities you should invite them to.

If you have made a new friend, and you've taken the time to get to know them, you can get a feel for the types of things that would interest them. If you have known someone for a few weeks, you can often tell whether they seem the energetic, high-energy, and excitable, they might like to go with you to an amusement park. If you know someone who seems like they keep a calm demeanor, they are not very energetic, and they have a low, even tone of speaking, you could probably tell that something more low-key and something with fewer people might seem like the kind of things they would rather be doing.

7.   You are more receptive to the beauty in things.

You will often find that you're the one who points out the beauty in things to other people. The things that are around us contain a good deal of beauty. The people who are preoccupied with the struggles and bustle of daily life may be less able to see those beautiful things throughout their environment. Something about being able to point out that beauty and bring it to the attention of someone who needs it is very gratifying. The beauty in the world is there for us to take in and being the first to spot them is a little bit of a nice aspect of life.

8. Your intuition leads you to your goals more quickly.

   Your intuition can tell you a lot about the path that lies ahead of you. When you can see things about what is coming your way, you can take the appropriate measures to avoid or compensate for them.

9. Anticipating and meeting needs comes naturally to you.

   As someone who is empathic, you can usually detect what it is that someone will need. In the workplace, this can be exceedingly helpful. Telling what things a customer or client will need before they ask for them, having things ready for a boss or a manager, or just being able to go above and beyond in your job. Being able to anticipate needs is not something that an average person will do very easily. They will balk at being asked to do so because they "are not a mind reader." People who are in-tune to the needs, inklings, inclinations, thoughts, and feelings of others will usually be able to tell how they can impress someone in the workplace.

10. You often say exactly what the other person needs to hear, without realizing it.

    This one might be totally obvious to you by this point. Being able to know what's going on with someone often means knowing what it is that they need to hear. However, this doesn't occur to us in a very clear thought process like traditional problem-solving might. You will approach someone, it will occur to you to say something, and it will often be the type of thing that the person needs or wants to hear. It wouldn't be something that you think, "I'm sure they would like to hear this, let's go with this." However, when you give your offerings of friendship and conversation with the person, and they will go on their way, the better for it.

11. It's easy to detect destructive patterns before they really take hold.

Due to your aptness for picking up on patterns, it can become clear to you when someone is adopting a new one. This eye for details can tell you when someone is heading down a new road, and whether or not that road is dangerous. For instance, you can see someone who is sad starting to adopt a new coping mechanism. To the person, it may seem like they're simply taking a moment to enjoy a large glass of wine. Taking a reprieve for themselves and getting ready to get back to another stressful day of work the next day. The next day, new circumstances present themselves, cause a new set of problems for the person, and they reach for another large glass of wine the following night, possibly two. You can see the escalation on a fairly immediate basis, whereas the person may take months to notice that they've been doing it every night.

12. You feel happiness on another level.

When you feel happy, you feel *really* happy. The higher frequency at which your emotions tend to run means that you feel an amplified version of them. Thanks to this, you will find that the things that make you happy tend to bring you a very significant amount of joy. If you find yourself breaking through something at work, or you find yourself coming up with a new creative idea, you could be completely ecstatic as a result. Bringing yourself that high level of happiness on a regular basis can make all the difference in your life and can impart a whole different hue to the scheme of your life. Do the things that make you the happiest and you will flourish.

13. You get hunches that tell you when things aren't going to go the way you want them to.

Just like your inklings of when someone has ill intentions, you have a mechanism within you that tells you when things look like they are going to go bad or have a result that is less than optimal. Knowing that these things are coming can help us to brace for disappointment and can help us to think of contingencies to improve the chances of things going well. When things go well after we have a hunch that they won't, it can help our ego to tell ourselves that we did a great job in staving off the negative. If we don't succeed, we can tell ourselves that we were right on the money with our hunch and we can take comfort in knowing that our internal meters are working precisely the way they should.

14. You're always the first to know if someone is upset.
   When someone walks into the room and they have a certain feeling about them, a certain dullness or edge to their vibe or energy, you can tell that they're upset. A good deal of people has figured out how to put on their game face or put up a good front while they are feeling bad. In spite of this, their energies give them away and their unsettled vibe will get through to you. You can get out in front of this by meditating, being a positive presence in someone's life, being nice to the person, or just acknowledging that something is wrong in their life.

15. You are more aware of how what you do will affect the people around you, cutting down on misunderstandings and conflicts.
   When you know how someone will respond to something you say or do, you can make adjustments so that the things you say and do will not negatively affect the people around you. Doing this can be exhausting, but it can also

be far less exhausting than the alternative of being caught up in some misunderstanding or feud as a result of saying the wrong thing. Being the peacekeeper of your personal circle can be tiring at times, but it can also save a lot of regrets, anger, tiredness, sadness, and other things caused by conflict. It's up to you to decide if you want to assume that role.

16. You can see from a distance, how arguments and conflicts will play out, so there is no need for you to get involved.
    If you have decided that the role of peacekeeper isn't one you want to assume, you can spot the arguments and conflicts before they're in your own back yard. If you spot that conflict from afar, you can keep your distance, let the involved parties discuss and come to their own resolution between themselves. If they don't achieve that resolution in a reasonable amount of time, and they need your help after the conflict has grown into something larger, you can decide if and how you would like to get involved to mediate. It's not your responsibility to resolve the conflicts of the people in your circles, but if you would like to assume that role from time to time, I'm sure you could do well.

17. You know just what will make a sick person around you feel better.

People who are sick and ailing will often have a good deal of emotional difficulty in the process. Being sick is not fun for anyone and the things that come with it can take an emotional toll. Thanks to this, you can often pick up on the things that could help someone in that position to feel better. Taking care of people is one of those things that come very innately to empaths and is something that they can do with ease. The things that they need can be as simple as an extra box of tissues or a pat on the head and reassurances.

18. You feel excitement over new thoughts or ideas in such a vibrant way, that it's contagious.

The really fun thing about being easily excitable about finding happiness more easily than others is that we have the ability to spread that happiness, that joy, that excitement to the people around us with ease. This feature of the empathic life is particularly fun because it starts a cycle that you'll love to watch. You get excited and feel lots of joy, you inspire others to feel joy, and you get joy from that inspiration. It continues on as you encounter more and more people throughout your life. Your friends and family better lookout; they are about to catch an infectious case of joy.

19. You are less likely to encounter danger because you can sense it more readily.

Like with arguments, people with ill intent, and things that could go wrong, you have a meter that tells you when there is danger present or imminent. Thanks to this mechanism, spotting that danger and avoiding it is something that can be done quite readily. Many people can get hung up on the subject of avoiding danger. They look for it, they take many precautions to avoid it, and they talk about ways to lessen it. While these are all a matter of prudence, the danger will still find its way through. For you, however, you have a radar that tells you when something that isn't safe if in your path. You can avoid that danger and keep yourself and others around you safe.

20. It's easy to get people to like you.

People gravitate toward you. You have a very calm and clean vibe that draws people in, making them feel at home with you. Thanks to this, getting people to like you is very easily done. You might need to work to feel close to someone, but people will generally feel much closer to you than you may realize, or than you might feel to them. Winning people over is a pretty useful talent and getting people on your side is always a good feeling in your life. Making friends with the people around you in life helps you to feel more open, to feel connected, and provides a good release for you. Get out there and make some friends!

21. You connect with people and animals much more readily. Your friendship with others isn't limited just to the people in your life. You will also find that the animals in your life will also gravitate toward you. Making friends with the people around you can be highly beneficial and can enrich your life more than you may have considered. Having animal friends provides a different, quite warm type of enrichment for your life that you may not have considered. If you haven't had pets in your life, you may be underestimating how meaningful it can be when a cat or dog chooses to curl up next to or on you and settles in comfortably. If you have had pets, you do know that joy, and you know how much it means to the animal as well. One of the best things one can do with this power to more easily attract and ingratiate animals is to give a very good home to one who is in need. Animal shelters are full of animals who are kind, loving, looking for a good home to call their own for the rest of their days.

22. Lie detection is an innate ability.
Because of the small details that you're apt to notice throughout your day and your interactions with others,

you tend to pick up on the little things that sound off when someone is trying to lie to you. In addition to this, you pick up on inconsistent details in the story behind the lie. If you know the person who is trying to lie to you, you're even more likely to be able to spot the things that would tell you if someone is lying to you. Say, for instance, your significant other untruthfully says, "I'm fine," but you know that isn't true. You know what they sound like when they say they are fine, and they sounded different. You will notice drops in pitch and tone, you will notice strange inflections and more that will show you when things do not line up.

23. You have a very high capacity for love and compassion. Love and compassion are two of the trademark traits for an empath. Being able to invest emotionally in the people around us is something with which others may struggle. Feeling loved and compassion on the levels that we do can enrich our lives, and it gives us power. Having more people in our corner that we can love, who we can do things for, and who we trust with the more sensitive areas of our lives is something to be admired. Rejoice in your abilities to love and your abilities to feel empathy and compassion for the people in our lives. It gives us strength, it gives us emotional energy, and it emboldens us to continue on.

24. You can tell when someone has bad energy that will harm you, making it easier to stay away.

    With your abilities to see people for who they are, identify the quality of their energy, identify the intentions behind the person, and to identify truthfulness, you can more easily detect the people around you in life who have negative energy. The negative energy that comes with ill intent will stand out to you in a way that screams to you that you should stay away. Avoiding people who stand out to you in this way will avoid a good deal of pain, heartbreak, difficulty, and trouble in your life. It's also a great way to protect the people that you love, who are not as attuned to this sort of stimulus.

25. Your compassionate reputation precedes you.

    People will often find themselves telling others about you. People who know you will not be able to keep themselves from telling other people who you are, what you do, what you've done for them, what they think of you, and they will convince others to meet you. Having people in your life who can see your gifts for what they are, and who can appreciate you for the things that you do each day, will give you more strength and will embolden you to continue just being you. In short, being you is the biggest advantage of being you!

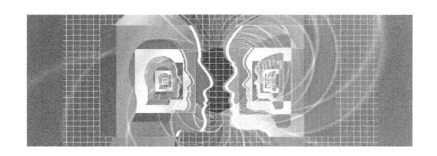

Chapter 5: Tips & Tricks for an Empath

Here are some simple things that you can do in your daily life to keep your batteries recharged, to keep you feeling ready to enrich your life and the lives of others, and to keep your outlook positive.

1. Create a mental bubble.

   Putting your guard up with people can be counter-intuitive. It can feel like the wrong thing to do, or it can feel like you're trying to shut people out of your life. These are both not the case. At least, they shouldn't be. Creating a mental space that is your own and keeping people from getting into it can be a really helpful mental exercise that can keep you from overextending. It can also help you keep the emotions of others around you from penetrating the most private and sensitive areas of your mind. Imagine a bubble of lightness around you. Imagine that bubble around the parts of your mind that you need to keep from yourself. The people around you can have access to the area outside the bubble, but the things inside the bubble are for you and the things you need to stay happy and healthy.

2. Create a space that is yours and only yours.

In your home, it can be possible for your belongings, your projects, your items to sprawl into the house. Possibly more important that this is that items from around the house that are not yours can make it into your space. Having a space that is specifically yours, that is only full of the things that you put there, and which is meant for you to use in order to recuperate and rest. All the most relaxing and helpful tasks that you take the care to do can be less effective if the space in which you do them isn't completely relaxing for you.

3. Spend some time alone.

The time you spend by yourself can give you the reprieve you need in order to recuperate from the things that impinge on your mental and emotional space on a daily basis. While you don't need to become a recluse or keep yourself from spending any amount of time with other people, some time for yourself is highly recommended. Spend time on your own, doing the things that you enjoy doing, things that relax you, and things that will give you more emotional and physical energy. Reading, coloring, taking care of yourself, cooking, singing, making music, studying, whatever it is that brings you the most fulfillment.

4. Utilize aromatherapy.

   Aromatherapy can be done in a number of ways. The most typical way is through incense or oil heating. Doing something relaxing while the scents you enjoy are flowing through the room is proven to help you relax, recover, rejuvenate, and re-center. Doing this in the time that you have for yourself can bring you more joy and can help you to get more out of the time that you take for yourself. Relaxing completely and getting the most out of the time you spend on your own is very important if you wish to recharge. See if aromatherapy is something that could help you to do these things.

5. Spend time with the folks you love.

   Investing time with the people we love can fill our emotional cup, so to speak. It can give us a lot of energy back, and it can help us to relax. Being around people we know, trust, love, and enjoy will do more for us than we might expect. Don't rush yourself through the time that you have together and take every opportunity you can get (aside from your time for yourself) to spend time with the people who make you feel safe, happy, and loved.

6. Yoga and/or meditation.

   Yoga and meditation are proven techniques for relaxation, recuperation, re-centering, and emotional rejuvenation. Taking the time to enjoy a quiet space, wherein you can focus on nothing but you and the replenishment of your emotional and personal resources, does so much for someone who is so emotionally busy. Take time to do so where it's convenient, even if that is only for several minutes each day. You don't need to block out your entire evening for yoga, you don't have to go to a studio downtown in the right clothes, spending an hour and a half listening to someone guide you through it, if that is not your type of thing. Spending ten minutes meditating, and a short amount of time in the morning to do a few poses and enjoying your own company can send you leaps and bounds in the right direction.

7. Seek catharsis.

Being mired down in a lot of emotions can cause you to feel like you're slogging your way through the day. If you find yourself feeling like you're weighed down under a large number of negative emotions, it can be hard to pull yourself out from under them. Catharsis is the sudden release of pent-up emotion. If you allow yourself to feel your emotions at their most vivid, allow yourself to become overwhelmed by them for a short time, and allow that emotion to escape for just a little while, you can release all the pressure they build up over time. Take the time to cry, to yell, to throw a couple of pillows, or whatever you need to do to fully experience those emotions. Once you do that, you will feel as though a weight has been lifted. Taking the time to do this every once in a while, can keep you from getting so mired in those emotions that you just can't cope.

8. Eat properly and keep yourself healthy.

Make sure that you get enough protein, you get enough vegetables, fruits, vitamins, and minerals. Not getting enough of these things can have as much of an emotional benefit as a physical one. Due to your empathic nature, you will have enough emotional curveballs thrown at you in your daily life. You owe it to yourself to do everything in your power to keep more from being thrown at you by something as fixable as eating properly. Just as important as this is getting the proper amount of rest. Sleeping well can keep you feeling healthy and can keep you on an even keel. Get as close to eight hours of uninterrupted sleep per night as you can.

9. Take charge of your happiness.

Cut the people out of your life who don't contribute to your well-being. Do the things that you know will make you happy. Take the chances to enjoy the things that are in your life. If you are able to do things to make yourself happy, then you absolutely should do that. Don't allow yourself to discount the importance of your happiness, the things that bring you that happiness, and the fact that you deserve to be happy. For all the things that your empathic gifts can do for people, for all the things that you do when you're too tired to be doing them, for all the hours you've spent caring for the people in your life, you deserve more than that amount of happiness in return. Take control of your life today!

10. Spend time in nature.

A lot of empathetic people have said that they feel very connected to nature. That they find great joy in being in the outdoors, connected to Earth, and doing things that keep them connected with nature. Spending time in the woods, in the garden, in the back yard, at the lake, in the park, the arboretum, the botanical gardens... Anywhere you can feel yourself being grounded in nature is a great place to start. Are there any places like this that call to you, or which sound like you would particularly enjoy? Try spending some time there in the next few days and see what it does for you!

11. Set firm boundaries.

Keeping your boundaries is what will keep you sane. If you're able to allow people to come into your life, in any capacity, whenever they want, you'll find that you will become exhausted, overwhelmed, overworked, and overloaded more quickly than you can imagine. Make sure that you set boundaries that will keep you comfortable, which will allow you to take enough time for yourself, which will allow you to keep enough energy for yourself and the things you need, and which will help you to stay happier for longer. It helps if you think of boundaries less as ways to keep people out, and if you think of them more as ways to keep your sanity, energy, and happiness in.

12. Identify the things that drain you and the things that energize you.

There are tasks we can do that give us energy and there are tasks we can do that take energy from us. It is imperative for you to find the distinction between those two types of things. Fill your life with the types of things that replenish your energies and try to limit the things that drain them. It is fair enough that the things we need to do from day to day can drain us. This would be things like going to the bank, dealing with bills, working on our credit, dealing with doctor's appointments, and taking our kids to school. These are not things that give us energy, and they're not things we can avoid. We can, however, insist on a balance between the things that give us energy and the things that give us energy. This is an important task.

13. Be willing to reevaluate your perspectives on others.
Knowing that someone is toxic or who has negative energy can be a great advantage in the life of someone who is highly sensitive, or who is empathic. It is also possible for people who have been through severe emotional trauma to exhibit toxic tendencies that can make them lash out at others. In order to move on from these people, or to help them if that is what we think is necessary, we need to be able to admit this. We need to be able to tell ourselves that toxicity is bred through more toxic behavior and that there is an end to this cycle. It is not always on us to provide that end, so be very judicious when deciding if this is something you want to do.

14. Keep an eye on the nature of your thought patterns.
You need to keep an eye on the patterns of thought that pass through your mind. Since you're an emotional and intellectual sponge, you will often adopt emotions and thoughts that you might not have had otherwise. Be sure to keep an eye out for the way your thoughts are playing out. A negative thought process can lead you down a rabbit hole of pain and sadness. It's important to be able

to pull yourself out of the middle of a negative thought pattern, interject positive and affirmative thoughts to take you in the right direction. Don't be a victim of someone else's thought patterns.

15. Employ positive affirmations.

Positivity in your life is a huge deal. Staying on top of the negative emotions that can come and go is quite important. Using affirmations in your daily life can help you to stay on top of them. It can impart positivity into your thought process in small measure, throughout your entire life. Try posting affirmations throughout your workspace, your home, your personal space, your phone, your journal, and anywhere that you'll see them with any regularity. Doing so will more or less pepper your whole life with positivity, and who doesn't need that?

16. Practice gratefulness.

Using your journal or just talking to the people around you, taking time to find reasons in your life to be grateful can be a great way of showing you more and more positives in life. Positive thinking starts with intentions of imposing that positivity in your life. By insisting that we be grateful for several things throughout each day, you will suddenly begin to see reasons to be grateful without even looking.

17. Forgive those who have wronged you.

    You don't have to let them back into your life or even tell them that you forgive them. However, holding onto the resentment, anger, hate, disappointment, regret, and whatever other negative emotions come from that, will hurt you more than it will ever hurt them. Don't allow that person who has wronged you to continue to harm you by holding onto those emotions. By forgiving that person, you allow those negative emotions to disperse and leave your personal space. You allow yourself to make room for the emotions that are more positive, more productive, and more able to give you happiness. Forgive and allow yourself to move onto better things for you and for the people who are closes to you. They will want to see you happy.

Chapter 6: Frequently Asked Questions about Empathy

Here are the questions that are most frequently asked questions about empathic abilities, empaths, and their abilities? Let us take a look at them and the answers about them.

1. Do empaths have psychic abilities?

   The abilities that an empath has been centered on the emotional, mental, and connective abilities that people naturally have. These abilities are more or less magnification of these natural abilities and are a capability of the sort that can help one to make more firm connections to others.

   Empathic abilities are different than the ability to simply read the minds of others, predict the future, or other things that are commonly associated with psychic abilities.

2. What are the sensitivities of an empath?

   Empaths are sensitive to the emotions, feelings, and inclinations of the people around them. The things empaths can tap into will tell them how the people around them are thinking, how they're inclined, and will often lead them to conclude the same things as those people in their surroundings.

3. What are the differences between empaths and mystics?

    While an empath is someone who can pick up on the emotions, feelings, and inclinations of the people around them, a mystic is a person who investigates by reflection and self-surrender to acquire unity with or retention into the Deity or the infinite, or who consider in the spiritual apprehension of truths that are beyond the intellect.

    The two are quite different in their paths, but they both seek peace through connection and unity.

4. Is it possible to be in a happy relationship as an empath?

    Absolutely. There are some things that you need to ensure are respected, there are some things you will need to look for in an ideal partner, and you will need to be specific about the boundaries you keep in that relationship. That being said, having a romantic or intimate relationship with someone when you are empathic is completely possible.

5. Are empaths more susceptible to anxiety and depression?

Unfortunately, it has been found that the likelihood of these disorders and afflictions is increased in people who are empathic. This is thanks in large part to the magnification that empaths tend to have on their emotions and feelings.

It's important to take care of yourself and to seek help for the mental troubles if you suspect that you might have a condition such as this.

6. Is there a cure for being an empath?

No, these are natural abilities that are had from youth and are not an abnormality or illness to be cured.

7. What is the difference between being an empath and having empathy?

An empath is a person who is exceedingly sensitive to the emotions and sentiments of the people in their environment. There are a lot of aspects of being an empath that, when you see them listed out for you, might explain a good deal of the things you've been going through in life without having a name for it.

Having empathy and being an empath are two different things. Empathy is a natural trait that many people possess. The lack of it characterizes some known mental illnesses, so if you've found a lack of familiarity with the concept from the description and examples above, consider consulting with your doctor.

8. Are there different types of empaths?

Yes, the types of empath vary about as vastly as empaths themselves. There are a number of different types that focus on different specific qualities in the people around them.

Conclusion

Thank you for making it through to the end of Empath Learning: A Complete Emotional Healing and Survival Guide for Highly Sensitive People to Reveal the Dark Mystic Secrets, Improve Skills and Habits for Defeating Energy Vampires and Overcoming Psychic Exams! Let's hope it was informative and able to provide you with all of the tools you need to achieve your goals whatever they may be.

If you haven't done so already, your next step is to complete the exercises laid out in each chapter for you. These exercises will help you to understand the mechanisms at work, will help you to find healthy coping strategies, and will help you to heal from past traumas or incidents.

If you have completed these exercises, your next step is to read the following book in this bundle! That is Empath Protection: A Psychic Survival Guide for Understanding Narcissistic People, Setting Boundaries Around Dark & Mystic Personalities, Sustaining Your Emotional Energy and Achieving Healing.

The second book in this bundle will serve to aid the empath in healing from the emotional trauma of a narcissistic relationship, how to spot narcissistic people before they become a problem, and how to cultivate meaningful relationships and help them thrive with the power of empathy.

Thank you very much for reading and please share the information you found helpful with friends and family who may also benefit. Finally, if you found this book useful in any way, a review on Amazon is always appreciated!

EMPATH PROTECTION

A Psychic Survival Guide for Understanding Narcissistic People, Setting Boundaries Around Dark and Mystic Personalities, Sustaining Your Emotional Energy and Achieving Healing. Tips and Tricks

By Crystal Gift

Table of Contents

Early Detection of Narcissistic People
Early Detection of Toxic People

Conclusion

Introduction

Congratulations on downloading *Empath Protection: A Psychic Survival Guide for Understanding Narcissistic People, Setting Boundaries Around Dark and Mystic Personalities, Sustaining Your Emotional Energy and Achieving Healing. Tips and Tricks* and thank you for doing so!

The following chapters will discuss many aspects of the life of an empath: someone who, as highly sensitive as an empath, has a good deal of unique challenges throughout life and personal relationships. It is the goal of this book to provide practical tools the average empath can use to forge a path ahead in life after an encounter or relationship with a narcissist has made that seem impossible.

The narcissists in your environment don't dictate your worth as a person, and they can't hold onto you forever. You have the power to live a happier life without them, and you have the capacity to bring other compassionate people into your life who can contribute to your emotional health and well-being.

This is a very popular subject with many published works to offer answers for empaths and those who know them. Thank you for choosing this book out of that vast number. It is our sincere hope that you find the information in these pages to be of use to you and that you can find answers within it.

Happy reading!

Chapter 1
The Empath and the Narcissist

What Is an Empath?

An empath is described as someone who has a higher sensitivity to many different things. The most common thing they're known for being sensitive to is the emotions of the people around them. Other abilities of an empath can clue them in much more than how the people around them are feeling, but few are as well-known or as widely used for self-growth and development.

There are actually several different types of an empath, and each one carries its own unique traits, as well as some traits that are shared commonly throughout each type of empath. It's important to note that empaths are simply people and that we are as varied and as individually unique as any other group of people in the world. We may have similar characteristics, like any group you encounter, but empaths shouldn't be categorically dismissed or granted specific things.

It is likewise important to note that while empaths are born having specific traits, we are not born *skilled*. We are born having the sensitivities that we have, and there isn't anything that can change them—but like any other talent that is had from birth, practice makes perfect, and skills must be honed.

As an empath, you will always be sensitive to a good deal of things in your environment. What you *do* with that sensitivity is another matter entirely—and knowing what to do with that sensitivity is something that will come to you more and more as you gain practice with using them.

The different types of empath could be listed out in their specificity, but a more accurate representation would be a very large, very odd-looking Venn diagram. There are so many different ways in which someone can be in-tune with the people around them, and there are many people who experience or exhibit the characteristics of several different types of empaths.

This can make it quite difficult for someone to look at a list of the different "types of an empath," in the hopes to put a label on the types of abilities they have. The most effective way to understand yourself as an empath is to get the information on what the most common traits of empaths are, see which of those traits you see within yourself, and work on honing the skills while working to diminish the drawbacks that can come with being highly sensitive.

As for the subject of a label, it might be easiest to avoid using one for the time being. If having that distinction is important to you, being able to say that you're an empath or a highly sensitive person with intuitive abilities is an ideal broad-stroke description for it.

I've listed the most commonly shared traits of empaths here so that you can take a look and see if these fit you. If you find that you identify with a good number of these, you might be an empath. Don't despair, however, if there are some items in this list that just aren't you.

We are all unique people with unique tendencies and abilities. You can be an empath without having all of these traits. If you find that you don't have a lot of these abilities, but you do have some, it can indicate a higher level of empathetic sensitivity that is somewhere between basic empathy and highly sensitive. There is absolutely nothing wrong with either outcome.

89. Strong emotional content on television has a profound impact on you.

    The thing about being in tune with the emotions and sufferings of other people is that it isn't limited to the people that you can touch. It's not limited to the people that are right in front of you.

    Thanks to the digital age we currently live in, many of our friends and family are only accessible by a digital means. Because of this, our empathy is forced onto those channels, and we learn how to pick up on the things that someone is thinking or feeling through that lens.

This could be a reason why seeing someone dealing with something on a screen, in text, in movies, in pictures, etc., do still affect us in a very real and very monumental way at times.

90. People are always asking you for advice.

Empaths often conduct them in such a way that signals other people as to our abilities. Thanks to this, people tend to know that they can rely on us to provide sound advice, or at the very least, lend an ear.

Think of it like having an invisible, yet perceivable beacon over your head that flashes, telling people that you know how to give great advice.

One of the things about this particular ability that required the practice and honing that I mentioned is being able to rely on yourself for advice. Many empaths struggle with being able to analyze the problems of others and give sound, usable advice while struggling with their own problems. Perhaps even more frustrating is that many of these problems are usually similar in nature to those that we've solved for others.

This is where that practice really comes in handy. We'll explore this in the exercises and journal prompts given in this book.

91. Intimate relationships can overtake all of your thinking, and the energy you get from them flows throughout your entire life.

I'd like to start by saying that starting and cultivating meaningful personal relationships as an empath is absolutely possible. There are things to consider, to be certain.

For instance, it should be noted that someone who is empathic will often have the need to discuss problems as they occur and resolve them on a fairly immediate basis. Someone who has a "wait and see," method of resolving problems would often cause severe anxiety in this type of person. This is not always the case, but it is quite common.

The emotional energy that an empath picks up from the people around them has a fairly profound effect on them, and it can tend to envelop the empath's entire thought process if they are concerned enough with it. Thanks to this, being closely involved with someone can seem overwhelming or like it's putting so much accessible emotion into their life that it can permeate every aspect of the person's life.

This is what makes boundaries in personal relationships so important. As an empath, you would do well to insist on a physical space where you can be on your own, and where the emotions of others, no matter how connected they are to you, may not enter. Personal boundaries will give you space in your life to get a reprieve and do the things you need to heal, recuperate, grow, and flourish.

92. Your sensitivity could be mislabeled as anxiety or shyness.
People who are very sensitive can get overwhelmed, we can feel like we need to recuse ourselves from the company of others, and we can seem a little bit edgy at times. There are more aspects to this, but it gives you a general idea of how these labels can be put on us, in spite of being quite healthy. Finding the right fulfillment, boundaries, spaces, and people can work wonders for the emotional, physical, and mental health of an empath.

93. Regardless of introversion or extroversion, you withdraw often.
This doesn't mean you are particularly a wallflower at social gatherings, but it could mean that you find yourself taking a couple of days to stay in rather than going out. It could mean that you take some time to read instead of going to a concert, or that you cancel plans you thought you'd be able to keep.
To take time for yourself is healthy, but one must do so in a measure that doesn't cut one off from the people and the world around one.

94. When thinking of leadership roles, you always assume that means putting the team first.

As an empath, you see the role of leadership as being a role in which you are completely responsible for the well-being and the success of your team. People who are otherwise focused might see leadership as an opportunity to get things from others, or to take credit for the work that is done by their team. Such things would rarely occur to an empath, which often contributes to their being such effective and admirable leaders.

95. The world you've created in your mind is rich and vibrant.
People who are empathic tend to spend a lot of time thinking, daydreaming, hypothesizing, thinking up hypothetical situations, and putting together characters and stories. Thanks to this, we have a very rich and vibrant environment in our minds.

96. Others find your very presence to be calming.
Thanks to your abilities, you often know what energies to give off in order to make someone feel at ease. This will draw people to you or make it very easy for people to relax around you.
Sometimes, the best compliment you can be paid is for someone with severe insomnia to say they got their best sleep in days, simply because you stayed the night with them.

97. Hunger very quickly turns into anger, sometimes even before hunger.

Thanks to your heightened sensitivity to feelings, urges, inclinations, and the things that are going on in your body, your blood sugar can crash a little more quickly than it can for some of the others around you. If you find yourself getting "hangry," with any sort of frequency, try keeping a granola bar or some other snack in your bag for times when things really start to bear down on you.

Keeping yourself fed can also help to lessen the effects and frequency of sensory overload.

98. You're highly sensitive to wardrobe malfunctions.

Things like scratchy fabrics, stiff tags, tight underwear, wrinkly socks, and loose waistbands can tend to bother you throughout your entire day. Many people have the ability to tune out the annoyance of such things as this, but those who are highly sensitive may have less of an ability to do something like this to get through their day.

A good rule to live by when you're getting dressed is that if it bothers you a little bit while you're getting ready in the morning, it will bother you ten times more once you're in public.

Try to go with clothes that fit well, fabrics that are comfortable and breathable, and socks whose elastic is still working quite well.

99. Criticism is painful beyond reason.

Even if the person who is offering the criticism is going so out of a concern for you and the desire to help you to improve, it can feel like a slap in the face when the answer isn't automatic approval.

100. You feel an overwhelming love for pets, animals, or babies.

You might find babies, animals, and cute things to be *so* cute that it's overwhelming. You might get so excited when there is a baby or an animal in your presence, that nothing else matters or even registers with you. This is a common trait for an empath to have.

Since empaths are more receptive to beauty and innocence, babies and animals check both of these boxes and stand out to empaths for these reasons.

101. You're exceedingly perceptive, and minor details don't escape you easily.

Thanks to your sensitivity to certain things and your ability to pick up on the things around you, you could be pretty detail-oriented. You could find that this eye for detail is an extreme advantage in the workplace.

102. You're prone to jumping or startling easily.

There is often a lot going on in the mind of an empath. Due to this, it is easy for a sudden noise or loud jolt to affect you a little bit more than some others might be.

103. Once startled, you may be shaken for a while or experience "aftershocks."

Sometimes, after we get startled, we can notice little shivers or quakes through our bodies after we've been through a loud startle or scare. This is your body anticipating another scare and letting off energy that it's building up to stave off danger.

Take some time to close your eyes, relax, focus on the immediate environment, and get yourself ready to deal with the things that you're working on. Most startles won't happen again!

104. Stimulants are very effective in short measure.

Caffeine hits fast, and it hits hard for some empaths. Coffee can be used sparingly and to a very effective result.

105. Depressants are very effective in short measure.

Things like alcohol hit very quickly and very hard. It's best to use alcohol sparingly, and it's best to drink in moderation.

106. It's easy for you to get a feel for where someone is coming from when telling you something.

For instance, when someone approaches you about a situation, you might immediately get an inkling for what they're about to say about it. It's important to hear people out and let them tell you everything they have to say, even if you think you know what they'll say.

107. You do a lot of introspection and deep thinking.

There is a lot to process when so many emotions and thoughts are passing through your mind over the course of your day. It makes sense that you would need to take time to sift through all of them and process the important parts. Just take care not to do this in the middle of social interactions or meals with others!

108. Pain sets in more easily.

Being highly sensitive does dial up the volume on so many things. Unfortunately, this can also affect your threshold for physical pain.

109. You ask the big questions in life and seek a lot of answers about the status quo.

People who have so many thoughts and feelings passing through their minds throughout the day do have the capacity and the thirst to know more things about life, each other, and the way things are.

Empaths will often find themselves looking for answers to questions that others might not even think to ask.

110. You find cruelty and violence to be abhorrent.

Empaths are exceedingly receptive to the feelings of others and are very sensitive to seeing things of a violent or harmful nature happening to the people around us. Our empathic abilities tend to make us feel the things that we watch people going through in our environment. It's best to remove yourself from these situations if at all possible.

111. You feel ailments or illnesses as someone you love is going through them.

This trait is one that can be seen as a downside—because of how sensitive we are to the struggles and emotions of the people around us that we can actually develop an illness or a condition that is being experienced by someone near us. Compartmentalization is important for this reason, and being stronger about what you allow to affect you is a skill that will help with this.

112. Deadlines and time limits leave you feeling shaken or rattled.

Keeping to deadlines and time constraints isn't necessarily difficult for you to do from a work effort standpoint. However, you might find that time limits on things tend to make you feel more harried, pressured, and less effective. It can seem like all the energy you originally had to work on your project is completely occupied by the time limit that's been imposed on you.

Things you should have easily been able to achieve otherwise, seem to be slammed up against that timeline and can only be accomplished with stress, a furrowed brow, and terrible personal care practices.

Don't allow yourself to skip meals to get to those deadlines; you need to eat, sleep, bathe, and breathe. Let yourself do those things.

113. Your greatest efforts are expended on not messing up.

Being so concerned with the task of not messing up is essentially a recipe for how to mess up. Relax, take a deep breath, and focus on doing your best. Don't allow this sensitivity to dictate the quality of your work or the richness of your social interactions.

114. Change is jarring or even upsetting.

Due to the empath's sensitivity to the things in their environment and all the small details, large changes or shifts can be jarring or upsetting for an empath. Knowing the changes are coming and having input on what those changes will do wonders to help the empath to adjust to changes, or to feel calmer when those changes take effect.

115. You find yourself feeling exhausted after having absorbed and processed the feelings of others.

Feeling your emotions requires a level of energy to be spent throughout each day. Feeling the emotions of several others in your day requires that many more times that amount of energy and it can exhaust you so much more quickly than you may realize.

This is part of what makes it so important to take time for yourself and do the things you know you need to do to recharge your batteries.

116. Sensory overload is much more easily achieved.

Unfortunately, with how sensitive we can be to every detail, every emotion, every bad vibe, and more around us—it can be easy for all of it to reach a boiling point. When someone experiences sensory overload, there is a very strong inclination just to shut it all down, put hands over the ears, stop in their tracks, and just wait out the overwhelming feeling.

This can, like many things, also be experienced in a number of different ways. What's important is that when sensory overload strikes, you come up with an exit strategy. You're able to calm your breathing, focus on one thing, or leave the area until you're able to calm down and resume what you're doing.

Shopping in malls or grocery stores is a pretty commonplace for such a thing to occur, as well as concerts, public transport, or busy restaurants.

117. You are affected by the general atmosphere of a room or "vibe."

"Vibe" may seem like a bit of a vague descriptor for the general feeling in the atmosphere of a place or person. However, what we mean is that certain emotions will leave a residual feeling in the room, and you will find yourself being affected by that from time to time.

For instance, have you ever walked into a room with a couple of people in it and gotten the feeling that someone was very upset or angry? That would be an example of the vibe of a room affecting you.

118. Beauty moves you deeply, sometimes to tears.

Beauty is all around us in the world. One of the benefits of being an empath is that that beauty isn't lost on us. We don't find ourselves missing out on how beautiful the things around us are, and we don't let it pass us by.

When we allow ourselves to experience the beauty of the things around us fully, it can be a very moving experience, and we can feel a very strong connection to that beauty.

119. You tend to adopt the feelings of others and feel them as though they're your own.

This is one of the more basic traits of an empath. Feeling the emotions and feelings that someone we care about or someone in our immediate vicinity is feeling. This comes along with the compulsion to want to help those people to sort through those feelings and work them out.

This is partially a self-preservation tactic, and partially a tactic that is done out of love for the people around us. However, you do things, make sure you're taking care of yourself as well.

120. Conflict can make you physically ill.

Knowing that there is unrest in your immediate vicinity or with someone that you care about can give you knots in your stomach, headaches, or even cold symptoms.

This is part of what makes us want to resolve things as soon as they come up. The longer we let them sit, the worse we tend to feel.

Resolving conflicts is one of the sharpest skills an empath can have, and I dare say this is out of self-defense and the need to survive more than anything else. Caring for the people involved in the conflict and wanting to help them feel better is a very close second.

121. You cannot see someone who needs help without desperately wanting to provide it.

Empaths have a very strong reflexive response called compassionate empathy. It means that when we see something wrong for someone, we roll up our sleeves, jump in, and take care of it. This is not always the best course of action.

People do need to learn how to solve their own problems in life, and people need to be able to do so without your assistance. You can't resolve the issues of everyone in your life, at every hour of the day.

If you did, when would you sleep? Eat? Work? Have fun? There would be no time left for you or your needs in the day. This is why it's so important to make sure we're spending our time as wisely as possible.

122. Occasionally, you will feel overwhelming emotions that are quite "out of nowhere."

This is one of the more basic traits of an empath. Feeling the emotions and feelings that someone we care about or someone in our immediate vicinity is feeling. It is possible for us to be minding our own business at the gym, the mall, on the bus, or at the store when we suddenly get unreasonably angry with no understanding of why.

It can be incredibly disruptive, and it can be exceedingly alarming to the people around us who aren't sure where any of it even came from.

As we hone our skills and we get better in identifying the types of emotions we can pick up on from those around us, it can give us a better sense of control on them and can help us to know which emotions are really our own and which ones we're just borrowing for a moment.

123. It's very hard for people to lie to you.

Lies come with a lot of little details attached to them. From the little twitches that people have that tell you they're dishonest, to the things that would make the lie make less sense, we are drawn to these little details.

As empaths, being made aware of small details makes it harder just to accept that things could happen to line up in a certain way and that the story went the way it was told, in spite of inconsistencies.

Detecting lies and being an intuitive response that tells you something is wrong, are things that come with being an empath. Listen to those feelings, as they're often correct.

124. You have a "big heart," and will often give too much of yourself.

In general, people with empathic abilities can tend to be kinder and more forgiving than people with a basic level of empathy. As a result of this, we can tend to give more of ourselves to the people around us who need it.

It's possible for someone with heightened sensitivity to lessen their own needs and put the needs of others in front of their own. As a result of this, the empath will find themselves more frequently exhausted, stressed, and even feeling neglected because no one is taking care of them the way they are taking care of others.

It is imperative that the average empath set boundaries for what they can give to others and keep to them. This way, they will be able to ensure they always have enough energy for the things they need, as well as the things they want to do to help other people in their lives.

Give some of yourself, but not all.

125. You seem to be a walking target for "energy vampires."

Energy vampires have a very difficult time creating energy on their own. They have a difficult time generating positivity, staying productive, keeping their energy levels high, and they very rarely (if ever) give others energy.

Because of their dearth of energy, they tend to suck it from the people around others, using it to stay alive, upright, and somewhat happy. Some energy vampires know that they're doing what they're doing. Some are completely oblivious.

Thanks to the energy that you naturally give others, people who are looking for that kind of arrangement will find themselves drawn to you. The energy that you exude and the positivity that you instill in others is something they crave. It would be prudent for the average empath to avoid this sort of person.

126. You feel that you know, without asking, what is going on around you.

    Being able to pick up on the vibe in the room around you or pick up on the emotions and inklings of the people around you gives you a general idea of what is going on before you even ask. You might find that you have the uncanny ability to predict the outcome of the situation in front of you, or what someone is about to tell you as a result of this.

127. You're an effective communicator and listener.

    Talking with others and listening to what they have to say is, for some empaths, a joy. Connecting with people, listening to what they have to say, and talking about the things that you both have in common can give the empath a lot of fulfillment and enjoyment.

    As such, you tend to listen to what the other person says with a genuine interest and acknowledge the things that they say to you in a way that lets the other person know you're actively listening. This is not as common a trait as it could be, and when people find it in others, they tend to really enjoy it.

Not all conversations and conversationalists are the same, and some are more enriching than others!

128. You have mood swings.

Being sensitive to emotion and susceptible to feeling a wide range of them can mean that your mood seems to be all over the place. It's important to take stock of things when your mood changes, ask yourself what caused the change, assess if the emotion is yours, and is appropriate and move forward accordingly.

As you gain more practice with this, the process will go more and more smoothly, and you will have an easier and easier time with it.

129. You have a trustworthy magnetism.

Being great at communicating makes people feel more open with you. This is part of seeming more honest and trustworthy. People who clam up or don't talk as much, or who can't keep a conversation going can tend to keep people from feeling comfortable or at ease with them.

You will often find that you're the person that someone asks to keep an eye on their laptop while they go to the bathroom at Starbucks, hold their place in line, or help them with something on the street.

130. You might reach for addictive substances to escape the other traits of an empath.

There is no question that the average empath has a lot of things to bear and that there is a lot of stress that can be involved with that. Unfortunately, with this territory and with the heightened sensitivity about the things going on around you, addictive substances can have more of a draw or more of an appeal.

If you're using such a thing as a crutch or as an escape, it is advised that you seek help to stop or that you find other ways to support you through the tough times that won't do damage upon continuous use or practice.

131. You're very creative.

The empath's capacity for detail, beauty, original thought, and imagination create a perfect storm for creativity. Many people who feel very deeply or who are perceptive of the feelings of others will turn out to be quite creative with some medium or another.

If you haven't looked into this for yourself, consider looking into some creative means that interest you, as well as seeing how you like it!

132. Clutter and a crowded space make you uneasy or stressed.

Your mental space has so much in it with great regularity. Thanks to this, physical clutter around you tends to send your mind into a flurry much more quickly than it might do for others around you. The need for an open, clean, orderly space is justified when so much is going on internally.

Exercise: How to Tell if You Are an Empath

There is a relatively simple list you can go down that will give you a concise answer to this question. For each of the questions below, answer yes if it applies to you. For every question that you answer with a "yes," give yourself one point.

You will find information on scoring at the bottom of the questionnaire. Read through the questionnaire and answer honestly before looking at the score information, and you will find that you will have a more honest, accurate assessment of your abilities and your tendencies.

41. Have I been labeled as shy, overly sensitive, or introverted?
42. Would I rather drive myself somewhere, so I have a way to leave before others?
43. Does it take me a long time to recover after spending an extended period of time with an energy vampire?
44. Am I easily startled?
45. Do I eat more than I need to when coping with stress?
46. Do I prefer to do one task at a time, rather than overwhelm myself by multitasking?
47. Am I socially reclusive at times?
48. Am I afraid of being smothered in intimate relationships?

49. Do I find nature to be recuperative or restorative to me?

50. Do I prefer small groups or even one-on-one interactions with large parties or gatherings?

51. Do I get mental overwhelm from people who talk continuously, loud noise, or odors?

52. Do I have a low threshold for pain?

53. Do I have a strong reaction to caffeine or medications?

54. Am I anxious or overwhelmed with any sort of regularity or frequency?

55. Do I need a recuperation period after being in large crowds?

56. Do I often feel like I do not fit in properly?

57. Do I have chemical or skin sensitivities that are exacerbated by scratchy clothes?

58. Do I seem to absorb the feelings of others?

59. Do I get sick over conflicts?

60. Do I feel more at ease in small-scale settings or cities than in large ones?

If you scored:

1-5: You are empathetic toward people but may not be an empath.

6-10: You have moderate empathic tendencies.

11-15: You have strong empathic tendencies

16-20: You are definitely an empath.

What Is a Narcissist?

A narcissist is someone who seeks gratification from vain or egotistical admiration of their own idealized self-image. This means that they look for fulfillment through admiring the qualities that an idealized version of themselves have. They take pride in their appearance, their abilities, and their accomplishments like the rest of us, but they find the more power and gratification in positive feedback about these things, whether it's from themselves or from other people.

It is important to note that being self-centered does not automatically mean that someone is a narcissist. There are specific things that you can look for in a narcissist that will tell you what their motivations are, what they're looking for from the people in their lives, and where their priorities lie,

Narcissism is the center of a personality disorder that is characterized by needing to be at the center of attention, needing to be involved in many things, and even sabotaging others so that they are seen or presented more prominently in the grand scheme of things. Narcissism can manifest in a lot of ways, and it can be a little more insidious than one might initially realize.

Many of us are familiar with the story of Narcissus from Greek mythology. Narcissus fell in love with the reflection of his own face in a reflecting pool. Depending on how familiar you are with the typical endings of tales from Greek mythology, you might be able to guess how that worked out for him in the end.

Being so preoccupied with yourself that you're disinterested or unconcerned with the trials and difficulties of the people around you can lead to more troubles than it can solve. As you can guess, the empath and the narcissist are somewhat of a dichotomy.

The unfortunate truth here is that the fact that their personalities and their concerns are so largely polarized—this doesn't keep these two types of people apart. The narcissist will see what the empath can do for them and will gravitate toward them. While the narcissist is not inherently an energy vampire, there is still a great deal to be gained by the narcissist by having an empath in their lives.

Recognizing a Narcissist

The behaviors of a narcissist will usually be the way to tell if someone is a narcissist. There are a lot of traits to look for, but if you can find several of the following traits in someone, it might be time to put some distance between yourself and that person.

Narcissists, by their very nature, tend to make poor friends and they tend to cause a lot of trouble for the people who are closest to them. The traits they exhibit with the people close to them will tend to wreak havoc on even those with the thickest skin and the strongest of constitutions.

For an empath who is involved with a narcissist, it can be catastrophic. Empaths tend to do the most they can to please the people they care about, and they deal with the emotions that those closest to them are feeling. With a narcissist, this would mean going above and beyond, only to be met with further criticisms, then feeling angry, anxious, insecure, and hateful immediately thereafter.

If there is someone in your life that you suspect might be a narcissist, take a look at this list of traits and see if there are at least 5 that you can see in that person. If there are, then you might want to reevaluate the position of this person in your life.

The Traits of a Narcissist

1. Envy is a huge focus of theirs, and they assume that everyone is envious of them.
2. They do not or cannot respect the boundaries of others.
3. They believe themselves to be superior to others.
4. They are not effective communicators.

5. They are a perfectionist in a way that demands the people around them be perfect as well.

6. They tend to exaggerate their abilities.

7. Attempts to get them to take responsibility for their actions result in blaming others and deflection.

8. They are typically obsessed with success and creating an image of success for all to see.

9. They have an overblown or an inflated sense of their own importance.

10. They thrive on having control of the situation and of others.

11. They tend to be overly sensitive about their imperfections.

12. Their personal relationships are typically a mess.

13. They expect special treatment in most circumstances.

14. They typically come across as arrogant.

15. Criticism is met with extreme anger.

16. They feel as though they are owed or entitled to things.

17. A deep sense of insecurity hides under their façade.

18. They tend to take advantage of the people around them.

19. Empathy doesn't come very easily—if at all—to them.

20. They believe that they are unique or special in a way that makes them better than the people around them.

21. If they don't receive copious compliments, admiration, adoration, and effusive praise, they will take it badly.

NARCISSISM

Exercise: How to Spot a Narcissist

There is a relatively simple list you can go down that will give you a concise answer to this question. For each of the questions below, answer yes if it applies to you. For every question that you answer with a "yes," give yourself one point.

You will find information on scoring at the bottom of the questionnaire. Read through the questionnaire and answer honestly before looking at the score information, and you will find that you will have a more honest, accurate assessment of their tendencies.

1. Do they often talk about how jealous they are or how jealous other are of them?

2. Do they respect boundaries when you set them?

3. Do they talk about others as though they are "beneath them?"

4. Do they have trouble saying what they mean and then get angry when they can't get their point across?

5. Do they have an obsession with perfections that somehow extends to you and how you "reflect on them?"

6. Do they overstate their experience or abilities?

7. Do they deflect or blame instead of apologizing?

8. Do they often talk about being successful and "showing others?"

9. Do they tend to overstate their importance or involvement with certain things?
10. Do they insist on being in control?
11. Do they lash out or get mad when imperfections are pointed out?
12. Do they have trouble keeping the peace in their personal relationships?
13. Do they expect special treatment?
14. Are they arrogant?
15. Do they receive criticism with extreme rage?
16. Do they have a sense of entitlement about them?
17. Are they deeply insecure?
18. Does it seem like they're taking advantage of the people closest to them?
19. Do they rarely display empathy?
20. Do they talk about having unique traits that make them better than others?
21. Do they seem to need a large amount of praise?

0-5: They have some narcissistic tendencies and could stand to work on them.

6-10: They have a large number of narcissistic tendencies and should seek help from a professional.

11+: They are narcissistic and should be avoided if possible

Journaling Prompt

Is there anyone in your life that you think might be a narcissist?

What is it about them that makes you think this?

Write the answers in your journal. These answers are just for you.

Chapter 2
How Empathy Can Improve
Relationships

See Your Empathy as an Asset

Your empathic abilities and your ability to empathize with people more strongly than the people around you *is* an asset. It can take some work to see it that way, as it's an asset that takes work. It's like a gift that someone gives you that takes a lot of upkeep. For instance, if someone gave you a pony, it would be a big deal and a great gift! However, you have a lot of upkeep that you'll need to do for that pony now. Think of your empathy as your pony.

The empathy that is backed by emotional understanding is an invaluable tool in the workplace, in personal relationships, in your day-to-day interactions with others, and as an upstanding citizen. So much of the things that happen in the world could be vastly improved by the introduction and implementation of empathy.

In the business world, more and more people are finding that if a business is being run with empathy, it will have more success as it makes use of that empathy. Empaths are being seen as more effective managers and leaders, because they tend to put their teams' and their customers' needs ahead of their own, listen to what is needed from the people they're working with, and do their best to make sure that those needs are met on a regular and consistent basis.

Now, in a personal sense, empathy has a place in most—if not all—of our relationships. You will find that utilizing your abilities to understand, sense, anticipate, and respond to the emotions of the people around you will often inspire and help your relationships, trust, and rapport with people growing. People will often trust people who can completely understand them, and empathy provides that in spades.

Empathy can be seen as a strength for a great many reasons. One of those is that you get a much more rounded view of the world and what's going on in it. The people around you will have many feelings, many understandings, and many experiences will shape their concept and view of the world. As they share those with you, you will inevitably impart those into your own world view, giving you a more accurate and comprehensive look as you expand and gain more perspectives.

Thanks to the ways in which empathy makes us stronger, more effective communicators, it makes us stronger and more effective friends and partners. Being friends with someone you can't communicate with on any level seems nearly impossible. Being friends with someone you can communicate with effortlessly is basically a given. For instance, it would be odd to see two people who were very effective at communicating with one another and understanding one another, only for them to go their separate ways with no liking for each other.

How Can Your Abilities as an Empath Help You?

Using your abilities as an empath, at first, is as simple as simply living your life and talking to the people in your life. As you do so, people will find ways to give you a reason to flex your muscles, so to speak, and use those abilities to help them—asking you to solve the occasional problem, as well as asking you to hear them out on something, solving problem, resolving conflicts, organizing, creative solutions, and more.

These are all things that can come up for you throughout your life as an empath. People are and will continue to be drawn to you for the abilities that you have to improve their lives and their personal situations vastly. People will charge a pretty penny for personal problem resolution, but you're right there, and you're willing to help them through it, so why should they just ask you to throw your hat in the ring and give your two cents on what's going on in their lives at that particular moment.

So, you know, with pretty reasonable certainty, what you can do to help the people around you in your life with your gifts as an empath. One of the things we've been talking about throughout the books in this bundle is taking time to help yourself and taking time to correct the things in your life that might have been neglected during the times when you've been so selflessly helping the people around you in life. But how do you do that? How do you flip the script and use your empathic abilities to help yourself in life?

Understand when someone is of ill intent and remove them from your life.

Removing someone from your life because you know they cannot help you to grow, or that they will work against you is the most valuable thing you can do for yourself. It can feel cruel at times to cut people from our lives, especially if we feel like we have the capability to help them to change for the better. However, with narcissists and people who have a mental illness, fixing the things that cause them to act the way they do is something between them and their doctor.

It can help to see the person as a hole in the middle of the road. The hole in the road is covered with some leaves and full of water, so it looks like it might just be a puddle. However, if you drive through it, your card will fall in and sustain irreparable damage that will certainly total it. So, what do you do with the hole? Do you pull over, siphon all the water out of the hole, fill it, and repave it? Or do you drive around it?

People who are narcissistic or who have ill intentions toward you or those in your personal circles have no place in your life. They don't deserve that space because they will only use it to cause harm or discord. You would do well to listen when your abilities are telling you that the person is an emotional liability and that you shouldn't allow them to remain in your life.

This is one of the move valuable things your empathy can do for you. Life is plenty hard enough with everything that goes on in times of normalcy. We don't need to invite people whose only intention or hope is to make that even harder on us.

Talk yourself through your anxieties.

When your friends are feeling anxious, what do they do? Do they call you and tell you everything they're dealing with, why they're feeling anxious, and why they're concerned that anxiety is justified? What do you say when people call you for this reason? Are you able to tell them the reality of the situation they're in, help them to see solutions, and put their mind at ease? Are you able to help them to laugh and see the positive sides of things before the end of your conversations?

This is something that our empathic tendencies grant us the ability to do. It's one of the things that make us very helpful to have around and very relaxing to talk to when things are going awry in the lives of the people we love and the people we care about. The thing we often fail to realize is that we can do this for ourselves as well. The problem-solving capabilities that we have aren't limited to everyone but us.

It can help to do this with a journal if you aren't comfortable or if you don't have a space in which you can do this out loud. Journaling is so helpful in such a large number of ways, this one included. Having a record of the things that we've guided ourselves through and the things that we've come through can really give us a valuable perspective on how far we've come when we're feeling down, and it gives us a private environment in which we can mull through the thoughts that are passing through our minds.

We've constantly dealt with so much, and it can really help to clear some mental room if we write some of it down and allow the journal to hold onto it for us.

When you're journaling, you can lay out all the aspects of the problems that you're currently facing, how it's making you feel, why you think it's making you feel that way, and what you think the solutions could be. Once you've done that, you can read back through what you've written with the voice of someone completely different from yourself.

Listen to the problem as though you have never heard about it before, and as though it's coming from someone that you care about very deeply and wish to help. Once you've done that, do your best to give that person the advice you know they need to hear. On top of that, give them the assurances they need in order to get through everything they now have laid out ahead of them. Be as honest as you can be, even if the things that need to be done sound unpleasant or difficult.

Once you've done this, you can work through any anxiety that comes up as a result of knowing that it is that you really need to do in order to reach a resolution on the problems you've just guided yourself through.

Being this kind of confidante and advisor to yourself can be an invaluable tool that can help you make sense of the murkier areas of life. There could certainly still be situations in which you need the advice or reassurance of the people around you, but having an extra pair of hands on deck couldn't hurt, right?

Help yourself to separate the scary feelings from what is actually happening.

When you're feeling an emotion that scares you, it's important to take a break. Call a time out and think about what that emotion is. Identifying that emotion is the first step to being able to work through it and process it properly. Once you've identified that emotion, you can identify what situation or stimuli in your life could have inspired that emotion to come on. If you don't have a valid answer, it could be that the emotion isn't yours, to begin with.

Let's address both outcomes of this scenario so that you always have a contingency for either outcome. The first scenario is that the emotion is yours. This is an organically produced emotion that came about as a result of something in your life that has some negative aspect to it. Now that you've identified the cause of the emotion, it's time to look at the problem itself and investigate where this emotion originated within the problem.

Talk through the problem with yourself through writing or voice, just to hear your version of how everything unfolded. As you listen to your own account of the problem, listen for things that would indicate that emotion coming about, or even things that seem to intensify that emotion within you. If you feel that emotion starting to bubble up, take a break.

The best way to get rid of an emotion that you're feeling is to let it cycle through. Experience it, feel it, let it run its course through you, and recover. Now, if the emotion is triggering a violent response, do your best to mitigate this. Throw or punch a pillow, go to the gym and take it out on a punching bag, or engage in a vigorous physical activity that could disperse that energy for you.

In whatever way that you decide to purge that need for a physical outlet, it's imperative that you neither hurt someone or yourself. Physical violence with a person or other living thing will not solve the problem, and it won't rid you of that emotion in any way either.

Now that you've let it all out, you can get back to the issue at hand and work through the thing that had caused you to feel that way. Be as analytical as you can and use the method from the last item to help you to work through the specifics of the problem. Doing so will help you to stop feeling that emotion that was threatening you before.

Now let's address the next scenario wherein that emotion is *not* yours. There is no problem you can identify that matches the emotion you're feeling, and you're not sure what to do with it. You cannot resolve an emotion that isn't yours, because there is nothing naturally causing you to feel that emotion aside from proximity.

The very first thing you'll need to do after identifying that the emotion isn't yours is to remove yourself from the space you are in. Leaving the person to feel their emotions and deal with them by themselves, or simply going to a different spot if your space is large enough and public. If you find that removing yourself from the area where that person is hasn't helped to diminish or eradicate the emotional response you're feeling—you'll need to let the emotion run its course.

You would do this in the same way that you would do it if the emotion was yours. Cry it out, feel the emotion, or work it out physically in whatever way the emotion calls for. Once you've done these steps, you should find that the emotion has dissipated, and you're left with only emotions that are your own.

Tell yourself the things you need to hear.

Sometimes, life throws us into situations that are uncomfortable. We get curveballs, we get situations that aren't fair, and we need reassurance when these things happen. The thing about being an empath is that we tend to rack up a lot of experience with telling the people around us the things they need to hear in order to move past that.

With the journal, or verbally, we can do the same thing for ourselves. We have had more than enough people tell us that we've said just what they needed to hear, to know that we know all the right things to say! So, this is another empathic ability we can turn in on ourselves and benefit from using.

Fully lay out the problem. Talk yourself through the long and short of it, laying out how you feel about each aspect of it, just as you would while talking to a friend who you're hoping will help you with this situation in your life. Be sure to spare no detail and talk to yourself like you've never heard this problem before in your life. This is how you will get the move organic responses and advice possible while talking yourself through things.

When you've heard yourself out, when you've gone through all the steps of the issue, you've gone through all the emotions attached to it, all the complications, all the nuances, and all the things that annoyed you the most, you can start to work on yourself.

The first thing to do is to acknowledge all the things that you've done right. Give yourself credit for taking the smart steps you've taken and let yourself feel the win of doing the right things in those aspects of the situation. Validate yourself and then move onto the things that could have been done differently.

Address all the situations that make us think, "I probably should have handled that differently," and be as gentle as possible about it. If you were talking to your best friend, you wouldn't be rude, and you wouldn't rub it in their face that they've made a mistake. You would calmly direct their attention toward the thing that should have gone differently, and you would tell them how they could handle that differently and more effectively in the future.

Doing things this way does point you in the right direction while validating you for the things you've done properly. When we can validate ourselves while still looking for ways to improve, we will find that more and more, as we find ourselves in similar situations, we will go for the solutions that are more appropriate.

Someone who is shamed or made to feel like they're less intelligent or valid for the things they did choose, will likely see very little change in their own behaviors and will likely see little success in similar situations as they continue to occur.

Be brutally honest with yourself about the things you're doing that don't work.

Being an empath doesn't mean we're right all the time. It doesn't mean we're kind all the time, and it doesn't mean that we're infallible in any way, shape, or form. We are human, and we make mistakes in every avenue in life. This is how we learn and how we grow. We make mistakes, we think about them, and we do better in the future.

However, it can be difficult in the times when we feel like we do so much for others, we give so much of ourselves, and we go through so much each day. It can be difficult not to be lenient with ourselves and make concessions for ourselves and excuse non-productive or unhealthy behavior.

It's so important to point out our bad behaviors to ourselves, though. It can be equally as important to notice when we're doing something that isn't going to lead to a positive result—being empathic means that we often have a pretty clear picture of how things are going to go in a situation based on the little details.

If we're doing something that's ineffective, unhelpful, rude, silly, or just a plain bad idea, we need to be able to be true to ourselves about it. We can't correct the behaviors and the problems if we're too busy ignoring them, right?

It takes a lot to admit when you're doing something that isn't serving you well, but I know that you can do it because you're very strong and you're very smart. You can figure out the things that will work better for you in the future, and you can make the changes that need to be made!

Identify the behaviors in yourself that you wouldn't tolerate in others.

It is absolutely possible for an empath to adopt toxic behaviors. You can think of yourself as an emotional sponge, and this will give you an idea of how possible it is for you to pick up icky things as well as happy things. What's important is to notice when you've picked up or developed a behavior that is not helpful or healthy.

It's not always a result of picking up on other peoples' emotions that we develop these toxic behaviors, so it's important to be vigilant when we feel like we've taken steps in the wrong direction in a given day. Going over your interactions of the day and processing how you responded, and if you could have done so in a more welcoming or positive manner.

Let's say that you were working a shift at a restaurant as a server, and you were under a lot of stress. Restaurants are very busy environments with a lot of hungry customers, and it's possible for emotions to run high when things get a little bit busy. Let's say that in one of those moments, a fellow server asked for your help with something and you snapped at her to say that you had just as many tables as she does and that you're not interested in picking up her slack.

This could have been a very quick interaction that you didn't mean as harshly as it might have sounded when it came out. Thinking back on that at the end of your day, you might be able to see how the person you said that to might have taken that to heart and felt badly about the job she was doing during that shift. That job is her livelihood too, and she depends on being good at her job to pay her bills, just like you. If she fell behind a little bit, she might have just needed a quick hand to catch up.

We're all human, and none of us are immune to making mistakes from time to time. None of us are immune to saying the occasionally very mean comment without realizing it, either. Once you notice that you've done something like this, you would do well not to sit on it. Don't wait, just pick up the phone and get in contact with the person to apologize.

You would demand that anyone else in your situation do the same, and you would demand that your co-worker from earlier deserved an apology immediately if you had overseen that interaction from a different co-worker under different circumstances. You would help the co-worker to see her worth as an employee and co-worker, and you would help her move past it.

This is why we need to hold ourselves accountable when no one else will. There's too much flippant cruelty in the world already, and we owe it to ourselves to impart the light and the positivity whenever we're able to do so.

Understand the way you're feeling and deal with it.

When we've had a particularly rough day, and we're down in the dumps, we can help ourselves out of them. We know what it is that leads from a cause, through emotion, and into the human response to that emotion. We understand why things make us feel the way they do, and we're able to tell ourselves what the solutions to those situations are.

In most cases, we don't tell ourselves what the solutions are to our problems because we don't want to know. We don't often want to do the work that we know we need to do in order to pull ourselves out of trouble.

It's easy, when you're feeling sad or when you're feeling bad for yourself, just to want to keep wallowing for a little while. Just be there, feeling the emotion, eating some ice cream, watching a sad movie and telling yourself that you'll do better next time without having to take responsibility for the current situation and why it went the way it did.

However, we know that this isn't a healthy way to deal with emotions, and we know that it doesn't solve anything. Now look, I'm not about to get myself booed off the stage here by saying that you're not allowed to be sad, eat ice cream, watch sad movies, and wallow for a little bit. What I *am* saying is that you need to follow that up with action.

As an empath, you will be able to tell yourself what that action is and how to get started on it sooner rather than later. If you do so, you will feel better sooner rather than later.

When we're feeling sad, it's hard to see the solution that requires more effort as the most viable and appealing one. Sadness takes a lot of energy out of us, and it can make us feel like sitting there. It takes all the wind out from under our wings, and it plants us firmly on our bums.

Looking at the avenue that requires immediate, decisive, and effective action is much more difficult when you're sad, but as an empath, you know that you can see that solution. Stop ignoring it or looking away from it and hop to it.

Give yourself the advice you'd give someone else in your situation.

Have you ever found yourself at a crossroads and not known what to do? Have you found yourself in need of some solid advice? Believe it or not, a lot of times, when we want advice, we're hoping that someone will just tell us what to do. We will often follow the advice given to us from other people because it removes the responsibility from the equation.

You take someone's advice and now if things go horribly awry, it's because you took that person's advice. This wasn't something you chose. This is just what your friend or family member said you should do, and you are in no way to blame for the fact that it went south faster than a bird in the winter.

However, you have the power to give yourself advice. You've given so much advice in the past—you have every ability possible to give yourself the advice that you know will be solid, will be sound, and will get you where you need to be in a hurry.

Write down all your thoughts, all your options, and all the possible outcomes of a situation. Once you've done that, read through it again, just like you've never heard any of it before, and make a decision that is proper for you, your well-being and the best possible outcome for the situation.

You will be wrong sometimes. You are human, you are not infallible, and you might make a mistake. This is okay, and you will deal with those things as they come up. In the interim, go forward bravely and be confident in the decisions you've made for your own life!

Use your tendency toward compassionate empathy to spring into action in your own life.

When we see things going awry for the people in our lives, we tend to have the inclination to jump right into the thick of it and give them what they need to pull themselves out of it. However, we have a tendency to put off the things that we know we need to do for ourselves in order to put ourselves into a better spot.

You are not any less important than the people around you in your life. You deserve to solve your problems before you solve anyone else's because you don't deserve to be saddled with your own problems and then someone else's at the same time!

If you see a situation where something needs to be done, let your compassionate empathy response work for you and spring you right into action on fixing that problem for yourself before it gets any bigger, or before another problem comes along to put it on the back burner.

Use your understanding of people to get you ahead in the areas where you want to excel.

Understanding people, what they want to hear, what they want to see in other people, and what they need can give you an enormous upper hand in dealing with people in life. Dealing with people is a very large part of life, and it's a very large part of getting into the jobs and careers we want, going the places we want to do, and doing the things that we want to do.

Using your empathy to know what the person in front of you wants to hear and knowing how to use that to your advantage can put you in places higher than you may have previously imagined.

Exercise: How Your Natural Abilities Can Help You

Think of ways that you can use the abilities listed in the section above to solve a problem that you currently have in your life.

Exercise: The Worth of Your Abilities

Pretend that someone did the things for you that are mentioned in the section above. Imagine that you had someone else in your corner with empathic abilities who did those things for you. What would you say to them? What would you do to thank them? What is your abilities' worth to you?

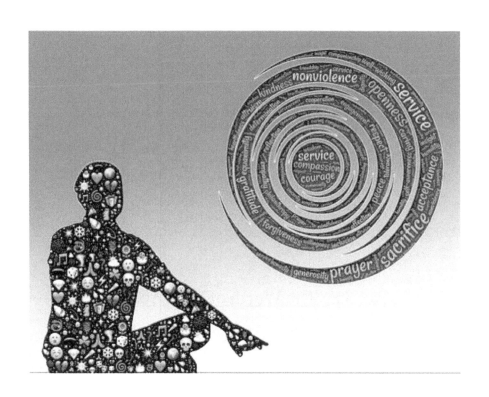

Why Communication Is So Important in Personal Relationships

You've probably heard it said that the secret to long-lasting, healthy relationships is communication. Why is that, though? Why is communicating with your partner such a fundamental part of building a life together? When you're communicating with someone, you're relaying your thoughts, feelings, and ideas to them. If the person is in communication with you and is understanding you, they're providing appropriate acknowledgments, and they're understanding what it is that you have to say.

When this works both ways, we get harmony going between both of those people, and we get those people doing things that work for one another. When two people are communicating properly, they *understand* one another. Understanding is the breeding ground for compassion and empathy.

If a couple doesn't understand one another, you will find so many arguments and hurt feelings. Two people who have no understanding between them cannot find any common ground, they cannot do things for one another that make them happy, and they cannot live a life that has any amount of harmony to it.

Empathizing with someone when you don't have any understanding of that person can be so much harder, and it can cause the upset feelings to get in the way of empathy ever even developing.

If a couple is in regular communication with one another about what each of them wants, about how they feel, about what they're dealing with, and they have an open forum for discourse and discussion on topics that come up, empathy blooms all on its own. You're able to know more about that person, how they will feel about things, how they will respond to them, and you'll begin to understand how they think before too long.

Having a partner who can understand and empathize with you can more appropriately give you what you need, make you happy, give you somewhere you can be heard, offer advice, provide the emotional support you need and so much more.

If a couple can get themselves to this place, their relationship has a much higher chance of thriving and flourishing.

Exercise: Utilizing Empathy in Your Personal Relationships

1. Think of a hypothetical situation in a relationship where having empathy could resolve a problem that one of the people is having.
2. Once you come up with that scenario, reimagine what would happen if there was no empathy between them.
3. Which one had the better, healthier outcome?

Journaling Prompt

Try to think of a situation that didn't quite go as well as you had hoped, which could have been resolved using empathy.

Write the answers in your journal. These answers are just for you.

Chapter 3
Anxiety Disorders and How to Overcome Them

The Effects of Anxiety Disorders

Anxiety is a broad term that covers a number of disorders that affect a person's sense of security and stability. These can cause worry, fear, nervousness, and so many other effects. These types of disorders can really affect every aspect of daily life and can make small things seem like the end of the world. It's terrifying, and it's exhausting for the person experiencing it. It's no picnic for the people who love them to see them suffering in that way, either.

In some cases, the reason for an anxiety attack or for a sudden flare-up of anxiety symptoms can be hidden from view. Things do tend to creep under the surface and cause issues from place to place. Why some social situations can cause anxiety and make one feel nervous, this is quite a bit different than having an anxiety disorder that can disrupt life in this way.

Persistent cases of anxiety and anxiety disorders can cause physical health complications and can have a serious effect on the quality of life for the person experiencing them. Unfortunately, anxiety disorders affect 40 million adults in the United States every year and are the most common types of mental illnesses among Americans.

How Can Your Empathic Abilities Help You Cope with Anxiety Disorders?

Let's go through some of the effects that anxiety can have, and we'll identify the things that you can do to combat them or cope with them.

A Strong Sense That Something Is About to Go Terribly Wrong

When you're feeling like something is going to go wrong, it can help to focus on the things that are okay. This is not a cure, and it might not be the right fit for you, but this is something you could try.

When one is experiencing a negative thought pattern that they can't seem to interrupt, it can help to stop what you're doing and focus on the reasons you have to be grateful, the things that are going well, the things that make you happy, or the things that you have accomplished.

Pick one of these things, or a mix, that you like best and spend some time listing out things that fit each category. Doing this for about 5-10 items each day either to yourself or in a journal can help you to center your focus on more positive things. While anxiety can be a wild beast to tame, we can interject some positivity and stability in small places, which does help to some degree.

By shifting your focus to those things, if even for a few minutes each day, can let the light shine in on you and offer a reprieve that some of us desperately need.

Panic Attacks

When you're in the middle of a panic attack, depending on the severity of it, it can be very difficult to think of anything or to regain any measure of composure. It can help, however, to write yourself notes to read when you're in the middle of an attack. If you find that you have trouble reading in those moments, you can put a recording on your phone.

Say the things that you know you'll need to hear in the middle of that moment and save it for a time when you need someone to speak kindly and reassuringly to you. Having these affirmations in the middle of our darkest moments can help us hold on through it and make it through the other side.

Depression

One of my favorite things to do to stave off or to combat depression that can come up from time to time is posting affirmations. I like to write the affirmations that make me laugh or smile and put them somewhere that I will see them. If I put them in random places, I have a much higher chance of seeing them in a moment when I truly need it.

The really cool thing about affirmations is that they speak to your subconscious. Your subconscious listens to the things that you say on a regular basis, and it forms its conclusions and imposes ideas based on them on a level below what we can be cognizant of. If we are constantly reading affirmations, our subconscious starts to pick up those sentiments and read them back to us at times when it deems it relevant.

Taking a few minutes to read your affirmations aloud each day and to tell yourself that things are going to be okay, that you are valid, that you are good, and that you are capable of great things, you will find that your subconscious will, at times, be a little nicer to you than it can typically be.

While we're waiting on our subconscious to pick up on the way we like being talked to, we can take the lead and be a friend to ourselves. As I've mentioned a couple of times, it's perfectly valid to come to yourself with the things that are bothering you. Lay them all out, no matter how valid you might feel the gripes are or aren't. Let your inner friend decide what's valid and what isn't. You just focus on saying the things that are on your mind.

Getting those negative thoughts out of your head and onto the page, or out into the air can alleviate a lot of pressure on your mind. When those negative thoughts are stuck in your mind, they're weighing you down and gumming up the works, so it's always better out than in. Just make sure the person listening is ready for it!

So, when you're talking to yourself, you can be completely candid about what things are going on that are causing you to feel down, or you can complain about the fact that even though nothing seems to be wrong, you can't get ahead!

Once you've said all you can say, you can kick your empath abilities into gear and respond to them the way you would respond to a friend who had just told you all of those things. Let yourself know that you're allowed to feel what you feel, no matter why you feel it. Let yourself know that it sucks that you feel so down and that you wish them well very soon. Let yourself know that you're glad you're getting it all out and being proactive about the way you feel.

When you're a friend to yourself, it's imperative to validate yourself for the things that you've done right. Seeking help, talking it out, taking steps toward a solution, doing the things that could resolve it, and whatever else you might have done right about the things that are causing you to feel down. I'm sure there are a few, you'll just have to look for them.

Remind yourself of the people in your life that love you, that care about you, and that want you to succeed in life. You are loved, you are cherished, you are cared for, and no amount of depression or anxiety is going to change that. The people in your life want the best for you and hope to see you succeed in your own time. They also want to see you happy and feeling well, so don't take the setbacks too hard, okay?

Think about the things that you've accomplished. Think of all the steps that you've taken, the progress you've made, the things that you've done that you couldn't have done a year prior. Look for the improvements and give yourself the validation that you deserve for them. If you are having trouble thinking of the things that you've accomplished, ask another friend. They will happily remind you, I'm certain.

Spending time saying things that are kind about yourself will also speak to your subconscious in the way that your affirmations will. Take a little bit of time to compliment yourself about things that you like. This could be from something as small as "my hair looks cute today," to something as big as, "I graduated college when I never even thought I would get there in the first place. I am absolutely amazing."

Talking positively about yourself gives you a little bit of positivity in the middle of your day, and it can re-center the focus of your subconscious onto positive things about you. Once this starts to set in, you'll start to have positive thoughts about yourself without even trying to do so. You'll find that you'll have a moment wherein you're wondering if you can handle something and your mind will say, "Of course I can. I'm amazing, remember?"

Irritability

Being irritable can seem like the top priority when you're in the middle of it. It can seem like there isn't really anything you can do except to be irritable, but you can actually do a couple of things. The first thing that you can do is take a breath and consider how the irritability you're experiencing is affecting the people around you.

If you're like me, anxiety symptoms will yield if I feel like I am hurting others with them. If I consider how I'm making other people feel with my irritability, I can snap out of it to tell the people in my immediate area that I'm okay, I'm sorry, and that I'm dealing with some anxiety at the moment.

Generally, if you do this, the people around you will understand, give you space, or try to help you work through it. If the people around you are aware that you are going through something, they are usually willing to do or give you whatever you need to feel better about it.

Being afraid to ask for help from the people around you can be harder than dealing with the symptoms from time to time. But if you practice asking yourself for help, it will gradually become easier to reach out or to develop a signal with the people around you for them to do whatever you need in order to help stave off the symptoms.

Another thing you can do—which is a personal favorite of mine— when you're feeling irritable, is to laugh at yourself. It can help to adopt a comical response to anger or irritability. If you find yourself getting so upset, flustered, and worked up, blow a raspberry. Really hard.

Can you stay mad? Can you stay mad when you've just done something so silly and off-the-wall? I generally can't, which is why it's one of my favorite things to do. I will usually begin laughing uncontrollably after a couple of seconds, and the anxiety will relent after that influx of endorphins.

If blowing raspberries isn't your thing, maybe try quacking like a duck, saying a funny word, making a silly voice, or thinking of a joke that never fails to make you laugh. As time goes on, you may need to adapt to find new things to make you laugh, but it's a great diffusion technique that I like to employ whenever I'm able.

Nervousness

Feeling nervous is one of those things that can be pretty broad, and it can come from a lot of different sources. Typically, when we feel nervous, we feel like we're anticipating something happening, sometimes we're not sure what it is, we don't feel like we can be at rest or relaxed, we feel a vibration of energy running through our bodies, and we might even feel a little queasy.

When you're feeling nervous, sometimes offering yourself reassurances about the things that are okay, about the things that are going well, and about the things that we have to look forward to can help us to feel a little more at ease.

In a time when you're not feeling anxious or nervous, take your journal and write positive statements about the way things are going. Write things that you know will help to impart a sense of calmness into things. Things that, if you were to read them aloud to yourself in your nervous state, could help to ease that.

Try also writing things that you have to be excited about. Nervousness is a feeling that has a high vibration to it and completely calming that vibration down can be a bit difficult. If you can replace that high vibration emotion with another high vibration emotion, you might have an easier time.

Try writing a list of things that get you excited in your journal. Remember to do this when you're feeling relaxed so that you are in the right frame of mind to remember everything and to put the right feelings into it.

When you're feeling nervous, you can read this list, and you might find that the excitement starts to wiggle its way into things and push that nervousness aside, if even just for a moment.

Insecurity

Being a friend to yourself is a great way to remind yourself of the things that make you amazing. The things that you can and have accomplished, the things that you're capable of, and the things that make you who you are. Feeling insecure can be the result of comparing yourself to people around you, and it can be a result of feeling like you don't measure up.

Comparing yourself to other people and feeling anxious or insecure about how you measure up next to them is a pretty guaranteed recipe for sad times. Try thinking about how you're doing now compared to how you were doing when you started.

Compare your progress on a current project to your progress from a week or a month ago and see how far you've come. Set yourself up for the wins you deserve and look at things from the perspective that you are a good person who deserves to feel good for what they've done, because you are, and you do.

Being insecure about the things that you've accomplished in life will only serve to set you back or to harm you emotionally and mentally. Make sure that when you're trying to gauge your success in life, you're basing it off of the goals that you had set for yourself, where you started, what you've been up against, how much you've put into it, and why it matters.

Reminding yourself of why you're invested in the things you're invested in re-centers your mind on the most relevant and meaningful things about the things you're doing. Rekindle the flame under your efforts when you're feeling insecure and remind yourself that you *can* do it.

Exercise: Mindfulness Journaling

Open your journal and write about what happened to you today. Be aware of what you're writing and be sure to pay attention to how you're feeling about each of the events as you're writing about them.

Make some observations about your attitude toward your day.

Exercise: Talk to Yourself as You Would a Friend

I'm not picky about the subject matter, but I want you to start practicing talking to yourself like a friend. You can do this verbally, in a journal, in a word processor document, in a messenger app, email, or text. Whatever works best for you is fine.

Treat yourself well and talk to yourself like you would talk to a friend going through the same things.

Exercise: Blow a Raspberry

When you're in the middle of a heavy emotion like irritation, anger, or frustration, do something silly to make yourself laugh and diffuse the situation.

Journaling Prompt

Have a written conversation with yourself about the things that are making you anxious. Give yourself the same advice and support that you would give to your best friend. How does that feel?

Write the answers in your journal. These answers are just for you.

Chapter 4
Escape and Healing from a Toxic Relationship

What Is a Toxic Relationship?

A toxic relationship is a personal relationship, either friendship or intimate relationship, that is characterized by frequent or semi-frequent occurrences of toxic behaviors exhibited by one or both partners. This is some kind of clinical description, but the long and short of it is that toxic traits and qualities have been exhibited by or brought out in one or more parties and there is a disturbing ratio of upset to happiness.

With any relationship, there is bound to be some measure of argument, upset, unrest, disagreement, or difficulty. When deciding if there's been too much wrong in a relationship, there are two things that are really important to measure in that relationship:

a) The degree of severity for the situations of disturbance
b) The frequency of situations of disturbance

These should be considered before weighing the good versus the bad. It's possible for a few little fights to break out between a couple and then never come up again, it's possible for the same to happen with a couple of really big fights. It's possible for two people to get upset with one another over something justifiable for an extended period time, and still bounce back from it if both people are of good intent, and who are both actively working toward a better future for one another.

There are certain characteristics of a toxic relationship that, if seen in large measure, should serve as red flags or indicators that the relationship is non-viable. There are a fair number of lines that should not be crossed in a romantic relationship and, if they're crossed, there may be no coming back from it.

In some cases, when the couples were able to reconnect after these crossed lines, it has been seen that they continue to break up and reconnect several times before deciding that the relationship is non-viable.

It is my opinion that if you can see more than three toxic behaviors being exhibited by one or both people in a couple, that the relationship is non-viable, that it should no longer be pursued, and that both parties would do well to seek help and start new with another partner when help was achieved.

As someone outside a toxic relationship, who can see that there is a difficulty inside the relationship, it can be a terribly sensitive subject that you feel a burning need to deal with, while still feeling like their privacy should be respected. In many cases, when a friend shows concern for one or both people in a toxic couple, that warning doesn't get heard or heeded. In spite of this, it is always worth a conversation with someone to see if they have noticed the same alarming patterns that you have noticed.

In cases when the person will not see the things that you see, providing examples of times when these behaviors occurred can be met by defensive or angry behavior. Toxic relationships can tend to instill insecurity and anger in both parties, whether that is a part of who they were before the relationship or not. This is the nature of something very nefarious.

Intimate relationships should serve as a haven for both parties. Both parties in a couple should feel like they have an open forum to say what's on their mind and be heard, should feel like the person opposite them is an ally, should feel like they are an equal partner in the couple, should feel like their feelings are every bit as valid—no more, no less—as their partner's, and should feel like they are truly a partner in the relationship.

If you aren't getting any benefit from the relationship, you're not happy, you're not well, you don't feel heard, you don't feel understood, you don't have a voice, you don't have the ability to choose who you spend time with, and you don't feel free, then I have something to say to you. *You aren't in a relationship. You are in prison.*

There is no point in being involved with someone who makes you feel like that. Any love you feel for them is not legitimately returned if they allow you to feel that way. This might sound harsh at first, but you need to understand that love is not ever characterized by control, anger, duress, pain, or lack of benefit.

Being with someone that you love should be a reason to celebrate and the person who loves you should be able to show you that they love you without anger, violence, danger, or denigration.

In this chapter, we will discuss the ways to identify toxic behavior, how to leave situations where toxic behavior is exhibited, how to say no to the things that don't contribute to the life you want, and how to feel okay when leaving such a situation.

There are a lot of delicate things involved with leaving a toxic relationship, and I want it known that I will never imply that anything about leaving a toxic relationship is easy. I will never imply that you don't love the person you're with and that there is absolutely no reason to stay with the person. If there was no reason, you wouldn't still be with them, would you?

What I aim to show you is that the toxic behavior is doing more to harm you than anything that relationship is doing to enrich you. I aim to show you that you are worth more than what that relationship is giving you, and I aim to show you that toxic behaviors are more destructive than we give them credit for being.

Let's take a look at some of the things that can serve as our indicators that something is wrong.

How Can I Tell if My Relationship Is Toxic?

They keep bringing up things you've done wrong in the past.

It may not seem to matter to them how much you've done rectify these mistakes, how much you've grown since you made them, or how many times you've apologized for them.

The fact that they have had to make concessions for you in the past is enough for them to feel like you owe them for life, and they will hang it over your head as long as you will allow them to do so.

They're frequently dishonest with you.

From small things about what they bought at the hardware store the other day to big things like where they got the money for the new television they've purchased; they can't seem to be bothered to tell you the truth about anything.

They might feign remorse for this the first few times you catch them, but after a while, they will stop responding to questions about the lies, or even attempting to cover them up.

This is a sign to you that they don't respect your role in the relationship or your right to know what is going on with them, with the relationship, or with anything they don't want you to know about.

They're unfaithful.

One of the common things they can tend to lie about is where they stayed last night, why they didn't come home, what happened after they left the bar, why they didn't call, and more.

If you have caught them being unfaithful on multiple occasions and no matter what tears are shed, what is said, or what is done thereafter, they keep coming up, then they're not ever going to stop. They will continue to step out on the relationship as a matter of disrespect and self-indulgence.

The harder you push for them to feel remorse and for them to change their behaviors, the further it will push them into that behavior.

DISCLAIMER: This is NOT my way of telling you that this is your fault or that you should stop pushing for them to respect you and your relationship. I am saying, however, that this is a blatant display of disrespect and a sign the relationship is over.

You've been compromising your standards for acceptable behavior to make allowances for them.

If there are things that you told yourself you would never put up with any partner no matter what, and your partner has been doing exactly those things, your standards have slipped. The things we hold as acceptable behavior in a relationship are indicators of the levels of respect we feel we deserve.

If we get to a point at which we feel comfortable with putting up with someone calling us names in front of our children or our friends, then we have lost a good deal of respect for ourselves. Concessions for this type of behavior will only ever lead to more of it.

You feel like you might be stuck with them.

There can be so many reasons that someone feels like they need to stay with someone who is abusive, toxic, or generally a bad partner—things from having children together, to feeling like we have nowhere better to go.

However, it should not matter what your prospects look like outside of that relationship. If the person is someone that you love, if they are kind, respectful, understanding, communicative, and is good for you, then you wouldn't feel like you were stuck.

Feeling like you're stuck with someone has more to do with the person opposite you in a relationship than it does with the circumstances outside of it.

There always seems to be some new problem, argument, or "drama."

In a relationship that seems to be something new and exciting every time you turn around, there is never any opportunity for rest, growth, emotional recuperation, or anything else.

There's not even any time to enjoy the company of the person you're spending your life with. There's not any time to love the person you're supposed to love.

People who are "drama bombs," who seem to sow discord everywhere they go, who seem to be a walking slap fight, and who aren't looking for peace in any real sort of capacity, then this person doesn't have the ability to have a relationship with anyone on any level.

They do not show you that they respect you through words or actions.

Someone who is an equal partner in a relationship will do their best to show you that they respect you. They will compliment you, talk about your strengths, defer to you on the subjects that you know the most about, ask for your input and opinions, and they won't encroach on the space that you have set for yourself or the boundaries that you have set.

People who denigrate or belittle you in front of others, who buy things with your money, who walk all over you, who refuse to tell you anything about the relationship, who talk to others about what you're doing wrong in the relationship—they are showing you that they do not respect you.

All activities in the relationship seem to be centered on needing to fix the relationship.

A toxic relationship doesn't seem to have any "regular days" or moments of reprieve. You can never have fun being in your relationship or doing things with one another because all your effort is centered on what you can do to keep the peace that day or fix the relationship.

Who can plan a weekend away when they're busy wondering when their partner will yell at or insult them next?

It's a wonder anything gets done at all in a relationship that's full of fighting, disrespect, anger, sadness, distrust, and toxicity.

You feel like they're going to come down on you for any little mistake you make.

If you can't do anything but worry about the mistakes that you could possibly make, you're going to make a lot of mistakes. This kind of pressure creates a terribly vicious cycle that can't be stopped easily.

When the person who is supposed to be a source of support and strength for you, is making you nervous, upsetting you, making you feel like you can't do anything properly, something is wrong. They shouldn't be cutting you down and making you feel like if you live up to his assessment, you are scum.

This is emotional and verbal abuse, and it should not be tolerated in any measure, for any length of time.

You can't say anything without fearing or receiving judgment.

It's impossible to be an equal partner in a relationship when you can't open your mouth and say what you're thinking without worrying that you're going to be openly mocked or judged for it.

This is a behavior that is meant to keep you silent, and which is meant to make you feel like a low life when you do speak. This is a tactic that keeps you in line and keeps you from feeling like you can get bold and say the things that are on your mind with any sense of confidence.

There are very few happy moments.

With the exception of mental blocks and things that go wrong in our day to day, the moments in our relationships should largely be positive. We should feel safe, happy, and calm around the people we love.

If your relationship has only very sparing moments of happiness and light, then this is a relationship that inspires sadness and depression. It can be impossible for anyone to feel loved or happy in a relationship that is almost all doom and gloom.

Lack of Support

Our partners are meant to give us support in our ambitions, endeavors, our daily struggles, our daily victories, and our lives in general. We should be able to turn to them for reassurance and for calming down when we're a little too excited or keyed up.

When we can't rely on the people closest to us for this, and when we can't talk to them about the things that are most important to us without feeling like we're going to be made to feel bad or wrong for it, we have no support.

Having no support in life makes every endeavor we undertake infinitely harder.

They don't take no for an answer.

If the person is insistent on getting the things that they want, regardless of how it will affect you, make you feel, or what it would require of you, they do not care about you.

Every person should be allowed to set their own boundaries and should be allowed to say no to *anything* that they either do not want or cannot do. People who do not respect this are not relationship material.

You can't seem to do anything right.

Making mistakes is one of the things that abusive partners tend to dwell on. They talk about them a lot, they compare everything you do to mistakes you've made, they wait for you to mess up, and they assume that you will mess up regardless of what you're doing.

If your partner is talking about your mistakes, missteps, slipups, drawbacks, troubles, difficulties and shortcomings more than they talk about your successes, strengths, achievements, accomplishments, and abilities, they are waiting for you to mess up again so they can talk about it. The intention here is *always* to make you feel terrible. There is no other reason.

They undermine you or insult you in front of others.

It is impossible to find your own self-respect when you're being torn down in front of the people you know and love, and even in front of strangers. This is embarrassing, degrading, troubling, and heartbreaking.

No one should have to endure humiliation at the hand of the person who's supposed to be their partner in life. This is a form of verbal and emotional abuse.

They are physically or verbally abusive.

If your partner has ever laid a hand on you and intentionally hurt you, there are no other criteria on this list that need to be met for you to be 100% certain that this person is not relationship material.

Physical abuse is inexcusable, and it can lead down a terrifying road that is not recommended for anyone. Seek help for leaving if you need it. Leaving should be made a priority in such a case—all extenuating circumstances should be addressed with the help that you get.

You don't feel worthy when you're with them.

Worthiness should never be a question in any relationship. If you don't feel like you are worthy when you're with this person, then they have not shown you common decency and respect. You should be afforded the opportunity to feel like a respectable and worthy person in your interactions with them.

If they ever say anything that makes it seem like you're not worthy, like you're not on their level, like you're not equal to them, or like you're less of a person, this is denigration and a lack of respect.
You are valid, you are worthy, and you deserve respect.

They make no effort to act as a partner or lover with you.

Physical affection and emotional affection are such a huge part of any intimate relationship. If your physical advances are consistently refused, and if you are denied any measure of love or affection from your partner, there is very little opportunity for you to get anything fulfilling or enriching from your relationship.

While relationships should never be solely about what you're getting out of them, you should be getting love, affection, respect, and some degree of fulfillment from it. These are *basic* traits of a relationship and should, in no way, be compromised or substituted.

They never go to great lengths to make you happy or to do anything for you.

A lack of effort on the part of your partner can be hard to see. If they're not putting forth any effort in the relationship, to make you happy, to do something for you, or putting effort into your life together, then you will be the one left doing everything.

If you're going to be the one doing everything, it will make more sense to marry yourself, as you'd save money on groceries.

They seem to be jealous or envious if you have anything they don't have.

Your partner shouldn't be comparing the things that either of you has or doesn't have. They certainly should strive you have at least as much, if not more than you at all times. If this is something they are doing, and they refuse to let it go or to let you have something they don't have, then they are controlling and toxic.

There is little to no follow-through on promises made.

In a lot of toxic relationships, the toxic partner will make agreements to get the argument, interrogation, or nagging to stop. They will agree to things that their partner wants, just to get out from under the magnifying glass, so to speak, but have no intention of following through.

This leaves the other partner feeling let down, sad, upset, and betrayed. These are all very valid responses to being lied to and to not getting the things that were promised to us by our partners.

You find yourself making compromises or changing your opinions to fit what they want.

The will of a toxic partner can often be something that is enforced with the threat of temper tantrums, angry fits, verbal abuse, or worse. Thanks to this, it can feel like we need to consent to what they want, in spite of how it makes us feel, just to avoid the wrath of our partner.

People who behave in this way do so to get what they want from the people around them. It is rather a childish behavior that is far more alarming in someone who is an adult. This is because they can tend to lash out in more dangerous ways.

Your relationship can never seem to get the break it needs in order to be good finally.

"If we could just catch a break, I know things would be better. I know they would treat me better if they weren't so stressed about the things that are going wrong around us. If we could just get one break, then they would stop being so abusive, and everything could go back to being good again."

This is a false hope that a lot of people have, thinking that stress is the reason their partners are lashing out, acting toxic, and doing things to make both of your lives harder. It's a nice thought that things could simply go back to being good if everything was suddenly good again, but it's rarely ever true.

Negativity seems to hang over every interaction.

Something as simple as asking your partner how their day was could result in some insults, a snide comment, or some other negative response. If there is so little positivity in the environment surrounding this person that chances seem slim that they'll answer this question without a fight, there is no hope to interject any positivity into it. Trying to do so could even result in an even more negative environment, with more anger than there was before.

Any love in the relationship is coming from you.

Don't be the only source of love in your relationship. Hold back any affection for a span of about five minutes, then try to hold a conversation with your partner about something pertaining to your relationship. How do you feel? Did you feel any love coming from them? Did you feel any love in that conversation, their words, and their concept of your relationship?

If not, then it could be time to make your exit.

They are passive-aggressive or sarcastic with you very often.

Few questions need a snarky or rude response, but some people will use them with every opportunity they get. This can put a lot of strain onto a relationship. Being passive-aggressive is a great way to make someone feel like they're on edge, and to make them feel like their intelligence is inferior. This is precisely the intention behind someone who does this with any sort of regularity, particularly in front of others.

Narcissism is a key trait of theirs.

We discussed Narcissism in a previous chapter, and this book is geared toward helping you to leave the narcissists in your life behind. If you find that your partner exhibits those narcissistic tendencies laid out in the first chapter, it's time to start planning the way in which you will separate yourself from this person.

Narcissism comes with its own terrible set of specific traits and repercussions. Narcissists are not people who can hold a sustainable relationship, particularly with empaths, who are so susceptible to that type of behavior.

They are almost always angry or likely to become angry at the smallest thing.

Living under this kind of anger all the time can cause so much stress for the people in the house. No one feels like they can say or so anything because they fear to incur that wrath and that anger.

No one wants to be yelled at, and no one wants to be yelled at for the benign things they do in their day-to-day. If you can't tell what's going to set off the person, then you never want to do anything at all. The very concept is exhausting, and no one should need to live in this way.

They are openly critical of you and your choices.

Making you second guess every choice you make instills insecurity in you that will span across your entire life. It will have you questioning even the most basic decisions that you make for yourself, and it will have you feel like whatever decision you make; you've probably done it wrong.

In addition to how exhausting this is, it chips away at your self-respect. Can you respect someone whose everyday choices and decisions you can't even trust? On top of this, it leaves you aware that your partner also does not respect you. Without respect, it's impossible for a true partnership to form.

They chip away at your self-worth.

With the things they say, the jokes they make, the jabs they take at you and your choices, the example they make of you in front of your friends and family, the things they say leaving you aware that they don't respect you, and questioning your worth in the relationship—they're constantly chipping away at your self-worth.

Someone who doesn't think they are worth anything, and who doesn't think they're worthy of something better, will not ever demand to be treated better. They will never demand that the abusive partner rise to the occasion and give them the respect they deserve.

You have no privacy.

You aren't allowed to have boundaries; you aren't allowed to say no; you aren't allowed to have anything that is only yours, and that is only meant for you and your eyes. This is a type of abuse that strips you of everything that's yours over a long period of time. If you have nothing, then you will get used to it. You will get used to things being bare and meant for your partner. Someone who does this to people wants to make sure that you never ask to have things for yourself.

You have no autonomy in the relationship.

Someone who works to strip your autonomy from you is afraid of what you will do with it. They don't want you to ask things of them, they don't want you to stand up to them for the things they do, and they don't want you to feel like it's okay to walk out.

Autonomy means being able to govern yourself, decide what things you're allowed to be, do, or have, and being able to dictate what someone in your life owes you or should do for you. Someone who works toward taking autonomy from other people is depending on you never taking back that autonomy.

You can't get anything resolved.

It doesn't seem to matter what type of things you try to bring to them to fix; they stonewall you. They tell you that you imagine things; they tell you that things don't need to be fixed; they tell you that there isn't anything wrong with what they've given you in life.

It doesn't matter how they spin it. One way or another, they will never be willing to go any work to change anything in the relationship.

The truth is, they know what's going on in the relationship and they want to keep it the way it is because they're on top. Either it's this, or they are afraid that they're the cause, and they fear help. Either way, it's a recipe for a stagnant relationship.

Spending time with them leaves you feeling drained, not enriched.

People who are emotional firestorms are not relaxing to be around. If you can't be sure when they're going to blow a gasket, or if you can't be sure what they're going to say to you next in an attempt to cut you down, then you are not in any sort of position to relax when this person is in your vicinity.

How are you ever supposed to get a decent night's sleep, a relaxing evening, or any sort of recovery in an environment with a person like this? How is anything supposed to be happy around this person? This is not the way it should be.

They don't trust anything you say.

In spite of the way they conduct themselves when you're not looking, they treat you like you can't be believed or trusted. This is similar to not being able to trust the decisions that you make. They don't believe you; they don't respect you, and they don't expect that you have the ability to do what's right.

On top of this, those who are dishonest with someone as a general rule, you will almost always find that they are not trustful of the person they're usually lying to.

You feel like you need to read between the lines in everything they say.

It seems like everything this person says has some other meaning layered into the things that they say. This is similar to being passive-aggressive or sarcastic. There's always some underlying intention in what they say, and if you get hung up on everything they say and what they really mean by it, you're bound to be utterly exhausted.

Putting your trust in this person can never seem like an option if you never know what they're thinking about you, about the people around you, and about your relationship with them. That's no way to live!

You don't feel safe when you're alone with them.

If you don't feel like you are safe when you're alone with someone, it could mean that you think they wouldn't protect you if something were to happen or it could mean that you think they would do something to harm you.

If you earnestly believe that your significant other would do something to harm you while you're spending time alone with them. That is not a relationship that you need to keep.

Seek help immediately and get help removing yourself from that person's life on an immediate basis. There is help available for people who are in situations like these, and it's imperative to reach for it because you never know when these things can escalate.

They're not making any efforts to learn or grow; they seem stagnant.

Someone who doesn't make any personal effort to change, better themselves, improve, grow, learn, or expand their horizons in any way for an extended period of time should seem a little odd. Most people will try new things, learn new things, read, or invest themselves in some sort of enriching activity.

Someone refraining from doing these types of activities and from growing in any way, it could be a sign that the person will not be doing any changing or growing to accommodate a more fulfilling or a better relationship.

You can't or don't ask for the things you need because there isn't any point.

If there is something that you need or want for your life, for your house, or in your relationship and you feel like there isn't even any point to asking for it, then you are most certainly in a relationship with someone who does not care for you.

The things that your partner needs or wants should always be open to discussion. Extravagant purchases should be curtailed, but aside from this, people should be able to get the things that they need from their partners.

One or both of you avoid spending time together.

If one or both of you would rather not spend time together, that should act as a fairly large red flag. People who are in intimate or romantic relationships should prefer to spend at least some time with one another on a semi-regular basis. Spending less time together will only serve to widen the divide between you, and you need to assess if this is something that you want to be doing.

If it is something that you want to be doing, then you should get proactive about it and just end the relationship to maximize the amount of space between you.

They need to be in control and become angry when they aren't.

Loving someone and controlling them are mutually exclusive, and it's imperative that partners realize this very early on in the relationship. If someone wants to have control over your comings and goings, the things that you have, the things that you do, the places you spend your time or anything else, this is not someone who wants to be a partner in your life. This is not someone who wants to love and support you, this is someone who wants to own you, and this is someone who will treat you like a possession.

Your behavior is worse when they're around.

People who are abusive to us or who treat us badly can make us feel terrible at every turn. Over time, this will build up, and we will have negative energy that just rolls up to the forefront whenever that person comes around.

As such, when someone who is badly treating you comes around, your speech, your behavior, and your overall demeanor can come across as far less pleasant than you may generally be.

As empaths, we are people who deal with emotion more than most other people. We are not typically very good at quelling, sheltering, or hiding those emotions. As a result, someone who loves you might hate the person you turn into when you're around a toxic partner.

Their presence makes you upset.

When all that negative energy comes bubbling right up to the forefront when they're around, you're bound to feel pretty upset about it. Especially as an empath, you will feel that ball of negative energy inside you always. You will feel it rattling around until your partner comes back.

When they come around, you'll get angry, you'll turn into your negative self, and you might end up pushing that anger down to keep from upsetting them. This is unhealthy and can cause a lot of health problems for you.

You're never sure where you stand or where the relationship is going.

If you're not sure what role you play in your partner's life, how they describe you when you're not around, what they think of you, if they want you around, or if your relationship is something you're supposed to be trying to prolong.

How are you supposed to do anything useful in this situation? How are you supposed to know which direction is up and which way is the best to go about your business?

This is more confusion on top of the confusions that a toxic relationship can already cause for you.

They demand everything and give nothing.

Controlling partners will often demand that things be done in a very specific way. They might demand that you go above and beyond to do things that will appease them. When the table is flipped, however, they will make no efforts to do these types of things for yourself.

They will give as little as humanly possible while demanding that you toe a very thin, very poorly defined line.

They make big decisions without speaking to you.

If your partner is making big decisions without speaking to you, they are indirectly telling you that you are not an equal partner in the relationship, that your input and approval doesn't matter, and that they have the right to do whatever they want without consulting you.

Your opinion, input, and consent should mean a great deal to someone who is claiming to be your partner in life. If you don't have a say in the big decisions, then you don't have a say in anything in the relationship at all. They will not step down from that decision-making position, and they won't allow you to hold stock in the relationship

You're not a team.

Partners who cannot make decisions together and who are not on the same page do not operate as a team. In order to operate as a team, you need to be aware of what the other is thinking—you need to feel like they care about your input, about you, your well-being, and the things that you have to say.

You have to look at things as a unified front, join together, come up with strategies for things, and make a single effort toward the things that you both want in life. If this can't be done, then you're not a team.

They tend to keep a mental record of everything you do wrong.

Someone who is waiting for you to mess up will often keep a mental note of the things that you do. Someone who aims to belittle you for minor shortcomings will do so with excessively collected information on very small, negligible mistakes.

They will use these as a basis to call you incompetent and to belittle you. This is not fair, and it will serve to undercut your confidence, self-respect, self-esteem, and the respect of those who hear this behavior.

They do not communicate with you or allow you to communicate with them effectively.

It is a toxic habit to stonewall communication efforts with one's partner. It is possible for them to maintain their control of you by withholding communication, or through occlusion that is achieved by withholding communication.

If they refuse to let you communicate with them, it shuts off accessibility, and it keeps you from ever reaching mutual respect and understanding on any topic. This is a way of keeping you from being equals in the relationship and should be seen as a red flag.

You aren't able to fully relax around them.

Spending time with your significant other should be a time when you can be calm, recover some of your emotional energy, feel safe, and relax. If this is not something you can do with your partner, then where can you do this? If you and your significant other do live together, are there any times of the day or night that you can spend being relaxed?

You shouldn't have to plan your schedule around your significant other's sleep or work schedule, just to get some time to be calm and still.

Exercise: Toxic Relationship Checklist

In the last six months, or since their most recent therapy session (whichever is soonest), how many has your partner exhibited? (If the answer is more than 5, your relationship is toxic. If the answer is more than 10, you are in physical danger in that environment.)

How to Safely Make Your Exit

Leaving a relationship is never easy. Personal relationships require a lot of emotional investment, and in a lot of cases, we come to love the person before it's time to leave. Breaking up is something that will often be painful and will come with some logistical curves.

When leaving a toxic or abusive relationship, there is a safety concern, and there are some steps to follow to make sure that you're completely supported through the entire process. You will need to make sure that there are certain things in place as you go so that you can get the support you need throughout the process.

Seek help.

Depending on what kind of person you are, what your support network looks like, and what you prefer to have on your side, your options might differ. Whatever you're most comfortable with utilizing for help in this scenario is ideal.

Unfortunately, there isn't any outfit that is as prolific as Alcoholics Anonymous or Narcotics Anonymous to introduce you to and keep you on a detailed plan to keep you on the right path. What you can do is utilize the help of someone who can act as a sponsor for you while you're dealing with everything that comes with making your exit.

There is no way to overstate the value of having someone who you can call when you're not sure where else to go, someone who can talk you through the most worrying or alarming parts of the process, and someone who can remind you why you're on the path that you're on. Being sure that you're doing the right thing for you and your health can do so much to keep you going in the right direction.

Express yourself and your feelings.

Going through something like this is no small feat, and it's not something that has a low emotional impact on someone. It's important when you're going through the process of leaving the toxic influence in your life to talk about how you're feeling.

This is especially important for someone who feels things as deeply as an empath, and for someone who is bound to feel the fear from the people around them because of it. Leaving someone who is toxic to you is scary enough before the feelings of others are foisted off onto us by our empathic abilities, so it's important to offload some of that emotional pressure by talking about it.

Whoever you choose to talk to about these things is your prerogative. Depending on the person, you could prefer to talk to a professional, a friend, a co-worker, or some other person in your life. If there is no one you think you'd like to speak with, you should at least write them out in your journal. Allow yourself to talk through all the finer points of what's going on in your mind, how you're feeling, and get them out of your head.

Remember that the space taken up in your mind by emotions can be cleared to some degree by talking about them or otherwise expressing them. Offloading that emotion can free you up and give you more emotional energy and strength to deal with the things that lie ahead for you in your path away from the toxic person and in your everyday life in general.

As we know, life waits for no one and continues on in spite of the things going on for us as individuals. Things will continue to come up for you, bills will continue to need to be paid, events will continue to transpire, and you will need the energy to face and deal with them. Writing your feelings down in a journal, email, document, or talking about them with someone we trust is a great way to prepare us for all of that.

Decide what is best.

Only you know what is best for you. No one else can tell you that you aren't getting enough from your relationships and no one else can decide for you if it's time to leave. People can tell you that you need to leave and that it's for your own good, but if you haven't made the decision to do that, you won't fully commit to leaving.

When the people around us tell us what we should be doing and try to insist that we do what they are suggesting, it can make us act out of resentment. As autonomous people who can think for ourselves, it is imperative that we make the conscious decision to do what we know is right.

Only you can make the big decisions about your own life, decide to detach yourself from the toxic person, and make your exit from that situation. Someone can forcibly remove you from that toxic relationship in your life, but they cannot emotionally remove you from it. You have to be the one to make that decision and work toward that goal.

If you are removed from the environment where the toxic person is, forced to live your life apart from them, there is still that connection to them, and they will always have some power over you. They will always be able to draw you back toward them. Decide what is best for you and run with it.

Make every effort to give yourself a positive environment.

As previously mentioned in this section, the emotions that are surrounding you will contribute a great deal to how you're feeling. You will find yourself absorbing the emotions of the people in your immediate environment because that's what empaths do.

Because of this, and because of the nature of the emotions that are bound to occur to you naturally, you will need an injection of positivity into your environment to help you through. Ensure that the people around you are aware that you need them to be positive for you. Spend time playing with the children in your family or with animals that you love, spend time doing the things that you enjoy with those closest to you.

Take the time to inject positivity in the way that works best for you. It's okay to ask the people around you to help think of ways in which to boost the positivity as well. With the help of our friends, family, and pets, interjecting more positivity into the middle of a tough situation is much more easily accomplished.

Make a promise to yourself and keep it.

When exiting a relationship, it makes sense that you will miss them in some capacity. The person played a very important role in your life, and it's okay for you to miss someone who hasn't been the perfect partner. You loved them, and you did your best to build a life for them. Leaving them doesn't mean you have to forget what happened, or that you're not allowed to feel that love for them anymore.

What it does mean is that the relationship was non-viable and that it's time to move on from them. It's best to find someone who you can be with that will help you grow, and it's best to build a life with someone who doesn't exhibit toxic tendencies.

To this end, it's important to promise yourself that you will not go back on your decision. Promise yourself that you will put emotional and physical distance between you and the person. Promise that you will not compromise on that distance and that you will not do anything that would indirectly compromise that distance.

You owe it to yourself to move in a good direction and move on toward things and people that will help you to grow and to thrive. In times when you feel like you might not want to keep your promise, remind yourself of the reality of what going back means. It means undoing the steps you've taken toward growth, it means putting yourself in harm's way, and it means you are making the decision to be okay with toxicity in your immediate environment from here on out.

You are leaving this relationship *for you*. You are not an incomplete person in your own right; you are enough. Relationships can be built with people who will build you up and inspire you to grow, or they can be made with people who will cut you down and keep you feeling small. You deserve the better of these two and, in spite of the hard road ahead, I know you can do what is needed to get to that point.

Exercise: Draft a Letter to Yourself

Write yourself a letter about what your promise is to yourself. Make a promise regarding leaving your toxic relationship, what it means to you, why you're doing it, and what your hope is for your future.

Keep this letter and refer to it whenever you feel uncertain about your decision to leave your relationship.

Feel free to add more positive content to this letter as time goes on. The stronger you get, the stronger your commitment to yourself and your own well-being becomes.

How to Say No

One of the biggest things an empath will struggle with is feeling like they can't say no when someone asks for something. How, when you know how much people need you, are you supposed to say no? If someone is asking for your help, how do you say no?

One of the things a toxic person can do when you attempt to cut them from your life is come up with an emergency that requires your sudden intervention. This is a tactic to get you involved back in their life as sort of a foot in the door. Once they have you back in front of them, they have more of an opportunity to ask you to stay.

If they are able to pull you back in for something such as an emergency, they will keep coming up with reasons to get back into your life and to get you back into theirs.

Let's go over some ways to keep yourself from getting back into a difficult situation.

1.   Don't agree to anything on the spot.
      When you're talking to someone, and they're asking you for your help, it can seem like a fine idea at the moment. It can seem like something you could easily resolve in order to get them on their way back out of your life.

However, once you're involved, you could find yourself in too deep to get back out. You could find yourself doing things that you don't want to be doing for the person, or you could find that they never needed your help in the first place, they just needed you to come a bit closer.

Put some time between them asking you and your decision-making. Tell the person that you'll need to check on some things or get some things in order before letting them know if you can help.

If you take the time to get away for the person, think about what it would mean to get involved with the person again and make your decision. If you need, get a friend to weigh in on it and let you know what they think about the situation. Sometimes, an hour or two can make all the difference.

2. Practice the different ways to phrase "No."

No can sometimes be a trigger word for people who feel the need to control us. Phrasing your refusal differently and framing it in such a way that softens the blow can make it seem like it's easier for them to take.

Think of ways in which you can say no that will sound kinder. This will also serve to soften the guilt response we can feel when denying help to someone who seems to be asking us for it in earnest.

It's important to bear in mind, however, that when a toxic person is asking for your help, there is always something more to it. They may thoroughly believe they need your help with this situation, but there is always something more. We'll list some phrases you can practice:

- "I'd like to help, but I'll be unavailable for this one. I hope it goes well for you."
- "I have a prior engagement that's keeping me from being able to help with this."
- "I don't think I would be the right person to help you with this. Someone else would be better suited for it."

3. Curtail your availability.

Modern technology has given us the ability to be in about a million places at once. The drawback for this is that you are at the beck and call of anyone who would like to speak with you. Between social media, messenger apps, phones, and everything that keeps us connected to one another, there isn't any communication you can send to someone these days that you can't reasonably assume they'll see within 24 hours.

Because this technology removes all the barriers between yourself and people who need something from you, the responsibility falls to you to put that barrier back into place. Establishing barriers is probably the essential tool in being able to say no to things. If you have a very rigid set of rules that you live by, you can rely on those to tell you when you're overextending.

The boundary on immediate communications can be maintained by setting your notifications to be muted past sometime in the evening so you can have time for yourself. This could be time to do chores and personal responsibilities, resting, relaxing, emotional exercises, prayer, meditation, or anything you prefer to put into your evening.

4. Be firm and yet courteous.

Being assertive doesn't mean needing to be rude. This is a very good thing since telling an empath to be rude to others as a general rule would be like asking a squirrel to ride a bike.

It's important for the average empath to know that you are not rude by being assertive in refusing to help them. You can tell someone, "I wish I could help you move this weekend, but I don't have the availability," and still be friends with them. You can tell them this and come to the housewarming with a lovely plant to wish them well in their new digs!

People who don't have the gift of being an empath do have the natural benefit of not worrying that their refusal will have negative repercussions with the person they care about. It appears to be a very empathetic response that tells us our use to people is directly proportional to their love for us.

I am happy to assure you, however, that this is not the case in a large number of relationships. Relationships that are predicated on exploiting your usefulness rather than on your feelings of mutual respect, affection, and familiarity are not as healthy and should, if at all possible, be avoided. You are person, not a tool; as such, your worth as a friend should be based on more than your "uses."

Understand tactics that are meant to get you to say yes.

There are a number of tactics in use by salespeople, organizations, and people to get you to say yes. It's important, as someone who has a hard time saying no, to be able to spot these. The more you know about the manipulation you face—the better chance you have of avoiding it entirely.

Here are some tactics that you might run into in your travels:

- Give Before Taking

  A technique that is common is to give you a little boost, a shot in the arm so to speak, before asking someone for something they actually want. So, this could look like someone coming to you and paying you a lot of compliments on your abilities and your proficiencies in life.

  From there, they see that you're flattered, and they might even ask you some questions about how you're able to do some of the things that you're able to do. Once you begin to explain some of the things you know how to do, the person can use that to appeal to you.

Using your own language and phrasing, they can make a strong case for why they need for you to be the person to help them with what they need. They can make their request sound like exactly the type of thing that you excel at doing. Once they've done that, it will likely feel to you like you're the only person who can help them with the thing that they need. Who can say no to that? You can.

With everything that's been laid out in this list, you can say no to anything that does not benefit you.

- Foot in the Door

  This technique employs the technique of getting you to say yes to something that seems benign and easily doable. Once they have your commitment to that aspect of what they need, they will expand the scope of what they're asking you to do.

  Of course, you have the option to change your answer and say no at any time, as you haven't signed any legally binding contracts and you're not under any obligation to do the things this person wants you to do.

  The reason this is effective is that it very intentionally rests on your distaste for going back on your word, or for backing out of a commitment once you gave your agreement to it. This is unfair, but it's a tactic that is commonly used.

It's advised that if someone begins to add conditions onto an agreement after you've already agreed to it, that you should just stop the conversation there, say "This is more involved than I had initially anticipated, and I don't think it's a good fit for me at this time. Thank you for thinking of me."

Cutting this off and not allowing it to grow into something more will save you a good deal of stress in the long run.

- The Advantage of Authority or Familiarity

  Another tactic that people use is to get someone that you know or respect to tell you that they think it's a good idea. In some cases, they only steer the conversation so you think that the person you admire, or respect would tell you that it's a good idea.

  This is a rather manipulative tactic, and it can be used by family, friends, salespeople, or people who simply would like for you to do something.

  In the event that someone is using this tactic with you, you can ask yourself how that person that you know and respect would respond if you told them, "That wasn't something I could comfortably or reasonably do, so I didn't agree." I find that this helps to alleviate the hypothetical pressure that this would impose on the

447

situation and will allow you to confidently tell the person in front of you that you're unable or not interested.

- Give a Time Constraint

  Putting a time constraint on an agreement is a way that some people use to add pressure to the decision-making process. As noted in the previous chapter, you saw that a time limit adds a considerable amount of pressure to any process for someone who is sensitive.

  Whether the person adding the time constraint knows this or not is unclear. The aim of this tactic is to get you to see the "buy now" response in your head, telling you to jump on the opportunity.

  It's bold of someone to assume that you want to jump in on the chance to do something for someone else, but believe me, stranger things have happened.

  With this tactic, you can simply say, "Thank you, I'll think about it and let you know." In most cases, the person will take this to mean that they won't hear from you in the future, but if you decide it's something you would like to do, you know that you're making the decision on your own terms.

5. If you must say yes or would like to, give a conditional answer.

   A great way to exert control over a situation in which you're giving your help to someone is to dictate some terms for the arrangement. This tactic is particularly effective in situations in the workplace. If there is someone who is shirking work tasks and looking for someone else to do them, this can help you.

If someone is looking for you to complete come tasks for them in the immediate term, you could tell them that, while you're willing to complete the tasks given, you will need some extra time.

Alternatively, you can tell them that you will do some of the tasks requested in the time they requested. This encourages people to look elsewhere for the help they need and establishes a boundary around you and your work.

6. Overestimate how much you need for yourself.

When someone comes to us looking for help and support, the assessment we have to make is of the time, emotional resources, and the energy that we have available. From there, we need to assess how much of those resources we need for ourselves and our tasks, what we have left, and if we're able and willing to spend them on the task being proposed to us.

When you're making this assessment, it's important to overestimate how much of those resources that you need for yourself. You need to make sure that you have more than enough of those resources to help you through your own life and overestimating what you need will keep you from overselling what you have to give and with burning yourself out.

7.   Do not confuse importance with urgency.

Someone running up to you with something that is urgent and needs to be addressed right away does not necessarily mean that it's important to you. The person who is having trouble could be important to you, but if you're unable to help, that doesn't make that person any less important to you.

Making these distinctions and holding to them will save you a good amount of trouble in your life and your relationships with the people in your life.

4. With a pen and paper, make a list of five scenarios in which someone is coming to you for some help, or your involvement that would not be workable, desirable, or helpful to you.

5. For each of those five scenarios, think of three responses that tell the person that you are not interested, able, or willing to be involved. Be as courteous as you'd like but remember to be firm.

6. Pick your three favorite responses from the ones you came up with and practice them out loud. If you have someone who can run through the scenarios you wrote in item one, so you can practice your favorite responses, doing so would greatly benefit you.

How to Feel Okay When Leaving a Toxic Situation

Leaving the environment where a toxic person can take a high emotional toll on you, but there are ways to mitigate that.

- Fill your environment with positive people.
- Maintain an environment of support for your situation.
- Be vigilant about self-care, whatever that means for you.
- Disallow yourself to feel regret or self-doubt about your decision with any regularity.
- Don't dive right into a new relationship.
- Express your feelings regularly.
- If you need it, get help from a professional.
- Share the story of what you experienced.
- Process feelings of shame about the relationship through writing or talking.
- Start new friendships.
- Rather than seeing yourself as a victim, promote an image of a strong person with great worth.

Exercise: Coping with Your Exit

Pick your favorite three items from the list above (more if you can manage it) and commit to doing them on a daily basis.

Journaling Prompt

Envision your exit from a relationship with a toxic person or narcissist. Write down the ways you envision it going and make contingencies for each scenario you envision.

Having that security can embolden you in your efforts.

Write the answers in your journal. These answers are just for you.

_____

Chapter 5
How Empathy Is Your Greatest Asset
The True Worth of Your Empathic Abilities

As an empath, your abilities will carry you very far if you allow them to. Your abilities to communicate and empathize with others on a deeper level than others can serve you so well in life.

As you gain more experience in using your empathic abilities, you will find their usefulness growing. You will find more worth in them as you get more used to using them, needing them, and even depending on them.

Hiding your empathic abilities, ignoring them, or trying to quash them will only serve to have you slogging through life with the involuntary empathic responses you naturally have. Embrace who you are and live your life to the fullest. Live to your own whims—you are more powerful than you know.

Your Empathy Is How Many People Identify You

Your compassion for the people around you is visible to everyone. It's because of this that we tend to attract people who need our energies and our talents in their lives.

When someone gets to know you on a deeper level, they'll find themselves thinking of your empathy and your abilities when they think of you. They'll come to be the things that people use to characterize or describe you.

Being empathetic with others and using your understanding of the people around you to help others makes you stand apart from most other people in the lives of those around you. Thanks to this, those things that draw others to you will come to be how they know you.

Embrace this and surround yourself with all the most positive and inspiring people you can find.

Empathy Can Resolve Many Situations if You're Creative Enough

From conflict mediation to effective leadership, there are few situations in which being empathic won't help you get ahead. As you come to gain experience with using your empathic abilities to help yourself and others, as you begin to hone your skills and strengths, you will find that you'll find more and more ways in which to use your empathy.

It seems to be a law of life that when you focus more on something and put importance on using it, you will find yourself gradually, yet exponentially improving in using it. You will think of scenarios you never thought possible, and you will find more and more reasons to use the abilities you've been graced with throughout this life.

Journaling Prompt

How can you use your empathy in a way you never have before? Write the answers in your journal. These answers are just for you.

Chapter 6
Using Empathy to Cultivate and Prosper in Healthy Relationships

Using Your Empathic Abilities to Find Others Like You

The abilities that you have at your disposal as an empath are more or less made to help you find others who are healthy for you and who like you. Our empathic abilities are as well-suited to helping ourselves as they are to helping the people around us. We just have to know what we're doing and what we're looking for.

Generally, when you meet someone whose empathic abilities are similar to your own, you will be aware of it very early on. There is something about empathic abilities that are magnetic. You will feel drawn to other empaths, without really knowing anything about them.

Listen to that magnetism and reach out to the person. Generally, when you introduce yourself to them, you will feel very calming energy from the beginning, and they will likely feel the same. From here, just be you and do the things that come most naturally to you.

Like others can do with you, starting a friendship with another empath can seem effortless. You sense the desire for friendship from both sides, you detect something genuine within them, and you feel calm with them. Thanks to these factors, starting a friendship with someone who shares your abilities is much simpler than you might think.

The same can be said if you're looking to start a relationship on a bit of a deeper level. People who are looking for a personal or romantic relationship and who are empathic will generally welcome you very warmly, just as they would do with a friend.
Be open to the vibes that others are putting out and put out your own vibes as well. You and other empaths will inevitably find one another.

Exercise

Make a list of the ideal traits that your best friend or partner would have. List out the things you would love to have in common with someone, as well as the things that you wish would differ.

Early Detection of Narcissistic People

Early detection of Narcissistic people can save you a lot of trouble and a lot of heartbreak. Paying close attention to the traits of a narcissistic person that are laid out in chapter one can help you to spot narcissists early on.

Let's take a look at how to detect each of the indications that someone is a narcissist.

Envy is a huge focus of theirs, and they assume that everyone is envious of them.

This will manifest in ways that seem benign at first. Look for a focus on what other people are doing and what they have. Some narcissists can come on a little stronger than others, but they will often be looking for the things that are going on with people around them.

They will often say something about getting something like what they have in the future, or they'll say things about how they could or should have that thing. The conversation will often come back to envy in some way.

Your assurances that they are better will often be met with statements of knowing, than with gracious ones. They will say they know they are better and will often resent the fact that it was ever a question that they're not.

They do not or cannot respect the boundaries of others.

They will ask you questions you're not comfortable answering and will use pleading or comments to push past your refusals. Let's say you're on a first date with someone and they ask you about some deeply personal habits. Having just met this person and not being comfortable with answering that type of question, you will politely decline to talk about it.

They'll say things like, "Aw, come on—no judgments here. I just want to get to know you, and I hate that social convention tells us that we can't be deeply personal with people right after the meeting." This is something to play to your empathy. You like getting to know people, breaking down barriers, and connecting. This statement is made to feel like a challenge to prove that behavior.

Further refusal to answer the question will result in visible resentment for your lack of cooperation with their whims. This lack of respect for boundaries and the insistence that they are heeded is based on their need for complete control of the people and situations around them.

If you sense this refusal of boundaries early on, it's an indication that this is the perfect time to make your exit. If you are in a situation that makes you feel like you cannot safely leave it, signal for help from someone nearby or feign an excuse that lets the person know someone is actively waiting for you to respond to them—a call from a friend or a text message. If you're in a restaurant, you can flag down a server or hostess on your way to the restroom, and they will typically assist you in making a safe exit.

They believe themselves to be superior to others.

Go out to dinner, and see how he treats the person serving your table. Does the person pick up on every little thing they do wrong and say things like, "How hard is it to _____?"

When empaths encounter people who think this way, it can be a natural response to break in with something like, "Well imagine if you were in their shoes. Think of how much they have to deal with at once, and they can get overwhelmed."

Narcissists have a much more limited capacity for empathy. When they are appealed to in such a way, they respond with things that make them appear very callous or cold. They will say things like, "I wouldn't know, because I would never allow myself to work as a waiter," or "They're only overwhelmed because of their incompetence."

They are not effective communicators.

Communication is built on the effective relaying of ideas to someone else and having those ideas acknowledged properly, then vice versa. If the person you're talking to seems unable to hold a conversation, or it seems very disjointed or off, it can be quite off-putting.

Communication is such a basic human necessity because it's what helps us to connect with one another and develop relationships. People who have no empathy or very little empathy will generally not put very much importance on connecting with people, because they do it so very rarely.

Connecting with people would probably seem like little more than a cliché or an ideal to someone who is narcissistic or who lacks empathy.

They are a perfectionist in a way that demands the people around them be perfect as well.

A narcissist will generally demand perfection in every aspect of their lives. Their clothes will often be exceedingly neat, and their possessions will often reflect their need for that perfection. When people of this type look at the people that they keep in their circles, they tend to view them as possessions.

Thanks to this warped view of human connections, they will often insist that the people closest to them maintain a certain standard, even if that standard isn't something the person would keep for themselves. This means that they will insist on excellence from the people closest to them because they fear that if others see something wrong with you, they will see something wrong with the narcissist as well. Since you are a possession of theirs, you are an indication of that person's taste in people and company.

This is a *very* warped view, and they might not even have the capacity to realize that's their motivation when dealing with people and insisting on their excellence. To the narcissist, it may sound or seem like they just want the best for you, and that it hurts them to see you slipping.

The way to spot this upfront is to monitor how they talk about the people closest to them. What are the observations they will make about those people? How do they talk about the sibling who doesn't quite have their act together? How do they talk about someone who has been struggling? Do they express concern for their situation, or do they sort of roll their eyes and say that the person is a mess?

This can be a hard one to spot at first, and it can look like several other things, but as time goes on, it will become more and more obvious.

They tend to exaggerate their abilities.

Because the narcissist is focused on the image of themselves that they put forward for all to see, they will embellish their abilities to some extent. Some people won't need to exaggerate their abilities, because their perfectionism has truly gotten them to the point of great skill.

When associating with other people, they will often inquire about the skills that others possess, only to follow up with the details of their own skills. The narcissist will not only jump at every chance to compare themselves to others—they will often create those opportunities in casual conversations.

If every story you tell about something you did results in a story about how they did something similar, only better, they might be someone with narcissistic tendencies.

Attempts to get them to take responsibility for their actions result in blaming others and deflection.

This is something that we often will not see in the narcissist until later into our relationships with them. It's not common for someone to insist that someone take responsibility for their actions if they don't know them very well, but some circumstances do happen, and it's prudent to be on the lookout for them.

Deflection of the blame for one's own bad habits is—in itself—a bad habit. If you notice this kind of thing in the early stages of getting to know someone, it's best to keep your distance from them and watch for the other traits in this section.

They are typically obsessed with success and creating an image of success for all to see.

Along with the overblowing of their abilities, insistence on perfection from the people around them, and for putting forth an image of superiority, the typical narcissist wants to be seen as successful and perfect. This is, of course, not possible because no one is perfect. This will not stop them from trying, and they typically don't apply that phrase to themselves.

The best way to detect this type of inclination in the early stages of knowing someone is by seeing how they respond to a minor failure or a minor hiccup in the plans they've made.

Sometimes, fate strikes and you're able to see this on the first meeting. For instance, if you're on a date with them and they had intended to take you to a museum that interests you. Let's say the museum has an unexpected water main breakage and needs to close down for the day, thus changing the entire plan for your date.

This is not a failure on the part of your date, but they could take it that way, and they could take it really hard. If your date seems more upset about the museum closing than you would expect someone to be about such a thing, it could be a bad sign. If they begin to talk disparagingly about the people who run the museum for ruining their plans, this could be a bad sign.

They have an overblown or an inflated sense of their own importance.

This trait is the one that makes people say things like, "Thank God I was here," "What would you do without me," or "If I'm not there to watch over things and make sure they go smoothly, something bad will happen."

They tend to use the overstatement of their abilities to get themselves put into positions from which they can exert control over others. A narcissist will always vie for the leadership role because it's the one where they can control others and take the glory of the accomplishments made by the group.

Look for things that make it seem like the person sees even the smallest contribution to any effort as the one effort that "sealed the deal," or caused success. Look for the person who will insinuate themselves when no one asked them to be involved, and you will typically find yourself face to face with a narcissist.

They thrive on having control of the situation and of others.

It can be a slippery slope for the "leave it to me," and the "don't worry about a thing," statements to turn into opportunities for the narcissist to assume complete control of any scenario. This is something that can be hard to spot at the beginning and can simply seem like they are just really good at making sure everyone around them is accommodated.

The real way to tell the difference is to try to make a change to the plan. Try to make a subtle difference in the way that things would play out to see what their response is. Choose something that wouldn't particularly change the overall outcome of the plan and see if they have a negative or a supportive response to it.

If they say something like, "just leave the planning to me. You don't have to think about anything, just do what I tell you," this is their way of warning you to stop getting in the way of their having control over things. If they say something like, "I'm not sure that would work because of _____," this just means that your idea might not fit into the plan. Knowing the difference here is key.

They tend to be overly sensitive about their imperfections.

Hypersensitivity to one's flaws is a characteristic of a number of different things. What really indicates the narcissistic personality behind this hypersensitivity is a response that is rooted primarily in anger and blame. A narcissist is never to blame for their own flaws, as far as they're concerned, and you are the enemy for bringing them up.

Their personal relationships are typically a mess.

Family and friends will generally have a long and complicated history due to having to deal with this person's narcissistic traits. This is one of the advantages of asking someone about their family when you meet them. It can tell you a lot about what their personal ties are like, how they regard them, and what the state of things is.

They expect special treatment in most circumstances.

This will manifest as a general disregard for being told what the rules are. They will generally still ask if exceptions can be made and will either respond with a smug tone when proven right or become angry when told to abide by the rules.

Look for requests for off-menu foods at a restaurant or requests for people to bend the rules on their account.

They typically come across as arrogant.

When someone is this occupied with their sense of importance and their sense of superiority, they tend to seem very arrogant to others. They may not even perceive of their arrogance, because to do so often requires humility and sense of how one is affecting others. This is not one of the strong points of the narcissist.

Arrogance can come across in a number of ways, but the primary thing about arrogance is that it's never subtle. This trait should reveal itself with quickness and should be unmistakable.

Criticism is met with extreme anger.

A quick response to anger should be alarming, especially if they're angry about something that is largely inconsequential. Criticism can make one feel angry, especially if it's phrased in such a way that makes a person feel less valid, or which insults them.

However, if someone is criticized on something small and it's relayed in such a way that is meant to help the person, it should be received with mild disappointment at the most. Someone who responds to these types of things with a loud kind of anger that causes them to yell, throw things, or worse, it should be taken as a bad sign.

They feel as though they are owed or entitled to things.

This is part of what tells the narcissist that they're entitled to special treatment or that they're an exception to the rules of an establishment or arrangement. They will usually present the idea of doing things for them as an opportunity or a benefit, rather than a chore or favor.

Look out for the things said to people who are bringing them things and pay attention to false gratitude. When someone says thank you as a matter of habit, with no feeling behind it should be an indication of narcissistic tendencies.

A deep sense of insecurity hides under their façade.

This is the mechanism that causes them to leap straight to the defensive when the smallest criticism is made toward them. Being deeply insecure can come from a lot of different places, so this isn't solely an indicator of narcissistic tendencies.

They tend to take advantage of the people around them.

As mentioned previously, a deeply narcissistic person can tend to see people as objects. Because of their lack of empathy, they can take advantage of people that are around them. The tendency to use people should be seen as a very large red flag.

People don't use people by mistake.

Empathy doesn't come very easily—if at all—to them.

Lack of empathy is something that can come from a few different mental illnesses, not the least of which is sociopathy. While narcissism is different than sociopathy, they both have their fair share of alarming attributes. Someone who cannot empathize with others on any level should be avoided.

Exercise

Think of someone in your life who is narcissistic. When was the first time you noticed any of the traits listed above in that person?

Early Detection of Toxic People

While toxic people tend to share a number of similar tendencies with narcissistic people, the two conditions are not synonymous. Knowing the difference between someone who feels little to no empathy for people and sees them as objects to use in order to further their purposes has a different tone to it than someone who generally a terrible influence, who wants to be involved with many people to get things from them, and who tends to sow discord wherever they go.

They play the blame game.

You will often find that someone who is toxic will find ways to blame their shortcomings on the people around them or on situations that make no sense. Look for a flustered response to questions about reasons something didn't go a certain way. These explanations will typically be nebulous, harried, strange, and convoluted.

Someone who is toxic won't be terribly concerned with providing you with enough information that you are at ease, so when you press further, you will often find that they'll ask you just to drop the subject and move on. Any future attempts to address the situation will be met with blame on you for continuing to harp on things that should just be let go because "I just want us to have a nice time."

They tend to be passive-aggressive.

Small jabs that are thinly veiled is one of the trademarks of a toxic person. Look for these when someone is attempting to avoid an argument, and someone else won't stop making backhanded comments to spur on more conflict. Toxic people thrive on conflict, as it keeps people distracted from noticing their behaviors, and it gives them more opportunities to ingratiate themselves to more people involved in said conflict. "Playing all sides" is another toxic trademark.

The way to spot this early on would be to see how they respond to negative people in their environment. If they blow the other person's negativity out of proportion and then make comments about them, but won't say anything directly to the person, this is passive aggression.

Not all who are passive-aggressive are toxic people. Most toxic people, however, are passive-aggressive.

They criticize others, whether they're standing right there or not.

Criticism can come in many shapes and forms, so you'll need to stay vigilant. Negative comments about everything from the way someone dresses to the way they are as a person can come from a toxic person.

Extended exposure to harsh criticism can lead to severely reduced self-esteem and worth. These should be avoided, if at all possible, and any critical comments about something someone cannot change should be immediately combatted.

When confronted, toxic people will generally back down.

They're manipulative.

People who are toxic will generally have some kind of "angle" when dealing with the people around them. They will never seek to spend time with people just for the sake of spending time with them. Toxic people are typically looking to get things from people or to do things that would create conflict so they can do more things behind the scenes.

If you are talking to someone and it seems like they're attempting to shift your line of thinking on something, try to spot why they're trying to shift your view. For instance, if someone is trying to get you to see their stance on something, this isn't manipulation. If someone is trying to change your opinion about a friend of yours, this is manipulation.

They're largely very negative.

This one can manifest in so many ways because negativity permeates every aspect of their lives. They will go into every situation with the mindset that things will go badly or that they won't enjoy themselves.

Restaurant experiences tend to be exceedingly awkward thanks to the way in which they approach the servers and other staff. They seem combative, impatient, and rude.

They tend to deal with emotional blackmail.

People who are toxic will tend to hold you as a hostage with guilt trips and reasons why your behavior is a betrayal to them. Even if they have no reasons to think that what you're doing is going against them, harming them, or pulling you away from them.

Toxic people will attempt to monopolize your time and sequester you from your other friends and family. This gives them a way to manipulate you without interference from others, gives them more ways in which to ingratiate themselves to you.

When you first get to know them, they will say things to make you think that they are your best chance at true friendship and companionship. They will say things to pull you into their circles.

This might not happen at the first meeting, but it will set in before too long, and it will become the norm if the behavior isn't met with a negative response, or if it isn't met with someone telling them they see what they're trying to do.

Exercise

Think of someone in your life who is Toxic. When was the first time you noticed any of the traits listed above in that person?

Journaling Prompt

Have you ever had a hunch that the person you were dealing with wasn't being completely genuine with you? Did that hunch ever turn out to be correct?

Write about how you would have done things differently, knowing that you can trust your hunches.

Write the answers in your journal. These answers are just for you.

Conclusion

Thank you for making it through to the end of *Empath Protection: A Psychic Survival Guide for Understanding Narcissistic People, Setting Boundaries Around Dark and Mystic Personalities, Sustaining Your Emotional Energy and Achieving Healing. Tips and Tricks*! Let's hope it was informative and able to provide you with all of the tools you need to achieve your goals—whatever they may be.

Understanding the differences between toxic people and narcissistic people, understanding what threats these people pose to your livelihood, understanding the personality disorders and the traits that characterize them, and understanding how to kick these people out of your life without fear, guilt, or shame is the greatest thing an empath can learn to defend themselves. Your livelihood, your survival, your mental prosperity, and your emotional well-being depend on your understanding of these personality disorders, their traits, as well as how to spot them when you first meet someone.

As an empath, helping people comes very innately to you, and it makes sense that you would be drawn to helping these people. It is your responsibility to stay safe while doing so.

If you haven't done so already, your next step is to complete the exercises laid out in each chapter for you. These exercises will help you to understand the mechanisms at work, will help you to find healthy coping strategies, and will help you to heal from past traumas or incidents.

If you have completed these exercises, your next step is to read the following books in this bundle:

- *EMPATH DISCOVERY: A Survival Guide for Beginners for Understanding the Empathic Brain, Discovering Your Dark Side, Embracing Your Emotional Skills and Getting Stronger Daily. Healing Modalities.*

- *EMPATH LEARNING: A Complete Emotional Healing & Survival Guide for Highly Sensitive People to Reveal the Dark Mystic Secrets, Improve Skills & Habits for Defeating Energy Vampires and Overcoming Psychic Exams.*

The bundle will serve to aid the empath in healing from the emotional trauma of a narcissistic relationship, how to spot narcissistic people before they become a problem, as well as how to cultivate meaningful relationships and help them thrive with the power of empathy.

Thank you very much for reading, and please share the information you found helpful with friends and family who may also benefit. Finally, if you found this book useful in any way, a review on Amazon is always appreciated!

Made in the USA
Middletown, DE
03 November 2020